CROSS OF IRON
The Nazi Enslavement of Western Europe

CROSS OF IRON

The Nazi Enslavement of Western Europe

Rupert Butler

ARROW BOOKS

TO JOYCE

Arrow Books Limited
62–65 Chandos Place, London WC2N 4NW

An imprint of Century Hutchinson Limited

London Melbourne Sydney Auckland
Johannesburg and agencies throughout
the world

First published in 1989

© Rupert Butler 1989

Phototypeset by Input Typesetting Ltd, London

Printed and bound in Great Britain by
Courier International, Tiptree, Essex

ISBN 0 09 95520 4

ACKNOWLEDGEMENTS

In the preparation of this book I am greatly indebted, as always to the staff of the Department of Printed Books at the Imperial War Museum, London, for its patience in supplying material, in many cases books on World War Two resistance which have long been out of print. The store of newspaper cuttings and eyewitness accounts of occupation in various western countries made available by the Institute of Contemporary History and the Wiener Library, London, were of particular value, and I would also like to thank Mrs Edda Tasiemka for allowing me to consult her unique private collection of wartime newspapers and magazines. The special collection of World War Two books held by Wandsworth Public Library was also useful. Felix Plottier, doughty survivor of the maquis of Haute-Savoie, eastern France, and his wife Joan gave me limitless hospitality and kindness at their delightful house in Bonneville and a treasure store of memories of life under Italian, Vichy and German repression. Translation from the French on this and other occasions was the difficult task of Joyce Rackham, to whom I extend my love and respect. Squadron-leader Frank Griffiths, DFC, AFC, ('Cromwell'), who crashed near Annecy and was looked after by the local maquis, supplied a vivid account of life in those days. Indispensable editorial assistance was provided with all her usual faithfulness by Vicky Clayton. I am also indebted to Peter Elliott and Gordon Leith of the Royal Air Force Museum, Hendon, and the staffs of the Luxembourg National Trade and Tourist Office and the Netherlands Board of Tourism. Acknowledgements are also due to Jean Bourgaux, Terry Charman, Robin Cross, Professor M. R. D. Foot, Andrew Mollo and Joe Rose.

'Jetzt es kein Kriegsspiel aber ein grausamer Krieg.'
(This is now no game, but war in all its cruelty.)
—warning given at the outbreak of World War Two
to Henri Frenay, leading figure of the French
resistance

SELECTED BIBLIOGRAPHY

After the Battle, No 56 (Battle of Britain Prints International Ltd, 1988)

Bird, Michael J., *The Secret Battalion*. (Frederick Muller, 1965)

Collins, Larry, and LaPierre, Dominique, *Is Paris Burning?* (Gollancz, 1974)

Dank, Milton, *The French Against the French*. (Cassell, 1978)

Deighton, Len, *Blitzkrieg: From the Rise of Hitler to the Fall of Dunkirk*. (Cape, 1979)

De Jong, L., and Stoppelman, Joseph W. F., *The Lion Rampant: The Story of Holland's Resistance to the Nazis*. (Querido, New York, 1943)

Dourlein, Peter, *Inside North Pole*. (William Kimber, 1953)

De Vomecourt, Phillipe, *Who Lived to See the Day: France in Arms 1940–1945*. (Hutchinson, 1961)

Flender, Harold, *Rescue in Denmark*. (W. H. Allen, 1963)

Foot, M. R. D., *SOE in France*. (Her Majesty's Stationery Office, 1966)

Foot, M. R. D., *SOE: The Special Operations Executive 1940–46*. (British Broadcasting Corporation, 1984)

Frenay, Henri, *La Nuit Finera*. (Opera Mundi, 1973)

Griffiths, Frank, *Winged Hours*. (William Kimber, 1981)

Gudme, Sten, *Denmark: Hitler's 'Model Protectorate'*. (Gollancz, 1942)

Hambro, Carl J., *I Saw it Happen in Norway*. (Hodder & Stoughton, 1940)

Haukelid, Captain Knut, *Skis Against the Atom*. (William Kimber, 1954)

Hayes, Paul, *Quisling*. (David & Charles, 1971)

History of the Second World War. (Purnell & Sons, 1966)

Hoffman, Percy, *Hitler's Personal Security.* (Macmillan, 1979)

Irving, David, *The Virus House.* (William Kimber, 1966)

Jackson, Robert, *The Fall of France, May–June 1940.* (Arthur Barker, 1975)

Jones, R. V., *Most Secret War: British Scientific Intelligence 1939–1945.* (Hamish Hamilton, 1978)

Lampe, David, *Savage Canary.* (Cassell, 1957)

Littlejohn, David, *The Patriotic Traitors.* (Heinemann, 1972)

Lottmann, Herbert, *The People's Anger.* (Heinemann, 1986)

Mabire, Jean, *Chasseurs Alpins: Des Vosges aux Djebels.* (Press de la Cité, 1984)

Moen, Lars, *Under the Iron Heel.* (Robert Hale, 1941)

Motz, Roger, *Belgium Unvanquished.* (Lindsay Drummond, 1942)

Myklebost, Tor, *They Came as Friends.* (Gollancz, 1943)

Neave, Airey, *Saturday at M19.* (Hodder & Stoughton, 1969)

Petrow, Richard, *The Bitter Years: The Invasion and Occupation of Denmark and Norway.* (Hodder & Stoughton, 1974)

Pool, James and Suzanne, *Who Financed Hitler: The Secret Funding of Hitler's Rise to Power, 1919–1933.* (Futura, 1980)

Rickard, Charles, *La Savoie dans La Resistance.* (Ouest-France, 1986)

Schoenbrun, David, *Soldiers of the Night.* (Robert Hale, 1980)

Simon, Paul, *One Enemy Only – The Invader.* (Hodder & Stoughton, 1942)

Wiggan, Richard, *Operation Freshman.* (William Kimber, 1986)

1

The thick icy fog of a bitter dawn broke over the airfield at Muenster-Loddenheide on the morning of 10 January 1940. Major Helmuth Reinberger of the Luftwaffe was only too conscious that the party he had attended the night before had been a particularly hectic affair. That would scarcely have mattered if, as parachute liaison officer at the headquarters of Luftflotte 2 under the command of General der Flieger Helmuth Felmy, he had not been due to attend a staff conference in Cologne.

Reinberger had intended to make the dreary journey by train but his sympathetic station commander, Reserve Major Erich Hoenmanns, suggested that he should be flown to Cologne instead. There could be no question of the severely hungover Reinberger piloting an aircraft himself. Hoenmanns agreed to do the flying. He had been a pilot during World War One and still held a current licence. Furthermore, there just happened to be the little Messerschmitt 108 communications aircraft available. True, there was no authorisation for such a trip but, since no one was likely to discover so trivial a bending of the regulations, that was not important.

As the aircraft snaked above the airport in that freezing January dawn, Reinberger shivered and attempted desperately to control waves of nausea. The only consolation appeared to be that the visibility, apart from a ground mist, seemed good. But what if anything should go wrong? For reassurance, he clasped the bulky yellow pigskin briefcase that lay on his knees and which was his special responsibility.

Surely, it now only remained for the weather to hold.

On 3 March 1939, in defiance of an agreement between Britain, France and Germany a few months earlier, the German Fuehrer, Adolf Hitler, set out to conquer Czechoslovakia. There had been two previous spectacular coups which amounted to blatant aggression: the first on 7 March 1936, when the Wehrmacht, ripping up the appropriate clauses of the Versailles and Locarno treaties, marched into the Rhineland. Then came the annexation of Austria, and when Hitler entered the country of his birth, the crowds strewed flowers in his path.

In all his adventures in the east, Hitler had enjoyed the indispensable neutrality of the Soviet Union, but the Fuehrer was under no illusions. On 9 October 1939, the generals were warned in a memorandum: 'We cannot count on Stalin leaving us to our own devices indefinitely. We must have freedom in the west.'

As for the people who lived in the west, it had been up till now a strange sort of war, one in which there was no fighting on land, while in the air, bombers carried nothing more lethal than crude propaganda leaflets. Only at sea was there any activity: U-boats prowled balefully amid British and neutral shipping in the icy immensity of the northern Atlantic.

But, in fact, Europe was sitting on a slow-burning fuse, even though Hitler had remained somewhat indecisive as to when he would apply a match to it. The German people were little wiser at the turn of the year. They had spent a miserable Christmas, with spartan food and absent menfolk; there was to be little warmth. A characteristic harangue from their Fuehrer was prefaced by a diatribe against 'the Jewish and capitalist warmongers'. He had gone on with vintage bombast to proclaim: 'United within the country, economically prepared and militarily armed to the highest degree, we enter this most decisive year in German history . . . May the year 1940 bring the decision. It will, whatever happens, be our victory.'

But even the seemingly unstoppable Adolf Hitler could not control the weather, which continued to be unrelievedly vile. On 27 December he had again postponed *Fall Gelb* (Case Yellow, the codename for the attack in the west) 'by at least a fortnight'. On 10 January the attack was set for precisely a week ahead; the onslaught would be at 'fifteen minutes before sunrise – 8.16 a.m.' Four days before that, it was intended that the Luftwaffe of Hermann Goering should have its moment of glory – in France. Belgium and the Netherlands would be left to sweat over their ultimate fate.

Plainly, Hitler meant business at last. German forces had moved up to their jump-off positions; unit commanders assembled at their respective headquarters for final briefings.

Then it was called off yet again. And the reason had lain in that yellow pigskin briefcase clutched so firmly by Major Helmuth Reinberger of 22nd Airborne.

For it contained nothing less than dossiers marked *Streng Geheime* (Top Secret). Their contents spelt out in chilling detail the intended destinies of a clutch of nations – France, the Netherlands, Belgium, Denmark, Norway and Luxembourg.

The Messerschmitt 108 carried aboard the proposed blueprint for the invasion of the west.

Any optimism felt by Major Reinberger did not last long. The weather had got worse. Furthermore, it was obvious that Major Hoenmanns was losing his bearings. Visibility narrowed by the minute and it was not long before Hoenmanns was admitting he was hopelessly off course. Without knowing it, he had been driven across the Rhine by the sharp easterly wind. The Me 108 was now in hostile territory.

The only possible lifeline would be a sighting of the Rhine, lying to the east. Hoenmanns struggled feverishly with the controls, but it proved useless, the engine was cutting out; there was nothing for it but a forced landing.

A swift decision was indicated. Hoenmanns selected a large snow-covered field, and there looming up was a dangerously solid-looking line of poplars. It was far too late to avoid them; all that could be done was to kick the rudder frantically and steer for what appeared to be a sizeable gap. A second later, the Me 108 was juddering violently, the trees slicing into the wingtips. Mercifully, the landing was successful. The plane came to rest just short of the far hedge.

The two men, suffering from little more than a severe shaking, had only one thought now. Those all-important documents must be destroyed, and at once. Precious moments were spent studying a map which showed that they had landed near Mechelen-sur-Meuse, just north of Maastricht, in Belgian territory.

Reinberger sought shelter behind the hedge, struggling with his cigarette lighter in a desperate bid to burn the incriminating papers. What happened next had a strong element of comedy. The landing had been witnessed by a Belgian peasant, who gravely handed Reinberger a box of matches. To the relief of both Germans, the papers were soon alight.

But the vital act of destruction was not to proceed uninterrupted. A knot of shouting Belgian soldiers arrowed towards the crippled aircraft. The quick-thinking Hoenmanns, conscious that Reinberger must complete his task, walked away from his colleague towards the approaching troops, his hands raised. With a bit of luck, they might be persuaded that there had only been one man aboard the aircraft. The ruse failed. One sharp-eyed Belgian had spotted the ribbon of smoke behind the hedge. Both men were promptly arrested by two Belgian privates, Rubens and Habets, who fired warning shots.

To make matters worse, the documents did not burn as rapidly as Reinberger had hoped. Most of them were captured intact.

At a nearby police post, they were questioned by a Belgian intelligence officer. To protect the men from the cold, a cast-iron stove glowed warmly in the room. During a pause in the questioning, Reinberger feigned exhaustion and appeared to be asleep. But he was watching his guard closely and noted, furthermore, that the precious documents lay unattended on a table. With a surge of hope, he leapt from his chair, grabbed the papers and attempted to stuff them into the stove. Captain Rodrigue, who was in charge of the command post, hastily put out the fire, burning his hand. He exclaimed furiously: 'It's always the same with you Germans. We treat you correctly and you play a dirty trick like this!'

Rodrigue's next action was to place his revolver on top of the papers. But Reinberger was not giving up yet. In a frenzy, he threw himself at the Belgian; Rodrigue had to tear the revolver away.

Reinberger had abandoned all reason and screamed hysterically: 'I have committed an unforgivable crime! I wanted your revolver so that I could kill myself.' Hoenmanns, who had remained docile throughout, attempted to explain his colleague's behaviour: 'You must excuse him. He's in real trouble. He's an officer in the regular army.'

But it is doubtful whether Rodrigue heard him. He was staring in open disbelief at some of the uncharred papers. Then he dashed from the room to contact his regimental staff.

The two Germans knew then that the last hope had gone.

Reinberger, soon in a state of terror, took refuge in lies. He reported to Luftwaffe headquarters through the German embassy in Brussels that he had succeeded in burning the papers to insignificant fragments, the size of the palm of his hand. It was a hollow move; the next day, 13 January, Belgium's German Ambassador alerted Berlin to considerable Belgium troop movements 'as a result of alarming reports received by the Belgian general staff'.

Any lingering doubts that the incident might be explained away were finally dashed at an icy interview between the German ambassador and the Belgian Foreign

13

Minister, Paul Henri Spaak, who proclaimed: 'The plane which made an emergency landing on 10 January has put into Belgian hands a document of the most extraordinarily serious nature, which contained clear proof of an intention to attack. It was not just an operations plan but an attack order worked out in every detail, in which only the time remained to be inserted.'

Such almost incredible carelessness by the Germans was viewed with suspicion by many of the Allied countries. Could the Nazis really have been so very lax? Could it be that the whole thing was a not particularly subtle plant to mislead them as to the date and place of an invasion?

Nevertheless, the documents, charred but still legible, were passed to the Dutch and French governments. Their representatives had more than a passing interest in them, particularly when they read 'General Orders of Luftflotte 2'. The document was, of course, incomplete, but enough survived to give a clear pointer to German intentions:

The German army in the west will . . . out its offensive between the North Sea and the Moselle, aided by the air force, through the Belgian-Luxembourg territory in order to . . . the most important parts of the French army and its . . . The area around Liège and . . . surrounded . . . Besides, our intention is to take over Dutch territory, with the exception of *Festing Holland*, with a grouping of troops . . . The 8th Air Corps and some of its troops must support a disembarkation operation made by 7th Airborne Division on the first day of attack. In close cooperation with the 6th Army (mainly positioned close to and west of Maastricht), it must support the progress of the ground force attacking the defence lines covering the Meuse basin and destroy the Belgian army west of that area . . . The fighter planes must gain air supremacy over the 6th Army's zone of attack.

The combined battle formation of the Luftflotte 3 shall take on the French air bases to prevent them from intervening in any battles fought on land. Next, the Luftflotte shall prevent French armies in the north from advancing towards the northeast . . . The 10th Air Corps, to get here with the Kriegsmarine, will concentrate on fighting the British naval forces.

The instructions for this operation were scheduled for Wednesday 17 January.

Hitler's reaction to the turn of events was predictable to anyone familiar with the towering rages of the would-be warlord. Even so, Hitler's anger surpassed anyone's worst fears.

Generalfeldmarschall Wilhelm Keitel of the Wehrmacht related after the war at the Nuremberg trials, where he was arraigned as a war criminal: 'When he was told about the incident, Hitler flew into a frenzied rage, the worst outbreak I have ever seen. The Fuehrer went into a trance, he was frothing at the mouth, he struck the wall with his fists, vowed he would have the guilty parties executed, and roared terrible oaths about the incompetence and treachery among the general staff. Goering, forced to bear the brunt of his fury, had not even recovered from it the next day . . .'

The hapless wives of Major Reinberger and Major Hoenmanns, who were in no way connected with what had happened, were both arrested and thrown into jail. General der Flieger Helmuth Felmy, commander of Luftflotte 2, was dismissed for the errors of subordinates.

The forced landing and the bad weather meant a postponement of Hitler's plans. The order went out: 'All movements to stop.' The Germans were hard at work, nonetheless. To the north were two other little neutral states: Denmark and Norway. These, it was reasoned, were plums ripe for picking.

2

Jens Lillilund was not by inclination a violent man. Reserved almost to the point of taciturnity, he was scarcely the type of which resistance heroes were made. But on the morning of 9 April 1940, he was fuelled by a novel emotion: a deep, smouldering anger at the sight of German troops in his native Copenhagen.

News had already reached him that Denmark had been rapidly overrun. He decided to have a look for himself. Indeed, there were the Germans looking remarkably relaxed on Langeline Pier, nonchalantly guarding the waterfront.

With difficulty, Lillilund kept control and peddled furiously away. But those Germans he saw striding arrogantly on the streets proved altogether too much. In what he was later to admit was a futile gesture, he aimed his bicycle at a knot of them. His response to the gutteral order *'Halt'* was to spit at the feet of the conquerors.

He was promptly arrested but, fortunately for him, turned over to the Danish police. The nervous authorities were not willing to antagonise their new conquerors needlessly. Lillilund was eventually released, with a stern warning not to provoke the Germans.

It was an injunction he forthwith resolved to ignore.

But *how?* A patient soul, he bided his time, studiously keeping out of trouble for as long as he could bear to. Then he saw the truck which the Germans had been ill-advised to leave unattended in Kongensgade Square. It contained hay for their barracks.

Jens Lillilund set fire to it. He had begun his resistance war.

In the early hours of the same day, the news editor of the *New York Times* was staring at a telegram which had just come in from the paper's Copenhagen correspondent.

It read: 'GERMAN TROOPS CROSSED THE DANISH FRONTIER AT DAWN AND TOOK POSSESSION OF COPENHAGEN. AT A CABINET MEETING IN THE SMALL HOURS KING CHRISTIAN AND THE GOVERNMENT AGREED TO YIELD BEFORE SUPERIOR FORCE.'

There was still time enough to rush out an extra edition and the news editor splashed over the whole eight-column front page a stark heading in thick type:

'DENMARK MURDERED'

The report was one of the first indications to the outside world of Hitler's assault in the west.

For six months it had seemed that the mighty German war machine had slumbered after the campaign in Poland. The Danes, in particular, were more than content at German inactivity. Memories went back to August 1914. Then Denmark had readily caved in to German pressure, mining the waters of the Great Belt, which had been within Danish jurisdiction and constituted one of the major nautical entrances to the Baltic. Denmark, by mining the Belt, had provided protection for Germany's naval base at Kiel until the war was over. King Christian X had justified the action by proclaiming: 'Denmark at the moment is in such a serious condition that one cannot play banque with one's country.'

The result was precisely as hoped: throughout the four years of World War One, Denmark remained neutral and untouched by battle. Now, twenty-two years later, this pleasant little country of four million, small and flat and therefore a gift to panzer armies, hoped desperately that it would be left alone.

Adolf Hitler also had his eyes elsewhere.

Norway would be the next objective. By gaining bases there, the British blockade line across the North Sea would be broken. Even more to the point, during the cold months iron ore from Sweden, vital to Germany's very existence, had to be switched to the Norwegian port of Narvik and brought down the coast by ship to Germany. German ore vessels would be sailing within Norway's territorial waters; their progress had to be assured.

But first there was the little question of Denmark.

The plans incorporated under the innocent-sounding codename of *Weseruebung* (Weser Exercise) became grim reality when German units fell upon Denmark on 9 April, exactly as scheduled. Simultaneously timed attacks were directed against Jutland, Copenhagen and the strategic island of Fyn. In Jutland, advance elements of the 11th Motorised Rifle Brigade and the 170th Infantry Division smashed across the border on a broad front. Resistance was feeble. No preparation had been made to block roads or mine bridges; in any case, Danish troops had little appetite for combat.

All too often, the pickings for the Germans turned out to be shamefully easy. The German advance had been greeted with blatant eagerness by pro-German Danes. They stationed themselves at crossroads, waving on the advancing German units. The allegiance of these particular Danes was not in doubt: many wore swastika armbands and greeted their conquerors with shouts of '*Heil Hitler*!'

Hitler showed himself the supreme realist. He needed the lands of Scandinavia, which is why the Germans were instructed to behave like liberators. There were harsh exceptions. Guards keeping watch over the frontier crossing at Krusaa in Slesvig were overpowered by men dressed as civilians. Three of them were killed; there were suggestions that the Germans were infiltrating fifth columnists. Local police, unwise enough to mount an investigation once the invasion was over, were told sharply to mind their own business.

Troops who garrisoned the Citadel, the ancient fortress

overlooking the harbour at Copenhagen and the site of the Danish General Staff headquarters, had been courteous to the German businessman who showed close interest in their activities, five days before the invasion. Indeed, a considerate Danish sergeant had escorted this personable tourist around the Citadel grounds. The visitor had been shown the General Staff headquarters and had been particularly interested in the two main gates leading to the fortress itself.

Generalmajor Kurt Himer, the German commander who had been given the responsibility of capturing Copenhagen, returned to Germany eminently satisfied with what he had seen.

The Danes, he was convinced, would be a soft target. And he was right.

When the German troopship *Hansestadt Danzig* arrived off Copenhagen, its progress was almost stately, as if the vessel was on an official visit. But vessels on official visits were not in the habit of carrying an assault battalion. Three combat companies were soon edging towards the Citadel, their progress barely noticed along dawn streets.

The only reported violence involved a hefty bricklayer who, on the way to work in the very early morning, encountered a solitary German, rifle in hand. He extended a burly fist; the German measured his length on the pavement. But the gesture of defiance was ignored.

The gates of the Citadel were unguarded; there were only two sentries. The entire Danish garrison surrendered without a shot.

With the Citadel secured, German troops closed in on the residence of King Christian X. Inside the castle, Premier Thorvald Stauning and Foreign Minister Peter Munch conferred. They urged swift capitulation. But General Wain Pryor, commander in chief of the Danish Army, argued stoutly that the fight must go on. The king, he urged, must leave with his ministers while there was yet still time. The struggle could be continued from the nearest military camp.

The seventy-year-old king, weary and confused, pleaded with General Pryor: 'Have not our troops fought long enough?' The swift riposte was indignant: 'They have not.'

Suddenly it all seemed sadly academic. The quiet skies were rudely shattered by bombers of the Luftwaffe screaming above the city.

Journalist Sten Gudme of *Politiken*, the country's largest daily paper, caught the sudden mood of fear: 'Are they going to lay the whole city in ruins? Will their bombload rain down on us the next moment? We had no idea then whether the Cabinet had decided to fight or surrender.'

What few in Denmark knew was that the German Minister to Denmark, Cecil von Renthe-Fink, acting on the instructions of Generalmajor Himer, had delivered an ultimatum. It acknowledged that German troops moving across the border into Jutland were landing on the principal Danish islands on the excuse that it was necessary to 'forestall a British invasion'. There had been a call on the Danes to capitulate immediately. And now leaflets from the aircraft were ramming home the point.

Anthony Mann, the correspondent of the *Daily Telegraph*, recalled:

The blow fell on me personally at 5.50 a.m. when I was still in bed in my Copenhagen flat. We were awakened by a mighty roar of engines: wave after wave of bombers, bearing sinister black crosses and swastikas, were flying in formation past our windows, almost at rooftop height. We could see the faces of the crewmembers, peering down through the plexiglass. At intervals of a few seconds, handfuls of pale green leaflets burst from each plane and floated lazily down to almost deserted streets.

Printed in extremely bad Danish, they informed the Danish people that Germany had forestalled an attack on Denmark and Norway by Churchill 'the greatest warmonger of the century', and had assumed the duty of protecting Scandinavia. Everyone should go quietly about his business and do what he was told.

At two o'clock that same afternoon, Himer and Renthe-

Fink called on the king. The elderly monarch, although inwardly shattered, rigidly maintained his dignity. Barely able to conceal his emotion, he proclaimed: 'The king and government will do everything possible to keep peace and order. Any friction between the German troops and Denmark must be eliminated. The country must be spared misfortune and misery.'

Himer was determined to match the king in dignity. He was, he explained smoothly, only doing his duty as a soldier. The Germans had come solely as friends.

Christian suddenly became embarrassingly servile, begging to be allowed to keep his bodyguard.

No objection was raised and the king noticeably relaxed. His last words to Himer were almost pathetically conciliatory: 'General, may I, as an old soldier, tell you something? As soldier to soldier? You Germans have done the incredible again! One must admit that it is magnificent work.'

Hunched at his desk in the editorial offices of *Politiken*, Sten Gudme anxiously grabbed the jangling telephone. The voice said: 'This is the German Legation. Press Attaché Frielitz speaking. Who is that?'

Gudme gave his name. Frielitz adopted a deliberately friendly tone; it might have been a conventionally social call.

'Good morning, Herr Gudme. I'm afraid that there can't be any more issues of *Politiken* or other papers until I let you know. I'm sure you understand. Will you please tell the other editors in your building?'

Then the line went dead.

Aksel Lannoe of the Danish Air Force was in the thick of events at Vaerloese airfield, Denmark's pitiably inadequate main point of resistance against the might of the German Luftwaffe. On that morning of 9 April, the airfield could

boast 21 obsolescent fighters, 27 spotter aircraft, one heli-
copter and 19 trainers.

Lannoe recalled:

'We had repeated "stand-bys" during the night and we were not
certain whether it was serious trouble or just an exercise. Our
planes were lined up in neat rows on the perimeter.

One aircraft, which had been ordered on a mission, began
taking off. At that moment, German aircraft came in at hedge-
hopping level and shot down the Danish plane at a height of a
few feet. Then they crossed and recrossed the airfield, firing
incendiary into our planes, which burst into flames. Our antiaircraft guns were useless because we had no ammunition.

When we tried to get into a brand-new shelter, we found that
the door was locked and the key had been removed. We threw
ourselves flat in the surrounding fields. A little later we received
a message telling us to "cease resistance".

There had been a time when the Danes were a warlike
people. Long ago in their history, they had battled their
way south into Italy and east into Estonia. They had overrun England and tightened their hold on Norway and
Sweden and the north. But that was some 400 years
before. Denmark had mellowed down the generations, and
the language had evolved a word to describe its people:
hyggelig, which signifies cosiness and comfort.

And now into the *hyggelig* country stalked the German
Wehrmacht.

It all seemed, at first, deceptively pleasant. The German
conquerors were prepared to be reasonable. What had
changed? Very little, if you judged by externals. There was
no German Reichskommissar in Denmark. King Christian
continued to live at Amalienborg Palace in Copenhagen.
The royal standard floated and Danish sentries in their
bearskins kept guard.

But Copenhagen had also become the city where police
cars careered through the streets in the small hours. Their
quarry, it was whispered, were English and French immigrants. Those rounded up were questioned, not by the

Germans, but by the Danes. It was reassuring to learn that prisoners were being sent to Danish jails and not to Nazi ones with their ominous reputation.

The king's appeal for order – 'an absolutely quiet and dignified demeanour' – had a tranquillising effect. The German troops who were chosen for the occupation certainly seemed to be an elite bunch; many could speak fluent Danish. They came either from Schleswig Holstein on the boundaries of Denmark, where Danish was an accepted language, or else from Austria. The Austrians had always been conspicuously friendly to Danes, and the tradition seemed to be maintained. The German supreme command issued a number of guidelines to the troops.

These indicated that seeking to educate the Danes in the tenets of National Socialism was a waste of time. The troops were told:

The Dane is freedom-loving and self-reliant. He has no idea of military discipline and authority.

Therefore: Give few orders, don't shout. It arouses in him a desire for opposition and is useless. Explain clearly and convince him. A humorous tone proves most effective. Unnecessary severity is wounding to self-respect and must be avoided.

The Dane loves a homely, comfortable existence. He may be won over by friendliness, small attentions and personal recognition.

The Danish businessman has a leaning to England. He abhors wars. Of Germany's National Socialist aims there is, except in a very few instances, no understanding.

Therefore avoid political discussions. The German language is understood by many Danes.

This document caused a certain amusement among a naturally humorous people. Yet another, entitled *Manual of Instruction in the Danish Language* also had its comic side:

Be so kind as to direct me to the mayor of the city.

'Good day, Mr Mayor! Will you show me the municipal cash box?

'If you do not hand over the cash box willingly, Mr Mayor, you will be shot.'

The tactics of Danish resistance in the early months of Nazi occupation were deceptively mild, ranging from gentle ridicule to studied indifference.

At first, the Germans were slow to get the message. An eager band of German musicians, smiling like young puppies desperately anxious to be liked, turned up to play in one of Copenhagen's main squares. The trouble was that their arrival always seemed to coincide with a parade of the Danish Guard, who insisted on playing loudly in the square since it was on the customary route to the royal palace.

Crowds became expert at turning up initially to hear the Germans, then teasingly peeling off to follow the Danes. Sten Gudme reported: 'There is always an empty space gaping in front of the German military bands when they turn up to play. It is a little ray of brightness in a hard and wretched year.'

Those who encountered their German conquerors on the streets were prepared to be polite, or even friendly. But a close look at shoulder lapels told a rather different story. Danes had taken to wearing a variety of buttonhole badges. These could consist of the king's portrait, the Danish flag, the Union Jack, the colours of the RAF or, most tellingly of all, the initials DKS.

They stood for *Den Kolde Skulder* (the cold shoulder).

News of DKS filtered through to London, and *The Times* reported: 'To the Danes belongs the credit of inventing a new order, unthought of by Hitler – the Order of the Cold Shoulder . . . and it expresses the feelings towards the Germans of about 90 per cent of the Danish population.'

Overtures of friendship were at first accepted, then spurned. The Germans, that summer of occupation, set up an academy for their own scientists and prominent Danish ones. It seemed a harmless form of collaboration;

the National Museum of Copenhagen received the German organisers civilly enough. Minister Renthe-Fink was installed to make the necessary arrangements.

He strode out smilingly to greet the guests for the opening ceremony. He did not smile for long. The Danish flag was ostentatiously flown at half-mast. In vain, museum officials were berated. Blandly, someone pointed out that one of the museum's oldest and most distinguished officials had died that morning. Surely the minister would not approve of any lack of respect?

The ceremony proceeded. Observers noted that Herr Renthe-Fink's smile looked as if it had been nailed on.

It was good fun, this German-baiting. Good fun for schoolboys in Elsinore who, when the Wehrmacht marched through the narrow streets singing '*Wir fahren gegen Engelland*' (We're marching against England), riposted with '*It's a Long Way to Tipperary*'.

But the humour, even for the naturally humorous Danes, had an air of desperation. On the surface, life did not seem too bad under the shadow of the jackboot. But elsewhere in the west the Wehrmacht and the SS prepared to scythe through Europe with the slash of iron.

3

That fatal 9 April had turned out cold and cheerless in Norway. Even so, the husky blond man with the bulging eyes and the shiny blue suit had spent most of the day sweating. He had to wait until evening before he could reach the studios of the Oslo broadcasting station and deliver his bombshell.

In a hoarse, guttural voice he proclaimed from the hastily scrawled text: 'Norwegian men and women! England has violated the neutrality of Norway by laying mines in Norwegian territorial waters . . . The German government has offered the Norwegian government its help, accompanied by a solemn assurance respecting our national independence and Norwegian lives and property.'

Norwegians were urged to desist from further resistance; furthermore, Vidkun Quisling informed his listeners that he had 'deposed' the country's legal government and now presented himself as the Prime Minister of Norway.

He continued: 'All Norwegians are hereby called upon to keep the peace of the realm and to preserve their presence of mind in this difficult situation. By united exertions and the goodwill of all, we will bring Norway free and safe through this serious crisis.'

Hitherto, the language had been bland. But now came the clear threat: 'I add that resistance is not merely useless in the situation which has now developed but directly synonymous with criminal destruction of life and property. Every official and every municipal employee . . . is in duty bound to obey orders from the new National Government. Any deviation from this will involve the utmost personal responsibility on the part of the offender and will be proceeded against according to the principles of justice and with the same consideration towards all citizens.'

With this single address, Major Vidkun Abraham Lauritz Jonsson Quisling made his mark on history; the epithet 'quisling' was given to collaborators throughout all the countries of occupied Europe.

But that lay in the future. Right now, Quisling sensed the whiff of power which he considered to be within the gift of his Nazi masters.

The man's background was respectable enough. He sprang from good solid yeoman stock in Fyresdal, a scattered village in the mountains of Telemark in southwest Norway. The family had been respected as pastors, farmers and professional men for six centuries.

He graduated first in his class at the Norwegian Military Academy and in his early twenties was posted to Petrograd as military attaché. The Russian Revolution of 1917 loomed; Quisling's sympathies then were pro-Bolshevik. Back home in Oslo he offered his services to the Labour Party, at that time a Comintern member.

His offer to set up a 'Red Guard' was spurned. Very well, he would form a party of his own. There was an ideal model to hand. In 1933, Adolf Hitler had come to power in Germany, his strident nationalism bolstered by strong-armed SS lieutenants within the National Socialist Party.

Quisling, with Hitler as inspiration, set about fashioning the Nasjonal Samling – the party of National Unity. But a bid to enter candidates in the Storting (the Norwegian parliament) turned out to be a humiliating failure. Only a scant two per cent of the votes cast went Quisling's way; even with Norway's system of proportional representation, he failed to place a single one of his followers in the Storting.

In a general election, Quisling stormed the country in a car built like a tank and equipped with a loud speaker.

Incensed voters, not caring for his particular brand of nationalism, broke up his meetings, clashing in the streets with the bullyboys of the Hird, Quisling's answer to the stormtroopers of Munich and Berlin.

By 1937, support had dwindled to a mere shadow. The figures were grotesque: in the local elections, fifteen-one-hundredths of one per cent of the votes cast in rural districts and six-one-hundredths of one per cent of those cast in towns. The Nasjonal Samling had become a thoroughly bad joke.

But in Nazi Germany no one laughed.

It was true that Hitler did not like rival fascist organisations on his doorstep; the mere whisper of challenge to his authority made him uncomfortable. But the Fuehrer had his own special plans for Norway. Quisling, the faintly ridiculous little man who looked like a provincial shopkeeper, was too important a potential ally to be disregarded.

Nazi Germany began courting Vidkun Quisling.

For the role of chief suitor, Hitler assigned Estonian-born shoemaker's son Alfred Rosenberg, who combined being adviser to the Fuehrer on foreign policy with an industrious, all-consuming hatred of Jews and Bolsheviks.

One of Rosenberg's racial fixations was particularly attractive to Vidkun Quisling. He dreamed of the establishment of a great Nordic empire which would exclude the Jews and other 'impure' races. Rosenberg, firmly in the grip of his fantasies, bombarded the Norwegian with Nazi propaganda and weighty philosophical treatises.

Rosenberg found his overtures falling on sympathetic ears. He sent an enthusiastic memo to Hitler: 'Of all the political groupings in Scandinavia only Nasjonal Samling, led by Vidkun Quisling, deserves serious attention.'

Mutual admiration was all very well. But Quisling was after a great deal more.

Reports had been reaching him from contacts in London that there were British fears that the Soviet Union, having attacked and subjugated Finland, might move into Sweden and Norway. Furthermore, there was a case for cutting off those vital iron ore supplies to Germany. There could therefore be no delay – Germany must occupy Norway.

Quisling told Rosenberg confidently: 'I have many supporters among top officers in the Norwegian Army.' Anxious to press his advantage, he outlined a bold plan which amounted to nothing less than staging a coup within Norway. He proposed that a number of hand-picked Hird members should be hurriedly trained in the Reich under the command of 'experienced and diehard National Socialists who are practised in such operations'.

The stormtroopers, safely back in Norway, would seize some of Oslo's strategic points. At the same time, the German Navy, with contingents of the German Army, would be on hand at a selected bay outside Oslo to answer a special summons from the new Norwegian government, of which Quisling, naturally, would be Prime Minister.

It was all very well, however, working out paper schemes. They would prove a waste of time if they did not find favour with Hitler. And they did not. The Fuehrer was in a cautious mood. Two interviews with the German Chancellor brought Quisling something decidedly less dramatic than a blessing for a coup: the leader of the Norwegian fascists would be provided with funds to combat British propaganda and strengthen his own pro-German movement.

Rosenberg also preferred to proceed by stealth. A special agent, Hans Wilhelm Scheidt, was assigned to Norway to work with Quisling. A small security-screened knot of officers of the Oberkommando der Wehrmacht (OKW) began work on what at first was called Study North.

The project's name was later changed to *Weseruebung* (Weser Exercise).

Hitler's summons went out on 21 February to the commander of 21st Corps, General der Infantrie Nicholas von Falkenhorst, a professional, nonpolitical soldier who had earned his spurs in the assault on Poland a year before.

Hitler fixed 9 April for the attack. It was a formidable

29

proposition. Norway's terrain was heavily mountainous. The internal communications were poor, which did not augur well for a rapid advance. A study of the country's history, however, put Hitler in a more cheerful frame of mind.

It was true that Norwegians had fought bitter border wars against the Swedes, but that was back in 1814. In the remaining years of the nineteenth century, the country had gone soft and antimilitaristic. In the 1930s, with Norway crippled with economic depression, sympathy for what was regarded as a stuffy military caste sank still further. There would, the Fuehrer was convinced, be little military resistance in 1940.

For an invasion fleet, however, it was a different matter; there was the very real threat of interception and destruction by heavier units of the Royal Navy. Strictly in terms of strength, Britain had the power to crush the German invasion even before the first Wehrmacht soldier set foot in Norway.

The first battle was, inevitably, a sea engagement between British and German fleets. In the balance hung the fate of Norway.

Narvik is an attractive town, sitting in a stubby peninsula flanked by the waters of two fjords. It is also the port and railhead to receive essential iron ore from Sweden. Elderly Konrad Sundlo, a Quisling sympathiser in command of the local garrison, faced an impossible situation.

Norwegian units had been charged to resist any invasion to the last bullet, but bad training, poor leadership and weak morale had left them with little stomach to fight. Sundlo had only 400 troops to man the town's perimeters and the key machine-gun and antiaircraft emplacements. The harbour itself was doomed when torpedoes smashed into the hull of the defending ship *Eidsvold*. It had split in two and sank immediately. Then German destroyers moved into Narvik's inner harbour. The *Eidsvold's* sister ship, *Norge*, opened fire; it was quickly sent to the bottom by torpedo attack.

Generalleutnant Eduard Dietl, a Bavarian crony of Hitler since the early brawling Brownshirt days, was able to walk ashore unopposed after he and his men tied up their launches along Narvik's waterfront.

His greeting to Colonel Sundlo was cordial. Admission of honourable defeat, he argued, was the only course. What would be the point of further bloodshed? After all, the rest of Norway were welcoming German troops as friends and protectors.

The last statement was patently a gigantic bluff, but it made Sundlo hesitate. Certainly, his orders had been plain enough: the Norwegian High Command had ordered him to fight and throw the Nazis into the sea. But now he hesitated. The situation had, after all, changed. Germans seemed to be ashore and digging in.

Eventually, he capitulated, saying: 'I hand over the town.' Not a shot at that stage had been fired. But, as it turned out, Germany's hold on Narvik was precarious; the British counterattacked fiercely later.

As early as noon, five principal Norwegian cities and ports and the big airfield along the west and south coasts – which run for 1,500 miles from the Skagerrak to the Arctic – were in German hands.

It was idle to pretend that the supremely successful invasion of Norway had not been a remarkable triumph for German arms. Hitler was ecstatic, proclaiming: 'The campaign was not only bold, but one of the sauciest undertakings in the history of warfare.'

In dizzy euphoria, the Nazi warlord instructed that Quisling was to receive full support and, in all negotiations with Norway's King Haakon, he was to remain the country's Prime Minister.

As for the capital, its inhabitants read in the newspaper of heavy fighting in the Oslo fjord. German aircraft streaked over the city at agonisingly low level. Plainly, Oslo was going to be blitzed. The population were told on the radio to evacuate forthwith.

The Dutch newspaper *Nieuwe Rotterdamsche Courant* reported:

At the entrance to the underground the people were struggling madly to get down into the tunnel; there are no other public shelters in Oslo. Some people sought shelter in the park near the Palace, all were distracted with fear, dismay and doubt. Others, again, fled or tried to flee from the town, trundling prams, on trucks, storming the stations, where every bit of rolling stock was loaded to the limit and sent away from the town, to the country.

Oslo fell to little more than a phantom German force dropped from the air at the local undefended airport.

Despite Hitler's endorsement, Vidkun Quisling was not altogether happy. By no means was he favoured by everyone in the Third Reich. He was known to be Rosenberg's man, and the party 'philosopher' had plenty of enemies within the Nazi hierarchy. There was a very real risk that Hitler could be persuaded to change his mind over the appointment.

It galled Quisling that his Nazi friends had not seen fit to give him advance notice of the invasion. But the important thing was that Hitler was firmly in control. He decided to take a look at the situation in Oslo. At the War Office, some old army cronies received him warmly. Encouraged, he moved on to the offices of his own Nasjonal Samling party. There things were even more promising: assurances were received that Germany would be delighted if Quisling, as saviour of Norway, was to form his own government.

It was enough encouragement. The radio address to the Norwegian people was drafted hastily. Its effect was nothing less than devastating. The supreme failure among the country's politicians, a man popularly regarded as a pompous windbag given to ludicrous nationalist vapourings, was taking upon himself the mantle of dictatorship. To the Norwegians, the very idea was as grotesque as it was shaming. They were not alone in regarding Quisling's new role with dismay. The German Foreign Ministry representative in Oslo, Dr Curt Brauer, a punctilious, old-fashioned diplomat, was in a painful quandary. Quisling, a man apparently without popular support, was the self-proclaimed Prime Minister of Norway. But what was to be done about the previous Premier, Johan Nygaardsvold? The only way of solving the matter, Brauer reasoned, was to discuss it around a table in the approved manner. A call was put through to Quisling's secretary, suggesting a meeting in Brauer's office.

Quisling now showed his greatest weaknesses; rank arrogance and a lack of tact. In a sudden flush of anger, he snapped at his secretary: 'Tell the German Minister that if he wishes to see the Norwegian Prime Minister he must call on me.'

Brauer obeyed meekly enough. He found Quisling and his underlings comfortably installed in the luxurious Continental Hotel. Quisling's effect on the veteran German diplomat was electric. Brauer, for once abandoning the niceties of diplomacy, rang German Foreign Minister Joachim von Ribbentrop in Berlin.

There was no mincing of words. Brauer reported: 'The man is incompetent, has no political sense – and, far worse no support!'

Ribbentrop's first reaction was delight. Here was a golden opportunity to score off Rosenberg, whom he detested. Even so, it would not do to disown Quisling without Hitler's blessing.

To Ribbentrop's dismay, Hitler, still flushed with the success of his engagement in Norway, would have none of it. All reservations were brushed aside and Hitler demanded: 'Why not Quisling?'

Further support from Ribbentrop was now out of the question. The Foreign Minister was Hitler's mouthpiece; if the Fuehrer said so, then of course Quisling must stay. Brauer reflected bitterly that he might just as well have held his breath.

Quisling, with his bumptious conceit, had previously been bad enough. Now he became intolerable. Flanked by his supporters he descended on the Storting building, demanding that the German troops occupying it should move out; space was needed for the new Norwegian government. As a move, it could scarcely have been more tactless. The swastika had already been raised over the building, and Hitler's bust reposed in the front entrance. The Germans were plainly the masters.

Quisling's little group was studiously ignored; the self-proclaimed Prime Minister stalked off in a huff. Consolation came from a whirlwind of activity as he set up a series of meetings with Norwegian businessmen, trade union leaders and public officials.

In vain, Quisling tried to interest them in the merits of a Nasjonal Samling government with, naturally, himself as the head. Everywhere he met rebuff and ridicule and, most serious of all, downright hostility from the army he had tried so assiduously to court.

King Haakon, who had fled from Oslo and was with his ministers outside Elverum, to the northeast, flatly refused the German demand for capitulation and his return to Oslo under a government led by Quisling. The alternative had been spelt out brutally. The weight of the mighty Wehrmacht would crush the face of Norway.

Haakon was deaf to threats and he proclaimed: '. . . I find that I cannot appoint Quisling Prime Minister, a man I do not know and in whom neither the people nor its representatives, the Storting, have any confidence at all.'

Quisling's reaction was to go ahead and announce a cabinet. His reward was a blunt judgement by General-major Bruno Uthman, German military attaché in Oslo:

'Quisling's proposed cabinet is a gangster government. Quisling is nothing more than a common criminal.'

Berlin had its first nagging doubts, and took a fresh look at the Nasjonal Samling party. It was soon discovered that Quisling's much vaunted movement could boast no members in parliament and drew such support as it had from malcontents with ill-defined dreams of a European new order. Moreover, a heavy percentage of supporters were still at school.

Frantically, Quisling tried to repair the damage. But it was too late. Hitler had been brought to realise that such an obviously detested ally would do Germany's standing no good at all. The Third Reich, it would be thought, had been duped all too easily by a charlatan.

After only six days as Prime Minister of Norway, Vidkun Quisling was sacked by his German masters. And, furthermore, sacked unceremoniously. The comfortable life at the Continental Hotel was over. Quisling's hefty bulk and outraged dignity found themselves literally dumped on the pavement, along with his Nasjonal Samling supporters.

Curt Brauer was not normally a vindictive man, but he relished offering a new job to Quisling by way of a sop. The post of Commissioner of Demobilisation was completely meaningless.

A wave of relief swept through Norway. But for Adolf Hitler, there was a fresh problem: there was now no Norwegian government with which to deal. It seemed a case for rather more drastic measures of the kind traditionally associated with the Third Reich.

As for Quisling, he was very far from regarding himself as a spent force. He skulked hopefully in the wings.

4

Josef Terboven was a tall, slim individual who in his youth had worn his hair slicked back to look like Rudolf Valentino.

This former bank clerk, whose job in Germany had been swept away in the economic blizzard of the 1920s, was a consummate main-chancer. He wangled an introduction to one of the country's most prominent industrialists, Emil Kirdorf, who in turn was courted by Hitler and the Nazis.

Kirdorf saw the personable Terboven as a likely front man to persuade the country's big-business brains to support the National Socialists. Funds for the purpose, some supplied by Kirdorf himself and the rest by a coal mine owner's wealthy widow who was also Terboven's mistress, suddenly ceased to be a problem.

Otto Strasser, editor of the newspaper *Berliner Arbeiterzeitung*, and one of Hitler's earliest allies, wrote of Terboven with a distinct trace of envy: 'I remember him as a rather hard-working party member who seemed to have a good deal of spending money on his person at all times. Since most of our members were poor, his frequent small gifts to them were not without effect – and at the first election he was voted leader of the Essen district. From this new position as one of the leaders in the Nazi party, Terboven did much to bring Hitler and the industrialists together.'

Before he became Gauleiter for Essen, Terboven had been appointed to the Prussian State Council and elected to the Reichstag as a National Socialist Deputy.

But Terboven wanted more than that. As was his wont,

he began cultivating senior influential figures, this time within Ribbentrop's ministry. Before long, Ribbentrop came to regard him as his protégé and set about finding him a suitable job.

This time there would be no nonsense from Rosenberg and his cronies. Terboven's brief was terse: 'The Fuehrer wants you to knock Norway into shape.'

Josef Terboven saw no reason why this process should not be carried out in the most comfortable circumstances possible. The money from Emil Kirdorf and his former mistress had given him a taste for the good things of life. He saw his new job in terms of a viceroyalty; what could be more natural than having his living quarters as Reichskommissar in the king's summer palace, with his working offices in the Norwegian parliamentary building?

The title of Reichskommissar signified that Terboven enjoyed the full backing both of the German state and the Nazi party. He lost no time in exercising his power to the full.

As in Denmark, the press was soon receiving a slap from the iron fist.

The existing staff of the Norwegian Telegraph Bureau, the agency which handled news from abroad, was summarily dismissed and replaced by Nazi journalists.

The guidelines for newspapers were rigid: there were to be no reports of German losses or British victories. Speeches by the king or members of the previous government were to go unreported. Foreign news was to be commented upon in a 'German spirit'; economic matters must be reported in 'progressive' terms, and there was to be much talk of 'improved conditions'.

It was time for the next step. On 14 June 1940, Terboven summoned representatives of the major Norwegian political parties to his office.

There the Reichskommissar proclaimed: 'A government must be formed that is sympathetic to Germany.' This seemed, at first, mild language to describe the proposed imposition of a puppet administration. But soon Terboven was shedding mildness for belligerence. He snapped: 'If Norwegians are not cooperative, then Germany will impose a government of commissars who will rush at you like bulls.'

Most of those who had to deal directly with the Reich-skommissar had already judged him pompous and humourless. Now he was shown to be brutal as well.

Furthermore, he was just getting into his stride. It was the monarchy's turn next.

It was true that King Haakon and his government were in exile in England, but the continued existence of a royal house, even one in limbo, was an irritating reminder of the old order. It could not be tolerated.

Within a week, the newly established Riksrad (State Council) had decreed that the previous government of Prime Minister Johan Nygaardsvold could no longer be regarded as in power. The decree added: 'As the king is resident outside the frontiers of the country, he is unable to exert his constititional function.'

It was a touchpaper for resistance.

First to catch the mood was King Haakon himself. Although he was now resident in England, he had been able to follow every twist and turn of the negotiations, thanks to sympathetic channels in the Swedish capital. Then came the demand from the Riksrad for the king to abdicate 'in consideration of the welfare of the nation and the future of the country'.

The response was swift. Over the BBC from London, the king stated: 'If I was persuaded that at this time I could serve best by abdicating, or if I was certain that at the back of the request stood a majority of the Norwegian people, I would, deeply as it would hurt me to separate myself from Norway, grant the request you present me.'

Then came the sting in the tail for the conqueror. The request, said the king, had been drafted under pressure from a foreign power and was therefore unconstitutional.

The press – Terboven's press – were forbidden to print

the text of the king's reply. Instead, there was condemnation: Haakon had failed his country in the hour of need.

Although there seemed to be no concerted campaign, the mood of anti-German defiance smouldered. Those with radios who had heard the king's message passed it on to their neighbours. It spread through cafés and bars and, by some bizarre quirk, gave a new lease of life to a game which had been highly popular in Norway a whole decade earlier – the sending of chain letters. It was the perfect method for mobilising opposition to any suggestion of collaboration. One such letter began:

Thou shalt obey King Haakon . . . thou shalt detest Hitler . . . thou shalt regard as a traitor every Norwegian who keeps company with Germans or Quislings at home . . . thou shalt despise treason and remember that its punishment is death.

Hatred was reserved particularly for Quisling's Nasjonal Samling party. Although Quisling was not now in the government, he remained a figurehead whom Hitler could not entirely bring himself to disown. The fascist-style party remained in existence; along with a strong, ruthless Gestapo and 330,000 German troops, it was a handy tool of repression.

Terboven's twin attack on monarchy and the political parties was quickly followed by moves against the clergy of the established Lutheran church. The order went out that the Norwegian state radio was to lard its regular religious programmes with 'sympathetic sermons' and talks by the clergy friendly to the regime. The confessional meetings of the Lutherans were protected by rigid privacy. Plainly, such heresy could not be permitted. Terboven moved to abolish this tradition. Any priest who rebelled against the edict would be imprisoned.

There were a number of clerics who bowed to the pressure, if only to the extent of praising Quisling at the start of their sermons and then blithely ignoring the Nazi threat. But this latest edict by Terboven was something different. January 1941 opened with a protest by the Lutheran bishops, who cited acts of terrorism by the Gestapo and Quisling's Hird.

It was no mere outburst of moral indignation. The bishops went into details. There had been an incident of Hird youths smashing their way into the Oslo school of business and beating up teachers and students with fists and clubs.

A sixteen-year-old Oslo youth had dared to appear on the streets sporting a paperclip in his lapel – the adopted symbol of Norway's solidarity against oppression. He had been hauled off to the Hird cellars, where he was stripped and lashed.

And there had been the case of the head of a students' organisation in Trondheim who had dared to refuse to post placards for the Nasjonal Samling party. The result was a sound beating.

The focus of hatred became Oslo university, where groups of dissenting students meeting in their favourite cafés ran the gauntlet of hustling and catcalls.

Students who forcibly ejected the Hird bullyboys were not allowed to enjoy their minor victory for long. The troublemakers, their uniform brown shirts torn to shreds, staged a march on University Square off Karl Johan Street, near the National Theatre and the main clutch of university buildings.

At first, the students watched the procession in contemptuous silence. Then came the sharp order in German: 'Attack!' The marchers tore into the crowd. Shoulder belts were removed, blackjacks swung. The students were all at once fuelled with a fury that overcame the vicious lashing from the blackjacks. They fought back and, within minutes, a number of Hird lay stunned and bleeding on the pavement.

Nor were the students the only defenders. It was early evening; the rush-hour was at its height and the opportunity for a scrap proved irresistible. Workers joined in with gusto, fists flying. The pent-up fury showed no signs of abating as a posse of police tumbled into the square.

To the astonishment of the students, the police made no attempt to protect them; instead, they formed a protective circle around the Quislings, who were swiftly marched out of the square.

There was a final insult to the decamping Nasjonal Samling members, when they broke into the Norwegian national anthem. The sound was soon drowned by one vast jeer from the crowd, rising into a roar.

After that, there was nothing the disconsolate students could do beyond dispersing.

But by the dawn of Norway's second spring of occupation it was clear that a new spirit stalked abroad. Throughout the country, a rash of duplicated leaflets appeared on city and village streets and in letter boxes. They were thrust into the pockets of workers on their way to work in trains and buses.

The forces of resistance were determined that the anniversary of German conquest was not to be forgotten.

The leaflets read:

Norwegians! On 9 April you must devote a full half-hour from 2 to 2.30 p.m. to thoughts about the fall of Norway. Spend this half-hour in your homes. Let not a single person appear at that hour in street, restaurant, store or any other public place. Surround with hatred and contempt those who would dare to disturb this half-hour vow of silence and thereby desecrate the memory of our fallen fighters.

The half-hour of silence was by no means the only form of passive resistance, even though the leaflets continued to pass from hand to hand, multiplied on typewriters and duplicators.

Germans who used trams in Oslo made the journey alone. As if in response to a single order, passengers stood up and left at the first available stop.

The Communist paper, *Ny Dag*, published in Sweden, proclaimed:

Persons who join Quisling's party are immediately cut off from

41

their friends as if by a magic rod, and they are everywhere met by unconcealed hatred and contempt. So great is the popular hatred for the stormtroopers that the latter hesitate to venture on to the street except in compact groups.

Such defiance, although a puny affair compared to what was to develop later, threw Josef Terboven into a paroxysm of fury. His anger only intensified the opposition. Terboven felt that some public and civic workers might be promising recruiting material. After all, this was the group that still had to run the country, and some form of cooperation might reasonably be expected. Most of these people presumably wished to go on doing their jobs.

But even here there was little comfort for the Reichskommissar. A special bureau set up to check political attitudes among civil servants produced a clear slap in the face – twenty-two organisations protested against Nazi enslavement.

Such form of anti-Nazi solidarity was bad enough. What was far worse was that the text of their protest was broadcast from London by the BBC even before it had reached Terboven's desk.

Now fury was replaced by something like fear. He knew that unless there was action, Berlin would step in and the palmy days of the viceroyalty would come to an abrupt and bloody end.

Gestapo agents instituted a dragnet, swooping down on the homes of dissidents. Those lucky enough not to disappear into Gestapo headquarters in Oslo were marched at short notice to the parliament building and treated to a harangue, while German guards, armed to the teeth, lined the walls. There were more arrests; those known dissidents who were left at liberty were warned 'not to create trouble'.

But all this, Terboven realised, was mere tinkering with the problem. Something far more dramatic was needed.

Meanwhile, the resistance organisations would be deliberately lulled into a false sense of security.

Far worse was to come.

5

An isolated corner of Rodert, near Muenstereifel, some forty miles southwest of Bonn, was a gloomy barely accessible spot, distinguished at the outbreak of war only by a knot of troop huts and antiaircraft gun emplacements.

Military maps at first designated the spot as 'Installation R' and then, equally anonymously, 'Installation F'. The final name, however, was to carry a suggestion of Wagnerian melodrama. As a tightly secure military headquarters for Adolf Hitler, this gloomy spot became known as '*Felsennest*' (Rock Nest).

At dawn on 10 May 1940, Hitler, flanked by his closest military confidants, strode to his own personal quarters, which consisted of a tiny bunker with one office, one bedroom, a few small rooms for aides and a kitchen and bathroom.

An air of tension had gripped *Felsennest* days before. A codename for the Fuehrer's arrival had been arranged: 'Whitsuntide leave approved'. It meant that Hitler's special train had arrived at Euskirchen station, where it would be met by the headquarters motor convoy.

At 4.38 p.m. on the day of departure the train pulled out of Berlin. A Fuehrer-Begleit-Bataillon (escort battalion) marshalled under cover near Euskirchen station shortly before 1 a.m. moving out to the square in front at 4.25 a.m. – the exact moment of Hitler's arrival. Five minutes later, the party was on its way to *Felsennest*. By 5 a.m. the Fuehrer was touring the entire installation, his keen eyes taking in every detail.

It is reasonable to hazard, however, that at least part of his mind was elsewhere. The codename *Danzig* had been flashed to all posts; at 5.35 a.m. on 10 May 1940, the German armies attacked in the west. A mere twenty-five miles away, the awesome machine of the Wehrmacht hurried over the Belgian frontier.

Along a front of 175 miles, from the North Sea to the Maginot Line, Nazi troops smashed across the borders of three small neutral states: the Netherlands, Belgium and Luxembourg.

Three days before, General der Artillerie Alfred Jodl, chief operations officer of OKW (Oberkommando der Wehrmacht) had written in his diary that Hitler, who had previously postponed the attack because of uncertain weather, had consented 'to postponement until 10 May, which he says is against his intuition. But not one day longer . . .'

Part of Hitler's anxieties, Jodl revealed, had been due to alarming reports from the Netherlands. News had filtered through of leave cancellations, evacuations, roadblocks and various forms of mobilisation.

As it turned out, there had been no need to worry.

Hitler had been able to spare only one division of panzers for the conquest of the Netherlands. But it had been buttressed to deadly effect by parachutists and troops landing behind flooded water lines which cautious souls in Berlin had believed would hold up the Germans for weeks.

The campaign in the Netherlands carried the distinction of being the first large-scale airborne attack in the history of warfare.

The aim of the Germans was the same as in Norway – seize the capital, together with monarch and government. But now there was a stumbling block: Dutch infantry, supported by artillery, ejected two German regiments from the airfields encircling The Hague. This certainly took the pressure off the capital, but it meant a severe haemorrhaging of reserve troops.

General der Artillerie Georg von Kuechler's 18th Army

had a formidable task. The drive from the German border was nearly a hundred miles and meant crossing bridges over two estuaries at Dordrecht and Moerdijk.

But first the bridges had to be seized. Airborne units – including one company landing on the river at Rotterdam in antiquated seaplanes – swooped down on the bridges before their Dutch defenders realised what had happened. Units were hastily improvised; for a time it looked as if the invaders were getting the worst of it. The Germans held on with the tenacity of a razor-fanged dog. All depended on one armoured division promised to Kuechler and which even now was smashing through the Grebbe-Feel Line, a fortified front to the east where there were a number of water barriers.

The Dutch pinned hope on French 7th Army, under General Henri Giraud, which had raced up from the Channel and reached Tilburg on the afternoon of 11 May. The Germans, however, luxuriated in air support and sophisticated armour; Giraud was pushed back. German 9th Panzer Division plugged the gap. Its forces poured across the bridges at Moerdijk and Dordrecht, arriving at the Bieuwe Maas across from Rotterdam. And, there, the German airborne forces held the bridges.

But the defence of Rotterdam held tenaciously. In The Hague, to the northwest, airborne forces were getting a bloody nose. With ill-concealed impatience, Hitler issued Directive No. 11: 'The power of resistance of the Dutch Army has proved to be stronger than was anticipated. Political as well as military considerations require that the resistance be broken *speedily*.'

A swift order was issued. Detachments of the Luftwaffe would be snatched from the 6th Army front in Belgium 'to facilitate the rapid conquest of Fortress Holland'.

Hitler went on to be even more specific: Rotterdam was to be obliterated as Warsaw had been during the Polish campaign of the previous year.

Rotterdam had been looking forward to 1940, but the expectation had nothing whatever to do with the Germans. Precisely 600 years before, the port had been granted its city rights, and it had been in a mood to celebrate. The Dutch are not generally associated with vivacity; Rotterdam is an exception, with crowded cinemas, theatres and nightclubs, the little waterfront cafés known to sailors the world over, added to the sights and smells of a rich and vital city.

On a bright summer's day the Germans set out to murder it.

A German staff officer from 39th Corps crossed the bridge at Rotterdam under a white flag and with a demand for the surrender of the city. Unless there was capitulation it would be bombed. The raid began as negotiations were under way.

For years, the Rotterdam raid was hailed as representing Nazi wantonness and terrorism at its worse. Yet, after the war, the tragedy was revealed as a direct result of confusion and error. Dutch commander Peter Scharoo protested to his German opposite number, General der Panzer Truppen Rudolf Schmidt, that the Nazi ultimatum carried no proper signature. Schmidt obliged willingly enough. But vital time was lost; the German's order to delay the raid disappeared along the chain of command. Schmidt had given Scharoo until 4.20 p.m. to surrender, but at three o'clock, the 100 Heinkel HE IIIs, the glazed-nose standard-level bombers of the Luftwaffe, were in the air. The pilots carried clear instructions that the mission was to be aborted if red Very lights were shot over Noorder Island.

Certainly General Schmidt had no stomach for the bombing of Rotterdam. Within minutes of his signing the ultimatum with his name and rank and the addition of *Kommandierender General eines Armee-Korps* (Commanding General of an Army Corps), the bombers roared in.

Schmidt cried out in horror: 'God Almighty! What will happen? It will be another Warsaw.'

And all at once he was acting like a man possessed, screaming for the Very lights to shoot into the air. Then he was frantically clawing at some bales of white cotton hastily seized from a department store and unfurled in the street.

But it was too late, far too late.

The leader of the German bomber wave which was approaching from the south spotted the Very lights and veered away. But the first three aircraft had already relinquished their lethal cargoes. The greater part of the bombing force proceeded with their mission. People fled to the cellars or flung themselves down on street pavements.

The howl of the sirens cut through the warning drone of the bombers, then there was the scream of falling explosives.

Water mains were fractured, gas pipes, the power network and the telephone system were annihilated. In one cellar under a small shop at the Oostplein more than thirty men, women and children were jammed so tightly that when the rear of the cellar was hit by a bomb, even those who had survived were powerless to help the wounded; their groaning was punctuated by the sound of still further explosions.

It was conceivable that fire appliances might have got through – but for the fact that the brigade building itself was a charred ruin. The efforts of individual firemen were valiant but hopeless. Splinters of burning wood and sparks drifted into the air. They set fire to curtains waving in the wind through shattered windows.

And there was the added cruelty of a strong west wind, which was soon spreading the flames like a whirlwind.

For the people of Rotterdam there were terrors beyond imagining. In front of one house, six corpses were scattered over the pavement like rag dolls. They consisted of an entire family. In another ruin, a small boy's head hung down, clamped between fallen beams; he had not been able to free himself. Elsewhere, a child's hand protruded from the rubble. Witnesses spoke of seeing a body plastered against the surface of a door, while another hung from a window.

There was a butcher who had sought shelter in his refrigerator, and three women who had taken refuge in a vault. The doors had buckled and they had all suffocated. Those who survived confronted fresh horrors. In a cellar beneath a shop at Oostplein the stairs had been cleared of larger debris. Something soft was encountered: the squashed head of a young girl.

At Bremen, the aircraft were loaded for a second strike. It never happened; Rotterdam surrendered and the aircraft were recalled.

For years after the war, it was believed that 30,000 people had perished in the raid. Total casualties were in fact around 900. But there were other statistics to spell out the tragedy: several thousand injured, 78,000 made homeless. Twenty-one churches and four hospitals were destroyed. Rotterdam surrendered, and then the Dutch armed forces. Queen Wilhelmina and government ministers had fled to London.

There was now an added threat. Utrecht, the Germans said, would share the same fate as Rotterdam. But the destruction of a second large city was more than General Hentl Winkelman could stomach. At 4.50 p.m. he issued the order to all commanding officers:

Germany has bombed Rotterdam today, and Utrecht is threatened with destruction. To save the civilian population and prevent further bloodshed, I believe it to be justified to order the troops under your command to stop fighting.

If the bombing of Rotterdam had indeed been due to an administrative muddle, that, predictably enough, was not something that OKW was prepared to admit. On 14 May, the German radio issued a special communiqué:

Under the tremendous impression of the attacks of German dive bombers and the imminent attack of German tanks, the city of Rotterdam has capitulated and thus saved itself from destruction.

49

The visitor to Rotterdam today will scarcely be able to ignore the powerful sculpture by Zakine which is called 'Destroyed City'. It is a powerful, jagged work, showing the figure of a man extending powerful arms to clutch at the sky as a symbol of defiance. But it is not just this affirmation of survival which strikes the spectator. For the stomach of Zakine's figure has been ripped out: the heart of a city raped and vandalised.

The surrender signed by Winkelman and Kuechler virtually ended the fighting in the Netherlands, which had lasted just five days.

The occupation of the Netherlands, however, was to last five years.

6

The freedom of the Dutch was slowly chipped away. On the surface, at least, little seemed to change during the first few months of occupation. Newspapers continued to appear. Amsterdam's main newspaper, *De Telegraaf*, was slow to change, except for the prominently displayed exchange rate between the Reichsmark and the Dutch guilder.

Neither, at first, was there undue worry at the appointment of Dr Arthur Seyss-Inquart as Reichskommissar for Occupied Holland.

It seemed hard to equate this mild, bespectacled young Viennese lawyer with what was known of the worst of the Nazi excesses. His manner was pleasant and cordial; he was known to be a diligent churchgoer, his service in World War One in a Tyrolean Kaiserjaeger regiment had been exemplary. The fact that he was Austrian was deemed the most favourable portent of all; the Austrians were noted, after all, for Tyrolean yodelling and the Strauss family. Plainly, there was nothing to be afraid of here.

Reaction might have been rather different if the Dutch people had known that Seyss-Inquart, as Reichstaffhalter (governor) of Nazi-occupied Austria, had made a speech urging the Austrians to respect the swastika, sacred symbol of the Third Reich.

More ominous were Seyss-Inquart's remarks at the time of Hitler's incursion into Austria in 1938:

We do not wish to plunge Jewish human beings and Jewish families into any material misfortune. In following our unchange-

51

able course, we neither wish nor enjoy individual hardships which it may involve. But neither do we seek to avoid their infliction.

During a visit to Linz at the time of the Anschluss – the union movement in Germany and Austria – he had proclaimed:

Austria is German and only German. The only guarantee for Austria's independence can be one given only by the German people. The spiritual Great German Reich is already a fact.

There could be no doubt about his first loyalty.

The dust of destruction had barely settled above Rotterdam before Seyss-Inquart was in full command in the Netherlands. The mailed fist would be kept wrapped in velvet for a while; a little flattery to the Dutch would not come amiss. Seyss-Inquart was determined, however, that his honeyed approach would be stage-managed in a manner appropriate to a conqueror: the people would be in no doubt as to who was master.

Of course, there would be full inaugural rites fit for a paladin of the Third Reich. The choice backcloth displayed a crashing lack of tact; the Germans opted for the ancient Ridderzaal (Hall of the Knights) at The Hague, where Queen Wilhelmina in happier days had opened the winter session of the States-General in solemn ceremony. Seyss-Inquart hoped that this would be interpreted as displaying a respect for Dutch traditions. Instead, right from the start it raised the ire of the Netherlands.

One detail in particular did not escape them: instead of Netherlands musicians in attendance at the Reichskommissar's inauguration, the entire orchestra of the Cologne Broadcasting System was transported to The Hague. The air hung heavy with Wagner.

In his speech, Seyss-Inquart declared that the Germans had come as the Netherlands' friends. And he added reassuringly:

We do not come here to suppress and annihilate a people, or to take away from it its liberty . . . The Germans do not wish to subjugate imperialistically this country and its population. Nor do they desire to force upon them their political convictions. Their activities will be limited by the necessities resulting from the state of war.

We are to build a new Europe based upon the foundations of honour and common labour. We all know that the ultimate purpose of our Fuehrer is: peace and order for all who are of goodwill.

If parts of the Netherlands was lulled into something like acceptance, the people of Rotterdam were not. Evidence of the ruined streets and shopping centre could not be smoothed away with conciliatory words. It was true that by the spring of 1941 German troops were no longer singing about invading England, and the subjugated Dutch could occasionally hear the encouraging note of English bombers passing overhead to attack the Reich. But it took an optimistic nature to believe in an Allied victory in the near future.

Yet there *were* stirrings of resistance, however tentative. They began as early as 29 June 1940 with the birthday of Princess Juliana's consort, Prince Bernhard, who often wore a white carnation in his lapel. All at once, white carnations flourished in the streets.

It was not much, but it was something. If it had only been the Germans whom the Dutch had cause to fear, resistance might have flowered earlier and more forcibly.

But the enemy was also within.

The rhythmic tramping of heavy high boots sported by black-shirted legions echoed through the sparsely populated streets of Amsterdam, watched by a small, sullen crowd.

At first, it seemed a mere token show of strength. Then all at once the procession wheeled away from the main thoroughfares, making for the Jewish quarter, which lay to the north. Jews on the streets were savagely beaten up, their homes attacked and looted.

The black-shirt cohorts then turned their attention to the trams, forcibly evacuating and ill-treating passengers. Other groups smashed and destroyed cafés and restaurants.

But the bullies responsible for similar incidents in a score of Dutch towns were not Germans. Anton Adriaan Mussert, ardent disciple of Adolf Hitler and Benito Mussolini, and leader of the Nationaal-Socialistiche Beweging – the NSB – had crawled out of the woodwork.

If it had not been for the war, there might well have been no moment of glory for this thick-set, balding municipal engineer from Utrecht who had plodded conscientiously up the ladder of the Dutch civil service. As with Vidkun Quisling in Norway, no one had taken his muddled political pretensions over-seriously; the NSB was a small right-wing party with a decidedly pedestrian chief and a caucus of disgruntled intellectuals.

At first, the German's reaction to Mussert had been condescending. The NSB had only 30,000 members; it by no means engaged the hearts and minds of the Dutch. Mussert's proposition to Seyss-Inquart that a Dutch government should be formed to consist of members of the NSB was politely declined.

As might be expected, Seyss-Inquart had no intention of submitting to a situation that might weaken his own power base. The hint of such a possibility kept him awake at night. He wrote hastily to Himmler: 'Mussert's political capabilities do not compare favourably with those of an average German gauleiter.'

Heinrich Himmler, as Reichsfuehrer SS and supremo of the German police, was also worried, but for another reason. He had kept an eye on the Netherlands as a source of racial material. If there was such potential it should be controlled by the SS, not by any pale, home-grown copy.

In the summer of 1940, Himmler had established at Munich an SS regiment, Standarte Westland, seeking volunteers from the Netherlands and Flanders. The level of interest had proved gratifying. Himmler looked forward to raising more Dutch and Flemish volunteers for the SS. But no one in the Netherlands, sympathetic or otherwise, was to have any ridiculous ideas of independence. Plainly, a truly reliable subordinate was needed to watch the situation on the spot.

Himmler's gift to the Netherlands was another Austrian, SS-Obergruppenfuehrer Hanns Albin Rauter.

The old Austro-Hungarian Empire that went to war in 1914 was an unwieldy structure of separate nationalities which crumbled to dust with the onset of an uneasy peace. Klagenfurt-born Hanns Rauter had served it as an officer in the Gebirge-Schuetzen-Regiment I in the Imperial Army. By the time he returned to Graz in 1918, Austria was a country in turmoil, seething with revolutionary unrest. There was the threat of invasion from annexationist armies of Yugoslavia, Poland and Hungary.

The burning spirit of nationalism was fuelled by a succession of student riots masterminded by the numerous 'free corps' (Freikorps) who fought off the intruders with a campaign of frenzied street violence. One of the most vicious and fanatical was the Styrian Home Guard (Steierische Heimatschutz), a paramilitary corps to whom Rauter had given total allegiance.

Throughout the 1920s, it stormed the streets with provocative marches and sustained violence against the hated Socialists. Above all, the Styrian Home Guard, from whose rank Rauter sprang as a prominent figure, was fanatically pan-German and anti-Semitic, dedicated to a last-ditch struggle for German supremacy amid the entrails of the ramshackle, doomed former empire of the Hapsburg rulers.

Its ideological platform moulded the future of Hanns Rauter.

In addition, one of its most ardent observers was the young Adolf Hitler, who had eked out a miserable existence as a third-rate commercial artist in Vienna and was nursing his own crude, ill-formed nationalistic and political ambitions. Hitler was to write of that time in his testament *Mein Kampf:* 'I achieved an ... understanding of the importance of physical terror toward the individuals and the masses.'

As a practitioner of bullyboy violence on the streets of Austrian towns and cities, Hanns Rauter was absorbing the same lesson.

By the late 1920s, links were forged between the Styrian Home Guard and the Austrian branch of Hitler's National Socialist German Workers' Party.

On 30 January 1933 the Third Reich, which Hitler boasted was to endure for a thousand years, was born in Germany. And Hanns Rauter was there, busily organising the total absorption of his Heimatschutz into the Nazi apparatus.

If if had not been for the outbreak of war in 1939, Rauter might well have become an obscure backroom figure, a mere technician of dictatorship. As it turned out, on 22 May 1940, Rauter was sent to the Netherlands as Hoehere SS und Polizeifuehrer Nordwest (HSSPF, Higher SS and Police leader) – 'Nordwest' being the pan-Germanic designation for the Netherlands.

An ardent casting director seeking a model to symbolise SS brutality in all its crudity and terror might well have chosen Rauter on appearance alone. Here was a tall, tough-looking butcher with an aquiline nose and a brutal countenance fractured by a vicious slash of a scar.

The title of HSSPF was no mere ornament; Hanns Rauter was Heinrich Himmler's personal lieutenant and that, in SS matters, meant total power. Rauter was to command all SS organisations in the Netherlands. These included the Ordnungspolizei (the ordinary German police force), the Sicherheitspolizei and Sicherheitsdienst (SIP and SD, Secret Police and Security Service), and all Waffen-SS units stationed there. He also commanded the entire Dutch police force.

Of course, it could be argued that Rauter's writ was limited. After all, Arthur Seyss-Inquart was his senior in the Netherlands; all orders would naturally have to be cleared with him. But behind Seyss-Inquart towered the infinitely more sinister figure of Heinrich Himmler, the erstwhile chicken farmer wielding absolute power in the police states of the occupied countries.

No one – and certainly not Arthur Seyss-Inquart or Anton Mussert – had much doubt of Rauter's main task. The Jews greeted his arrival in Amsterdam with suspicion and fear – suspicion in no way lessened by a period of ominous inactivity. In Germany there were the Nuremberg Laws of 1935, which deprived the Jews of citizenship, confining them contemptuously to the status of 'subjects', and which eventually went on to outlaw them so completely that shops, hotels, beer gardens and places of public entertainment invariably carried signs indicating that Jews were not welcome. But nothing of the kind happened, at first, for the Dutch Jews.

Their gradual disinheritance was being planned, nonetheless; the campaign, when it came, was launched with a direct assault on a fundamental tenet of Jewish belief.

On 7 August 1940 the Germans peremptorily prohibited the ritual slaughter of animals. No longer were cattle to be killed by severing of the arteries or bleeding. The generally accepted methods of stunning or shooting would have to be adopted. The first stirrings of discrimination had begun, and they grew apace.

The next stage was for Aryan and Jewish butchers to be separated. The Jews would no longer be permitted to serve gentiles; overnight, Jewish butchers lost eighty-five per cent of their trade.

It was, predictably, only a matter of time before *all* Jewish tradesmen came under the edict. By as early as

October 1940, the campaign had struck even deeper: entry into the civil service was completely banned to Jews and to gentiles married to Jews. Those who already had jobs could expect no further promotion. Then, at the end of one working week, came the next stage – a bald announcement under the signature of Seyss-Inquart: 'No Jews are expected to return on Monday.'

Into the decree were swept all Jewish professors, teachers, doctors and clerks.

That final Saturday which spelt the end of a livelihood for so many, certainly brought mass protest of a kind, but it was protest wearing a gentle face and expressed with flowers. Clinics, classrooms and workshops throughout the country were a riot of colours, decorated by non-Jews as tributes to those colleagues who had been forcibly removed. Children came with their parents to take grave, formal leave of their teachers.

Beyond the odd skirmish, blood had not yet spilt on to the streets. Rauter and his SS contingents, nominally responsible to Seyss-Inquart, held their fire.

But progressively the persecution worsened. Economic privation was the next stage. Mrs Alfred B. Spanjaard, a Jew from Amsterdam who survived two years' imprisonment in German concentration camps, recalled at the end of the war:

New decrees were issued daily. We were not allowed on certain streets. We couldn't ride in streetcars, our telephones and radios were taken away, we could shop only between 3 and 5 p.m., and we had to be in our homes at 8 p.m.

All Jews were ordered to bring their money, jewels and insurance policies to the Lippmann and Rosenthal Bank in the Sarphati Street, which the Nazis had taken over. There we had to make a complete accounting of our funds and valuables. We were allowed to keep 250 guilders and were told we couldn't spend more than 100 guilders a month for rent, clothing, food and medical expenses. It didn't matter whether rent alone amounted to more than that figure – that was the order. After the 250 guilders were spent, we had to draw on what was left of our funds at the bank. If we had nothing left, we were either supported by the Jewish community's pooled resources, or we died.

Then the so-called 'Koco Affair' burst on a shocked Amsterdam.

The two ice-cream parlours collectively called 'Koco' were popular meeting places for both Jews and gentiles in the non-Jewish quarter of south Amsterdam. What was worrying was not so much that the owners, Cahn and Kohn, were Jews, but that they were refugees from Germany. It was obvious that it could only be a matter of time before the establishments gained the close attention of the Nazis. Some form of protection was clearly needed.

Unfortunately, fledgling resistance groups at this time consisted largely of enthusiastic young amateurs. Some of them proceeded to deck out the parlours with a variety of primitive weapons, consisting largely of gas pipes encased in straps. One of the owners was encouraged to fix a special twenty-inch flask of ammonia to the wall.

The results were greeted with enthusiasm. After a few unsuccessful forays, the Germans left the 'Koco' alone. Encouraged, the resisters reinforced the parlours with fresh weapons. Here was something of an adventure, a game that had all the best elements of a Hollywood Western.

In a frenzy, the Germans returned to the attack. On 19 February 1941, a police patrol swept down on the parlours, only to be greeted by a bombardment of ammonia. The two owners, together with other Jews, were arrested.

Ernst Cahn endured a month of torture but refused to reveal which 'conspirator' had fixed the bottle to his shop. On 3 March 1941, he gained a tragic niche in the history of the German occupation of the Netherlands: he was the first in the country to be shot by a Nazi firing squad.

Dutifully, Hanns Rauter turned in a report on the incident to Himmler. The account was made deliberately lurid. Here, argued Rauter, was a fine example of the disorderly behaviour and lack of discipline prevailing among the Jews. There were graphic descriptions of a Jew 'gnawing through an Aryan's artery and then sucking out his blood', another had squirted 'poisonous fluids at policemen pursuing their duty'.

Such Jewish treachery cried out for retribution. It was the pretext for which the Germans had been waiting.

Within a few days, a series of lightning terror raids were unleashed. Enthusiastically assisted by Anton Mussert, around 200 Jewish men were snatched on 22 February and herded into synagogues which were promptly put to the torch.

Those who survived a little longer were sent to the concentration camp at Mauthausen, near Linz, which had been built by Himmler with the original intention of housing Austrians.

Three weeks after the men had been rounded up, their relatives received identical letters telling them that the prisoners had been 'killed trying to escape'.

The raids were to go on for the rest of the year and well into 1942. Jews, under the constant fear of arrest and deportation, killed themselves by the score.

Mrs Alfred Spanjaard was able to watch the raiders at work.

She related:

... I was approaching the Jewish Institute of the Blind on Amsteldyk, when I saw several trucks drive to the kerb. Gruene Polizei got out and dashed into the building. They came out dragging the blind, young and old. I stood there, I couldn't help looking. I retained my senses sufficiently to hold my bag so it would cover the *Jood* star over my heart. Otherwise the Nazis might have seized me too.

... The Nazis began throwing – literally throwing – the blind into trucks ...

A few days later I was passing the maternity hospital on Nieuwe Keizersgracht, when I saw the scene repeated. Nazis were dragging out mothers, some of whom had given birth only a few hours before, and throwing them into the trucks. Many of the women haemorrhaged and the blood began to drip through the wooden boards of the vehicles.

Opposition to the Nazis in the Netherlands began at a low murmur. Gradually it changed into the harsh clamour of sabotage and resistance. But there was still the long hard night of Nazi barbarism.

7

For a few short moments, the bewildered men of Belgium's 7th Infantry Division defending the eleven-mile front along the Albert Canal thought the bright lights cascading to the sea were meteorites.

Bewilderment was understandable: the perspex of the cockpits had caught and magnified the rays of the sun. The contours of the attacking force seem blurred from below.

The Luftwaffe aircraft were flying too high for the attention of the antiaircraft guns; nothing, it seemed, could stop the onward progress of the attackers, trailing behind them long parallel streams of whitish vapour.

Like a flock of starlings scattering at some mysterious signal, the planes dispersed momentarily then tipped their wings and wheeled towards their target.

That was how the Belgian infantrymen saw the German invasion of the west. It was a little after 4.15 a.m. on Friday 10 May 1940.

By the time the Dutch surrendered, the fate of Belgium, France and the defenders of the British Expeditionary Force had been sealed. After the bombers screamed their destruction of the Albert Canal, the avalanche broke. Its force was a vast, swiftly moving concentration of armour which had cut through the forest of the Ardennes that day and stretched back in three columns for a hundred miles, far beyond the Rhine. It had smashed through the French 9th and 2nd Armies, and was heading swiftly for the Channel.

Indisputably, the greatest and the most spectacular prize was the capture of Fort Eben Emael, which commanded the junction of the Meuse and the Albert Canal, Belgium's frontier with the Netherlands. The triangular-shaped fortress, resembling a giant segment of pie and constructed in a series of steel and concrete galleries set deep underground, its gun turrets protected by heavy armour, was fondly considered a formidable obstacle.

It did not take long for the Germans to shatter the illusion, for the entire structure was fatally flawed. It did not command the surrounding landscape, and its gun positions could offer no protection to the bridges of the canal.

Into the attack went the Koch Storm Detachment, formed at Hildesheim. The unit consisted of the 1st Company of the 1st Parachute Regiment, the Parachute Sapper Detachment of the 7th Flying Division, the Freight Glider Unit, a beacon and searchlight detachment and an airfield ground staff. These were buttressed by a towing unit of Junker 52s. To the parachute company went the responsibility for the capture of the high bridges of Vroenhaven and Veltwezelt.

The sapper detachment was under the command of Oberst Rudolf Witzig, a Westphalian veteran of the Wehrmacht from World War One. Oberst Witzig later wrote:

We were the only parachute unit comprised entirely of sappers, and all were volunteers. Among us were the best amateur glider-pilots from pre-war days when Germans already excelled in the sport of gliding. During the two years of the unit's existence, it had grown into a sturdy, close-knit community in which each man had confidence in his fellows.

So it was that in a light ground mist, through which the attackers could dimly make out the outlines of the fortification, nine gliders – two out of the total force of eleven were lost during the flight – actually landed on the fort, crippling the rooftop gun emplacements and periscopes.

Then it was the turn of the flame-throwers, with Belgian

63

troops becoming human torches. Charges were fixed to steel cupolas, to the guns of the casemates and even in the barrels of the big guns.

An almost mystic faith had been placed in Fort Eben Emael; it had mesmerised the Belgians into fatal neglect. The fort lacked mines or barbed wire; the garrison was deprived of infantry training; and there were no trenches round the casemates.

Attempts by Belgian infantry to dislodge the attackers were set at naught by waves of Stuka bombings and further parachute attacks. At noon on 11 May, after a bout of hand-to-hand fighting in the underground tunnels, a white flag was hoisted. One thousand two hundred dazed and demoralised defenders filed out and surrendered.

Gleefully, the propaganda machinery of Josef Goebbels went immediately into action. Hitler was later photographed with these bemedalled heroes of the Reich, who sported their battle smocks and paratroop helmets rather than the customary ceremonial dress.

As a moral blow to the Belgians, the loss of Fort Eben Emael proved devastating.

But the process of humiliation began on 10 May itself, some two hours after the start of the invasion. The windows of the foreign ministry in Brussels rattled from the explosion of bombs in nearby airfields and the air was rent with the constant roar of the Luftwaffe, as Vicco Buelow-Schwante, the German ambassador, solemnly intoned from a document: 'I am instructed by the government of the German Reich to make the following declaration: in order to forestall the invasion of Belgium, Holland and Luxembourg, for which Great Britain and France have been making preparations clearly aimed at Germany . . .'

The farce of diplomatic niceties in such circumstances proved altogether too much for the Belgian Foreign Prime Minister, Paul-Henri Spaak. He cut into Buelow-

Schwante's litany by saying: 'Hand me the document. I should like to spare you so painful a task . . .'

By the morning of 19 May, the mighty wedge of seven armoured divisions had driven westward north of the Somme; there was a mere seven miles separating the Germans from the Channel.

Hitler was delirious with undreamed of success; the 2nd Panzer Division had reached Abbeville at the mouth of the Somme. Generalleutnant Erich von Manstein, chief of staff at Hitler's Army Group A, had previously persuaded the Army High Command (Oberkommando Des Heeres or OKH) that a frontal conflict with the Allied armies on the flat land of Belgium would lead to a war of attrition like that of 1914–18. There was, Manstein believed, an enticing alternative.

Massive armour could thread its way through the Ardennes forest and over the Meuse. Ahead would be flat open country that was nothing short of a gift for tank warfare. Furthermore, terrain like this could be found all the way to Paris and the Channel. Manstein was a detached, icy professional, but he allowed his imagination to soar at the prospect of vast armoured thrusts, with panzer and motorised forces far outstripping all other transport.

The Manstein Plan, as it turned out, was no dream. By 13 May, a mere five days into *Fall Gelb*, German armour had secured four bridgeheads across the steep-banked Meuse from Dinant to Sedan.

The plan to hold the river was abandoned under the relentless pressure of the German advance; even so, the Belgians held out for seventeen days. On 13 and 14 May, the Germans broke through the French lines north of Dinant in Belgium and at Mézières in France. For the French 9th Army it was wholesale debacle; General Maurice Gamelin, the Allied supreme commander, ordered a general retreat. On Monday 27 May, messages from the French liaison officer at Belgian HQ reported that they had 'abandoned the struggle'.

King Leopold III sent an envoy to the Germans, proposing a ceasefire at midnight. Back came the reply: 'The Fuehrer demands that arms be laid down unconditionally.' They were.

Unlike the crowned heads of the Netherlands and Norway, the king refused to contemplate setting up a government-in-exile. He declared: 'I have decided to stay. The cause of the Allies is lost.'

In a speech full of bitterness, Premier Paul Reynaud of France went on radio to declaim: 'I must announce to the French people a grave event . . . France can no longer count on the Belgian Army . . . King Leopold III without a word to the French and British soldiers . . . laid down his arms. It is a fact without precedent in history.'

Supporters of the king argued that he had taken a perfectly legitimate decision, not as head of state, but as Allied Ground Chief. General Maxine Weygand, who became the king's superior commander and Allied Ground Commander-in-Chief, professed himself stunned by the lack of consultation: 'It was like a bolt from the blue. There had been no warning . . .'

The French rubbed salt into the Belgians' wounds, regarding them as a defaulting ally. A British war correspondent, Gordon Waterfield, listening to Reynaud's broadcast in a bistro, saw two women burst into tears, crying *Les salauds! Les salauds!* Parisians threw innocent Belgian refugees out of their homes or set fire to their wrecked carts. They had to endure heckling and intimidation.

The progress of the conqueror coincided with days which slipped past under blue skies and bright sun, and the perpetual starry nights. May and June would normally have been smiling times for the people of this rich, proud land. But in 1940, the heat of the Belgian summer served only to mock the endless columns of men and women bowed down with fatigue and an overwhelming sense of loss.

Ahead of the distracted columns on the traffic-choked

roads lay France, already in sight and in its death agonies. The provinces of the centre and south were in no position to receive a large influx of Belgian refugees. In stark statistical terms two million Belgians became homeless and the French had five million refugees of their own from the north.

The capitulation by Leopold III had been bad enough; the material privations were even worse. Belgium had previously snuggled within a cocoon of prosperity and comfort; the events of September 1939 to May 1940 had not bothered the country particularly. Within a few short days all complacency was shed: a reassuring daily routine was no more, the future for thousands appeared to be an endless walk over congested roads where there was little prospect of a roof or a bed or, indeed, the means to pay for either.

The German columns marching into Brussels encountered virtually a ghost town. There was barely a transport service worth considering; bridges had been destroyed by the Allies in their retreat.

The capital lacked water, gas or coal; barges sunk by Belgian troops blocked the main canals. Without the bridges, there was nothing for it but to cross the canals by lock gates not sufficiently wide for two-way traffic. Thus pedestrians were only allowed to cross for five minutes in each direction alternately.

Yet there were rich pickings for the country's new German masters. It was true that the country only covered an area of 12,000 square miles with a population of 8.5 million. Yet in the league table of foreign trade, Belgium occupied fifth place in the world, with exports that could touch £250 million and gold holdings estimated at £200 million.

All this, the Germans reasoned, pointed to the existence of vast reserves. Just how vast they made it their business to discover with maximum speed.

The swastika barely had time to cast its baleful shadow over Antwerp before a fleet of German trucks roared in to seize everything that was either edible or remotely of industrial value to the Reich. Under the sullen murmur of the guns, bills were posted throughout the port proclaiming:

All foodstuffs, raw materials and half-finished products are of primary importance to the economic life of the occupied countries. The British blockade will render these stocks insufficient; therefore, in the interest of the occupied territories, all goods enumerated below are to be requisitioned: foodstuffs, raw materials, half-finished products and all other commodities which are scarce or of which there are insufficient quantities.

By 3 p.m. on 18 May 1940 in Antwerp huge army trucks had been backed up to the warehouses, which were swiftly stripped of all merchandise. The contents of cases and bales were unchecked; the trucks sped off towards the Reich.

It was not crude looting. Everything appropriated was paid for. The owner was required to put in a bill for the confiscated merchandise. He received a bond for the entire value of the goods – to be redeemed, of course, by the Germans from Belgian coffers. The exchange rate was pegged at a level which made everything available at virtually half-price for the conquerors.

The Wehrmacht troops could scarcely be blamed for believing they had landed in paradise. By the time the first cold wave of winter arrived, woollen goods had become virtually unobtainable; the Germans had seized them all. Lars Moen, an American journalist working in Belgium, wrote in *Under The Iron Heel:*

They had rushed to buy warm woollen underclothing. . . . Women's stockings are equally scarce; every German soldier bought a few pairs of silk stockings for his wife, sister or girl-friend, not to mention silk underclothing of every description. When I left, two Belgian women out of three were going bare-legged. . . .

The German soldiers bought anything and everything, and

then purchased expensive leather luggage to carry what they did not send home via the army postal service. It was years since most of them had seen shops stocked with so much merchandise – some never had – and they made the most of the opportunity.

Many of them not only spent their entire accumulation of army pay in the shops, but wrote home for every bit of money the family could scrape together . . .

As for the 90,000 Jews in Belgium, life before the occupation seemed secure. There was flourishing employment in the clothing trade and other small businesses. Antwerp was also the focus of the diamond trade, largely in Jewish hands. The illusions of security were swiftly stripped away; within six months of the arrival of the Germans, the Belgian tragedy of deportation had begun.

For the Gestapo it was a triumph of organisation. Hermann Goering, when the Nazis seized power in Germany, had lost no time in securing control of the Prussian State Police, the forerunner of the Gestapo. He had an ardent disciple in Hamburg University graduate Rudolf Diels, who had hitherto been solely interested in carousing in Berlin beer halls.

The dissolute Diels now swiftly became intent on making a name for himself. The fate of the Jews was of the keenest interest to his superiors; plainly, there was profitable work to be done. Within four months of Hitler gaining power, Diels had helped fashion a draft law to regulate status of Jews throughout the Reich. This law would, it was proposed, be administered by the creation of a Jewish council, composed of the Jews themselves and answerable to the Gestapo.

Desperately, the leader of the council in Belgium played for time, seeking to negotiate the release of individual Jews. At first, the Gestapo seemed remarkably conciliatory, indicating that it might be possible to do business – at a price, of course. Jews could be allowed, at 25,000 francs a time, to make for Switzerland, transported by the Belgian

Red Cross. Reassuring letters were produced from Dutch Jews who had made similar journeys.

The council yielded up scores of Jews who, full of hope, prepared for the journeys. Most of them got no further than the deportation centre at Mechelen, staging post for a final journey to the concentration camps of the east. The Dutch letters had been faked by the Gestapo or written under duress.

The Gestapo found a healthy supply of collaborators who were prepared to act as intermediaries for the Jews. A fee of 25,000 francs was common. Those Jews who did succeed in fleeing the sinister shadow of the Gestapo in Belgium frequently turned over their jewels and possessions. Even so, there was always the risk of finding a Gestapo reception committee at the border with France.

The Jews who remained were easier prey. Wave after wave of Gestapo raids was launched on the Jewish quarters.

Tos Hakker, a Jew living in Antwerp, wrote:

The Jewish inhabitants were dragged outside and ill-treated. Ten minutes were granted to collect some clothes. Many of them, almost dead with fear, suffered themselves to be taken away without saying a word. . . . Vehicle after vehicle was loaded and driven away. No distinction was made: old and young, whether ill or healthy, everybody was dragged outside, many of them half-dressed. First the victims were taken by the Gestapo. They remained a full day without food or drink. Then came large closed furniture vans. . . . The human cattle were heaped up on them. . . . The raids went on regularly. Carts traversed the Jewish quarters and many a cowardly compatriot was willing to point out houses where Jews were living or places where many of them were hidden.

Many a cowardly compatriot. . . . Along with the other occupied countries of western Europe, the story of occupation was not just one of stoicism in defeat and defiance in resistance.

Collaboration was an ever present reality.

70

8

In the dark of the early morning of 10 May 1940, the Wehrmacht poured into the Grand Duchy of Luxembourg, the pathetically small postage stamp of territory at the back door of the mighty German Reich.

The complexion of the land constituted an irresistible gift to the invader. On the German side of the three rivers constituting its border with Luxembourg, the land rises swiftly to heights of hill and escarpment, growing wilder and steeper towards the north. There are thick forests with villages dotting the edge of streams crossed by some bridges. Direct routes from Aachen, Cologne and Koblenz to the north and northeast, from Mainz, Frankfurt and Mannheim to the east, Saarbruecken and Strasbourg to the southeast converge on the bridges. On the east bank of the rivers, roads course from village to village; along these roads and on top of the ridges the invader dug in his commanding concrete gun emplacements.

The previous night, around 11.45 p.m., the first messages had started arriving from the frontier: 'Important troop movements are to be seen on the German-Luxembourg frontier especially at Palzem on the extreme southeast.'

An eyewitness account, published after the war in *La Resistance du Peuple Luxembourgeois*, recorded:

As if by chance, one began to see groups of armed men wearing armbands with swastikas on them. They were members of the fifth column who had finally come out in the open and were awaiting their master. At the German legation, all the windows were lit up, as if an important meeting was taking place. Every-

71

thing indicated that the Germans were on the road ready for action. The messages from the frontier bore out events in the capital.

Invasion was imminent.

The people of Luxembourg had long learned to live with the threat. A decade earlier the smaller countries of western Europe had banded together to form the Oslo Group – Norway, Sweden, Denmark, Finland, the Netherlands and Luxembourg. It aimed to forge economic links and agree on some form of political consensus under the daunting shadow of its powerful neighbour.

By 1936, Luxembourg had already caught the scent of danger – Nazi Germany had reoccupied the hitherto demilitarised Rhineland. Two years later, Hitler had walked virtually unopposed into Austria and in 1938, after the notorious Munich agreement, had seized the Sudetenland of Czechoslovakia.

The threat seemed so palpable that Belgium had made ready to receive the entire Luxembourg population retreating from invasion.

And now it had happened. From its industrial southwest 47,000 Luxembourgers streamed into France, inevitably entangling with the hosts of French fleeing to the south. Another 50,000 sought refuge in the Ardennes; a third of the nation was on the move.

On the move also from his job as Gauleiter of Trier, conveniently placed for the Luxembourg border, was Gustav Simon, the Fuehrer's gift to Luxembourg.

It would have been a mistake to underestimate the little man with the soup-bowl haircut and an old-fashioned bank clerk's deference. The same colourless qualities, after all, were shared with Reichsfuehrer-SS Heinrich Himmler and, in terms of acquiring power within the Nazi hierarchy, they had done him no harm.

Simon was not simply a traditional bureaucrat. There

was a restless energy, fuelled by a fanatical devotion to the interests of his Fuehrer, one of whose more bullying tenets he was never tired of echoing: 'We can go to the limit of humanity if we restore happiness to the German people.'

The bustling little Gauleiter did far more than merely mouth the utterances of his master; within three months of the occupation, he had approved an order proclaiming that 'the language of Luxembourg and its inhabitants is, and always has been German. . . . The German language shall be the exclusive official language.'

With that single utterance Simon had railroaded the centuries-old Luxembourg tradition whereby the Grand Duchy had been bilingual in both German and French. Sturdy, independent Luxembourgers were not unduly worried; they were determined to continue with their old ways, no matter what the Germans said.

For his part, Simon reckoned it was time for the iron fist. He rushed out a shoal of decrees on what were termed 'measures of Penal Law'. The fourth of these, published in *Nationalblatt*, was couched in language of unambiguous pomposity:

. . . Any person undertaking any action calculated to interfere with the planned return of Luxembourg to the German Reich, either by the restoration of Luxembourg or its inclusion in a foreign state, likewise forfeits his life for this dishonourable offence against the nationhood.

Furthermore, the plotting of the above-mentioned crimes and any offer or invitation to participate in such treasonable activity is punishable by death, as also is the furthering of any such attempts of high treason and any communication with foreign governments with the object of preparing any such undertaking. . . .

The death penalty is also applied to any person who, whether at home or abroad, undertakes to assist an enemy power in any way or to hinder the war effort of the Reich and all its Allies. . . .

Simon also thundered in *Nationalblatt*: 'It is forbidden to use non-Germanic accents (i.e. acute, grave and circumflex) when writing in the language of Luxembourg. Offences will be punishable by a fine of 150 Reichmarks or imprisonment.'

In addition, the use of 'Monsieur' and 'Bonjour' was outlawed, as well as such French names as 'François' and 'Camille', consigned to oblivion, along with 'Jacques' and 'Dupont'.

The Gauleiter, who after these measures pronounced himself satisfied, proclaimed: 'Luxembourgers are Germans by race and language, and only by vicissitudes of history, the intrigues of the Great Powers and separatist movements, have they been torn from the German fatherland. They now wish to return.'

Such reassurances would doubtless satisfy Reichsfuehrer Himmler, who announced that absorption in Germany was a historical necessity, since Luxembourgers had become 'racially degenerated by their ancient contact with Belgium'.

The Luxembourgers, however, had no wish to 'return' to Germany and no stomach for Nazi occupation. Gustav Simon was prepared to meet their defiance with cold cruelty.

The unstoppable mobile columns on 10 May had continued their deep thrust into the very entrails of France. In the west Generalmajor Erwin Rommel's forces occupied Le Havre; after two days' rest came the order to slice through to Cherbourg on the Contentin peninsula. Hitler's forces had encircled the British Expeditionary Force, compelling it to evacuate by sea. The much vaunted Maginot line – the concrete and steel fortifications stretching from Luxembourg to Switzerland along the French border with Germany – had been bypassed with contemptuous ease.

But it was the loss of Paris which was the most bitter blow of all. Until the Germans reached the capital, the weather had been perfect; on 13 June, the leaves along the Champs Élysées had been a tender green. The majestic dome of the Invalides, containing the tomb of Napoleon, glistened in gold, and through the gateways of the Louvre could be glimpsed the vivid flowerbeds of the Tuileries Gardens.

Anyone seeking reassurance had only to glance at the tricolour flags waving serenely above the Chamber of Deputies and the Ministry of Foreign Affairs. Since the July day twenty-one years before, at the end of another war, when with a thunderous roll of drums and fanfare of trumpets a squadron of the magnificent Gardes Republicains rode through the Arc de Triomphe in front of France's two heroic Maréchals, Joffre and Foch – Paris had enjoyed its freedom.

On 14 June 1940, a single armed German policeman stood outside the Invalides. He wore a green uniform with helmet and jackboots, directing nonexistent traffic with a small stick. At the Place de la Concorde were massed tanks, guns, lorries, and ambulances. Two cameramen were filming Paris firemen busy on a high ladder, hoisting a Nazi flag on the facade of the Ministry of Marine.

As the Germans approached Paris, the fine weather gave way to drizzle and sullen skies. Early on the morning of that same 14 June, Oberstleutnant Dr Hans Spiedel, an officer on the staff of the 18th Army of General der Artillerie Georg von Kuechler, received two French officers who had come under a flag of truce. Their instructions were to give up the French capital. The bloodless and orderly entry into Paris was made by troops of the German 87th Infantry Division, led by an anti-tank detachment which speedily occupied the Hôtel de Ville and the Invalides.

There was no denying that the first troops to enter Paris had an impressive bearing. There was an element of stage management about it all; the Wehrmacht had deliberately prepared itself. The men were spruce and smartly polished, and could easily have been models for a recruiting poster. Soon, troops were drilling in the public squares and mounted bands were practising on the Champs de

Mars, and there was the bizarre spectacle of soldiers clad in shorts kicking a football in the Tuileries Gardens.

There was heavy emphasis on correct behaviour; officers were saluted by their men with scrupulous rectitude.

The politeness extended to the people of Paris. For a while, the Parisians allowed themselves to relax and even stopped groups of German troops in the street to ask what was happening. The Germans answered all questions with grave courtesy before getting on with what seemed to be their main leisure activity – taking snaps of the Arc de Triomphe or Notre Dame.

But there were ominous portents. 'Occupation money' was soon issued – notes which were legal tender, circulating only in France. Their value was set at four times the value of the franc; any shopkeeper unwise enough to refuse them found himself severely penalised. The 'occupation money' was spent lavishly with soldiers buying everything in sight. A Paris journalist, Paul Simon, who was to edit the clandestine newspaper *Valmy*, saw the unemployed at Vaugirard packing a Berlin-bound train with goods that had been gathered from every part of France.

Inevitably, there were those who later made conspicuous profits from the victory celebrations to the new conqueror. One of the first objectives of the Germans was Montmartre and the promise of 'Les Girls'. An estimated 4,000 troops swilled champagne in their victory; the first French fortunes of the occupation were made that night. One restaurant owner swiftly converted a three-roomed apartment into a 'furnished hotel' for the German troops and their girl friends. There was no coyness in proclaiming the riches of such instant collaboration; certainly not from a fashionable restaurant which sold nearly a thousand pounds' worth of champagne on victory night, and there were tireless whores whose weekly takings from then on averaged three hundred pounds.

Those who had decided to quit the city in the wake of the German advance could not believe it would be long before they were back to the old life. The scenes on the congested roads frequently resembled a holiday outing rather than evacuation from a potentially lethal foe.

An eyewitness wrote:

... The queue of traffic which our car joined at the Barrière d'Italie contained vehicles of every description – delivery vans, touring cars, heavy lorries, and even antique horse-drawn cabs. Big lorries contained whole families, who were passing round sausage and wine. Every time a queue stopped – about every 100 yards – people would scatter to the roadside and go into houses, returning with a hunk of bread or a bottle of water. The hot sun blazed down on the happy crowd – a paid holiday.

Paris, with its stone bridges arching above the clear waters of the Seine, was serenely beautiful under the pale blue of the summer sky. But it was also a city under the heel of the conqueror. There was a visit from the Nazi warlord; a gloating Adolf Hitler smirked like a gargoyle on the Palais de Chaillot.

Clearly, life would never be quite the same again, although it was hard to believe it at the smart racecourses of Longchamps and Auteuil. Here the women seemed as attractive and as fashionably dressed as ever. Only their escorts had changed. The men wore the well-cut field grey officers' uniform of the Wehrmacht or the blue of the Luftwaffe.

But the majority of the five million Parisians settling down to what was to be four years of occupation did not welcome the Germans. Least of all those with memories of just twenty-one years earlier.

One man above all stood out during the deliriously triumphant victory parade through Paris in July 1919. Maréchal Henri Philippe Pétain, Commander-in-Chief, rode through the Arc de Triomphe on a white horse, tall and magnificent in his uniform of horizon blue. For him, the crowds gave more than applause. Here was veneration for a national hero who had led his *poilus* through the sublime ten-month nightmare of the battle of Verdun and who had nursed and restored French morale after an army mutiny in 1917.

These achievements were indeed remarkable for a man who had sprung, not from an aristocratic or patrician background, but from peasant stock.

Such a background, it was said, denied him promotion for something like forty years. It took World War One, to change all that. Henri Philippe Pétain rose to be a Maréchal of France, a national father figure, drawing affection and admiration even from political opponents.

And now, not a generation later, here he was, head of the French government, sitting apprehensively in Bordeaux waiting for a telephone call that would bring him news of the German terms for an armistice.

The presentation of the terms, it turned out, was to be no mere formality across a green baize table; Adolf Hitler was determined to make the most of the occasion with a bold piece of theatre.

He chose for the setting the forest of Compiègne, where a delegation of Germans in November 1918, in a railway carriage, had signed an armistice dictated by Ferdinand Foch. Now the roles were reversed; France was to quaff the cup of humiliation to the last drop.

Hitler gave precise orders for the staging of the new armistice; the old railway carriage No. 2419D was to be taken from a museum and returned to the exact spot where it had stood in 1918. Hitler took the seat formerly occupied by Foch who had laid down the terms of the 1918 armistice to the Germans.

The Fuehrer had not finished with his elaborate theatre of revenge. Generaloberst Wilhelm Keitel explained that the site had been chosen 'as an act of reparatory justice'. The reading of the terms took fifteen minutes. Another of the historical parallels was rigidly adhered to.

In November 1918 Maréchal Foch had greeted the German delegation with *'Qu'est-ce que vous désirez, messieurs?*' The head of the German delegation, Matthias Erzberger, had replied that the group were there to receive the proposal of the Allied Powers for an armistice.

Foch had replied sharply: 'I have no proposal whatever to make.'

In other words, no discussion was permitted. In June 1940, in the same railway carriage, no discussion was allowed either. When Keitel had finished, Hitler threw a Nazi salute and left to the strains of 'Deutschland, Deutschland Ueber Alles'.

Pétain announced over the wireless on 17 June that France was asking for an armistice and that Hitler had drawn it up for signature on 22 June. This was greeted by the more optimistic French as a sign of possible reasonableness from the Germans. After all, where else had Hitler signed an armistice with a defeated foe? In all other occupied territories, conditions were dictated flatly on the basis of unconditional surrender.

Certainly, the terms of the armistice were harsh, but not, at first sight, humiliating. The country was to be spared total occupation. France was to be divided into occupied and unoccupied zones. But over *both* zones the French government's authority was to apply equally. No official text of the terms was published immediately, but in London the British produced a summary stating the main provisions.

Germany will occupy roughly all territory north and west of Tours in west-central France and will thus control Paris as well as all western seaports. All rights of occupation except local administration are to be maintained by the troops stationed there, with France to pay the costs of occupation.

These costs, as it turned out, were to be at a rate of four hundred million francs a day.

Despite earlier optimism, it soon became obvious that there was much about the German terms to stick in the craw. Even though there was no complete occupation, the country was obliged to turn over to the Reich all the anti-Nazi refugees in France and her territories. This struck at one of France's most cherished traditions, the right of asylum.

In addition, the French accepted Article 20 of the armistice agreement, stating that French prisoners of war were to remain in captivity. It had been naively assumed that this stricture would no longer apply once the armistice terms were signed. The German conquerors did not see it that way at all; a million and a half Frenchmen were condemned to rot in prison camps for nearly five years.

The French government was free 'to choose its seat in the unoccupied territory or even, if it so desires, transfer to Paris'. The French government did not so choose; instead, it opted for the spa town of Vichy in the south-central part of the country. It had the major advantage of a central position, good communications, including its own airfield, and ample accommodation in its many hotels. But it was not simply a matter of administrative convenience. Vichy had figured on the contingency plans of the French government long before the war; it had been considered a suitable alternative to Paris, should the battle front threaten the capital.

On 10 July the French National Assembly, meeting at Vichy, buried the Third Republic, which had been the longest living government since the Revolution. Pierre Laval, the political figure who was to become most identified with the policy of collaboration and was now Deputy Prime Minister, informed the Assembly that a 'national revolution' was in the making. 'Liberty, Equality and Fraternity' were obsolete irrelevancies. From now on it would be 'Work, Family and the Fatherland'.

Democracy had patently failed; the time had come for autocratic government by decree. The matter was put to the vote. Of the 666 deputies present, a mere 80 voted 'no'. By an overwhelming affirmative vote of 569 (there were 17 abstentions) 'the Vichy regime' was launched into history.

Hitler's provision of an Unoccupied Zone for France was a shrewdly calculated move. Talk had reached the Germans of plans for a French government-in-exile with its seat in North Africa.

Now that scheme was set at naught, with the country divided both geographically and administratively.

By no means were all members of the Vichy government pro-Hitler. Nonetheless, there were enough useful enemies of democracy who might reasonably be expected to cooperate in the realisation of the Nazi New Order in Europe.

Adolf Hitler had good reason to express himself satisfied with the way things were going. France, unbeaten for four years in the previous war, had been knocked out in just six weeks. His troops were masters of most of Europe, from the North Cape above the Arctic Circle to Bordeaux, from the English Channel to the river Bug in eastern Poland. German hegemony in Europe seemed assured.

The Franco-Italian armistice was signed in Rome two days after the German one. The bellicose Benito Mussolini's attitude towards France had been recorded long before in the diary of the Duce's Foreign Minister, Count Galeazzo Ciano. On 13 May 1938, Mussolini was being described as 'more and more anti-French. He said they are a nation ruined by alcohol, syphilis, and journalism'. Four days later, Mussolini was noted to be 'very worked up against France'. When the Italian leader launched into a shrill anti-French speech in Genoa, the crowd hissed, and a rash of anti-French sentiment broke out all over Italy.

In terms of actual fighting, however, Italian efforts were puny. Some thirty-two Italian divisions were, after a week, unable to budge a scratch French force of six divisions on the Alpine front and further south along the Riviera.

After the armistice, signed at 7.35 p.m. on 24 June, Mussolini was able to occupy only a small portion of French territory.

Six hours after the Italian armistice, the guns in France fell silent.

9

Not everyone had left Paris. Even during the first few days of the occupation, scattered groups of dissidents, many of them ex-soldiers, congregated in the cafés. Over the coffee and the Pernod, bewilderment was soon being replaced by a slowly burning anger. The journalist Paul Simon translated it into a course of action which, recalled later, seemed puny indeed. But at least it had been a start.

He had managed to lay his hands on a small rubber printing set that was, in fact, little more than a child's toy. Soon, a group of fledgling resistants were composing each letter into what was hoped was a pithy slogan. The words *Long live the Republic, in spite of everything*' seemed to strike the right belligerent note. It was printed on the most convenient material to hand: strips of gummed paper.

Simon later revealed: 'That night, returning home in the dark, we stuck our small slogans on maps at the metro stations, on lamp posts, and on shop-fronts. The next day, passing the same places, we each saw our handiwork being read. We mixed with the little groups of two or three and overheard some friendly comments. This encouraged us.'

A friend from northern Europe who had taken refuge in Simon's home brought some half a dozen rolls of the sticky papers. When those ran out, they used the kind of paper intended for protecting windows against bomb blast.

Soon, Simon's little group had expanded to five, each paying a monthly subscription of five francs, and, in true resistance tradition, adopting cover names.

One of the number, known as Boyau-Rouge, had a weakness for metro stations. He planned his campaign scrupulously, each day taking a different route and sticking slogans secretly on German posters and the handrails of escalators. Great satisfaction was to be gained from stuffing the slogans into the belts of German soldiers when the trains were crowded.

Another friend was responsible for a rash of adhesive labelling on the walls of cafés, on lamp posts, railings, trees and hoardings. People downing a quick drink in a bar suddenly spotted a label stuck to the bottom of the glass. Even a quiet stroll down the Champs Élysées or through the Bois de Boulogne provided no escape. There they were stuck on seats and on the barks of trees.

Many carried the blunt message *On les aura* (We shall get them).

But somehow these initiatives, although personally satisfying, lacked the sufficiently brazen touch. More spectacular acts of defiance were clearly necessary; Simon decided to extend his personal skills to the service of resistance.

Paris, he decided, would have its very own underground newspaper; its very title would breathe defiance in the face of humiliation.

Everyone in the group agreed on the excellence of the name *Valmy*, in recognition of a key victory during the French Revolution which had freed France of Prussians and royalists. A bow would thus be made to historic pride. Paris would go into battle with words – at this stage, the only weapon it possessed.

For such a newspaper to be printed in conventional form was obviously out of the question. It would have to be typed; reasonable enough if typewriters in Nazi-occupied Paris had not been as rare as printing presses. There were suitably sympathetic firms prepared to rent out machines in a good cause, but the business of making a smart profit could not be subordinated to patriotism. Almost overnight, prices from hire firms mysteriously multiplied. The rental was clearly beyond the slender resources of Simon and his group.

More direct methods were called for. An attractive sympathiser named Renée was employed as a secretary by a company doing business with the Germans. The solution was absurdly simple; at the end of one working day Renée strolled into a neighbouring office, lifted a machine and walked out with it.

The audacity of the move took the group's breath away. There was now sufficient encouragement to do something even more daring. By a stroke of luck an incredibly primitive duplicator had been secured, but stencils and ink were needed. Fortunately, Suzanne, also a resistant, worked for the Germans. Coolly, she and another member of the *Valmy* staff walked into the offices and collected the stencils. Simon confessed gleefully: 'We even took extra time to type the word *Valmy* on top of a stencil and we left smiling happily at the German officers we met in the corridors. But then Suzanne was an extremely pretty girl.'

Ownership of a typewriter and duplicator required a police permit. Production of each issue of *Valmy* was almost an open invitation to arrest; the clatter of machines could have alerted either collaborator or the police.

But *Valmy* survived and triumphed. In one of the earlier issues the paper was trumpeting:

CERTITUDES

Six months have elapsed since France laid down her arms and came to terms with the enemy, contrary to her pledged word. Today, one may assess from the unfinished history of the war some of the results.

To begin with, the armistice has not ended the state of war.

For the two million French prisoners it is still war; occupied France submits to a state of siege; the so-called free zone feels itself a military protectorate.

It has been claimed that to come to terms with the enemy was a necessity. Experience proves the contrary. Norway, Holland and Belgium, completely invaded, have continued the struggle to the seas or from vast colonial territories. Their lot is not harder than ours. If the French fleet and overseas armies had not abandoned the fight, under orders ... the Italian vulture would have its claws cut and Mussolini would be hiding in shame. Is that what it was desired to avoid? . . .

You, Frenchmen, have only this choice. To agree to uphold an order of life which is nothing but a welter of joyless misery, and to accept as final a defeat turned to surrender by men hating liberty and greedy for power. You do not want that.

You know that democracy still lives. It has known betrayal and besmirching, but it will not be attacked from now on without risk, for it is forging arms in the world's mightiest arsenal.

Valmy

For the time being, these arms were made only of paper. But the spirit of rebellion was contagious. It would spread further, to the other occupied countries of the west.

10

High above the battlements of Oslo's Akershus Castle the Norwegian flag fluttered in the winter breeze, but its presence had nothing to do with the defiance of a conquered people.

For on 1 February 1942, the unthinkable had become reality – Vidkun Quisling, whom many had thought still smarting under the contempt of his Nazi masters, was back in power, his new-found authority vested in the title of Minister President.

At the time of Quisling's ignominious dismissal as Prime Minister, Hitler, conscious that his much hated protégé might nevertheless be of future use, had insisted that Quisling be given an 'honourable position' and 'held in reserve'. The move by Kurt Brauer to give him the meaningless sinecure of Commissioner of Demobilisation had by no means drawn Quisling's fangs.

He had remained in firm control of his Nasjonal Samling party, a strong-armed ally that Josef Terboven realised he had need of. True, in 1940 it had been little more than a disreputable rabble, but the Nazis' hold on Norway had changed all that. Collaborators had crawled out of the woodwork in October 1940; by the end of that year membership of Nasjonal Samling had risen to 26,000, and it kept on increasing.

But with Quisling in the shadows, nominally at least, the credit for this could be attributed primarily to Terboven's icy presence. It was he who wielded ultimate power in Norway; his clout was far greater than that of General der Infanterie Falkenhorst or, indeed, even of the Nazi secret police.

It was not just a question of crude oppression or terror, although there was plenty of both. Terboven attacked Norway through its stomach. Germany looted Norway's larder; for the first time in living memory, beggars appeared on the streets of Oslo. In the land of the smorgasbord, it became impossible to buy an egg; milk was scarce; and there were acute shortages of poultry and cattle. As early as October 1940, Olaf Hansen, a Norwegian journalist who eventually escaped to London was reporting: 'Meat is not rationed, for the simple reason that there is not enough of it to ration ... You would have difficulty in buying a bar of chocolate in Oslo and there is practically no tobacco. All prices have increased by double since the German invasion.'

Newspapers in Oslo reported that only a flour substitute was available and that production of some form of powdered fish was expected. Even this was wishful thinking; the last supplies of fish were fast running out. Hansen reported: 'At the moment, Norway's great fishing industry is at a standstill because of the acute shortage of petrol. Nobody is allowed to use a private car in Norway. There are a few taxis left in Oslo, but the owners who have survived are permitted to run their vehicles on three days a week only.'

There were consolations of a kind. In the early months of the occupation, there were plenty of jobs, and all available labour was absorbed by the Germans' extensive building of aerodromes and barracks. Pay was more than adequate. But winter was soon casting its grey shadow and the employment figures plunged.

The effect on the middle classes was devastating. Long-established shipping firms shed their labour, along with import and export agencies. Scores of black-coated workers found themselves on the streets, and with the depression came the abolition of unemployment benefit.

Here was fertile ground indeed, for Quisling's Nasjonal Samling members moved in to fill vacant jobs.

Among the ranks of Hird youths there were plenty of

takers: fat wage packets could now be tucked into the pockets of crisp new uniforms.

Terboven, however, remained uneasy. This, after all, was a *Nazi* occupation of Norway. His masters in Berlin demanded a heavy injection of National Socialist ideology and expected him to supply it. The schools of Norway looked like fertile ground. The job was turned over to Ragnar Skancke, one of Quisling's close associates and an ardent Nazi.

Skancke's intention was to pull up Norway's education system by the roots and remodel it for the New Order. Revision of all textbooks on constitutional law and European history was demanded. German was to become the country's second language, in place of English. To discourage rebellion, pictures of Quisling glared down from classroom walls; anyone removing them was disciplined.

That was just a start; Terboven was determined that Quisling would earn his rehabilitation. Not that the architect of Nasjonal Samling had exactly been idle. With the improvement in the fortunes of his organisation he was soon looking to his friends in Berlin. But, as it turned out, there was no need to seek fresh favours. Hitler had begun looking fondly on Quisling once again, and there was an equally enthusiastic advocate in his old crony, Alfred Rosenberg.

Within Norway there was no such support for Quisling. Members of those organisations that had been absorbed by Nasjonal Samling retaliated by resigning or by dissolving their movements. These dissidents – known as B groups – were to form the nucleus of civilian resistance.

But they could not strike yet with any prospect of success. Furthermore, they were contending with a Quisling armed with awesome new powers.

Nobody was more astounded than the man himself when the summons came from Josef Terboven.

The Reichskommissar for Norway told Quisling: 'The time has come for you to have a public role in Norwegian politics. You will be allowed to form a new government.'

The words were carefully chosen. Terboven was imply-
ing that Quisling would not have a free hand to do precisely what he liked in Norway. He was to be first and last
a tool in an overall scheme to consolidate pro-German
appeal throughout the country.

It was necessary, Terboven realised, to feed Quisling's
considerable vanity; a colourful ceremony to mark his latest
elevation would not be out of place.

And so it was that on 1 February 1942 the Norwegian
flag was raised over Akershus Castle and the parliament
building to signify that now Norway had a government of
its own, led by Vidkun Quisling, who, at the elaborate
ceremony, stood to attention in his grey Hird uniform
in the presence of an honour guard drawn from seven
Norwegian regiments.

Hitler did Quisling proud. The Nazi hierarchy was represented by Martin Bormann, the Fuehrer's most trusted
confidant, together with the German Kriegsmarine and
Wehrmacht. The day reached a lavish climax at a sumptu-
ous banquet in a mansion in the suburb of Bygdo.

Quisling was not averse to luxury. The Villa Grandi was
considered eminently suited to his new-found eminence.
It was promptly requisitioned. The name Villa Grandi,
however, was not considered grand enough; Quisling had
it changed to Villa Gimle (Home of the Gods). What title,
after all, could be more suitable for Norway's undisputed
new masters?

Terboven claimed to be suitably impressed, but he lost
no time in telling Quisling that results in stamping out
opposition must be speedy and effective.

Quisling made up his mind to intensify Terboven's
relentless campaign against the teachers. Furthermore, he
would step it up in such a fashion that no one would be
left in the slightest doubt about the power of the Minister
President.

A new organisation, the Teachers' Front, sprang into
being. Quisling's newspaper *Fritt Folk* defined its purpose
with unambiguous crudity. It would, the paper empha-

sised, 'serve as a straitjacket for all those who are unwilling to do their duty to the state and to Norwegian youth' .

Quisling's warning was orchestrated with silky menace by Orvar Saether, the former chief of staff of the detested Hird who became the Front's first leader. Saether warned in a speech that, while individual teachers would not be compelled to join Nasjonal Samling, they would in time 'no doubt find it appropriate to do so'.

Quisling was by no means finished yet. Hot on the establishment of the Teachers' Front came a fresh decree forming a Nasjonal Samling Youth Movement. Quisling's eyes, as usual, were on Berlin. The young people's movement, Hitler Jugend, had proved a conspicuous success in Germany; the Nasjonal Samling model would ape it assiduously. Such a movement in Norway, Quisling declared, 'gives us control of 400,000 young, from whom we shall select those who are to be trained for membership in our party'.

For the teachers there was now a clear, if uncomfortable, choice. They would either have to bow to the demands of the Norwegian Nazis, or reject membership and be hounded out of their jobs. For days, the underground B organisation agonised. Its eventual decision was courageous and fateful: the teachers would be mobilised throughout the country for a mass action that would decisively reject membership of the Teachers' Front.

By a method of secret communication bypassing the German censors, letters were sent to teachers in the towns and villages of Norway. They were ordered in their turn to mail their rejection. So that the defiance would have the maximum effect, the members of the B group ordered the teachers to write in identical terms on precisely the same day – 20 February.

The reaction surprised even the organisers. The Teachers' Front was spurned by 12,000 out of Norway's 14,000 teachers.

It was a direct challenge to Quisling's rule and could scarcely be ignored. It was not merely a question of rebellion by the teachers, serious though that was. Plainly, there was an organised civilian resistance at work.

Saether ordered a series of sweeping arrests in Oslo, Bergen and Trondheim, together with other dragnets in smaller towns and cities. By the end of March, Quisling had more than 13,000 teachers under arrest; many of them were sent to the Grini concentration camp outside Oslo.

For 700 of them, a special horror was reserved. Quisling decreed that they were to be sent to forced labour in the Arctic, alongside the prisoners from the war in Russia.

Their initial journey, packed in railway cattle trucks, was to the rural concentration camp at Jorstadmoen. Physical harassment – gymnastic exercises at the double, belly crawls through slush, and constant hard labour on meaningless tasks – accompanied total isolation. Conversation and the writing or receiving of letters were forbidden.

It might have been thought that men and women more at home in school classroom or university library would have cracked under such a harsh programme of physical and mental humiliation. As it turned out, the action of those so cruelly oppressed was nothing less than heroic.

The harsh regime was kept up for fourteen days and nights, with the camp officials dropping the hint that membership of the Teachers' Front would bring it to an end.

Only fifty teachers out of 687 at Jorstadmoen gave in. They were promptly freed. One hundred and fifty other broken and dispirited prisoners found themselves back at Grini. The rest were marched to unheated cattle trucks and transported to Trondheim, packed aboard the *SS Skjerstad*, a creaking wooden coastal steamer built at the turn of the century and intended to hold only 200.

The conditions were so appalling that they enraged the Nasjonal Samling doctor allowed on board. He sent a personal message to Quisling:

SS Skjerstad, with some 500 teachers and guards and crew, is due to leave Trondheim. Many cannot lie down at night but must stand, as the ship has only room for 200 persons. Many of the teachers are very ill with pneumonia, gastric ulcers, asthma, bronchitis, haemorrhage and mental derangement. There are only two toilets for everybody. . . .

As if sensing the likely reaction from Quisling, the doctor ended his message by stating: 'Several of the teachers are willing to join the Teachers' Front.'

Appeal was useless. Quisling thundered that the teachers had been given their last chance to repent at Jorstadmoen; the ship must sail as scheduled. The *Skjerstad* left on 14 April for the Arctic port of Kirkenes, near the Finnish border. There was no let-up in the appalling, crowded conditions, with prisoners receiving only one hot meal a day. One teacher, crammed with others in the hold, wrote: 'A tiny gleam of light shone from above, but there was no fresh air. There was a fearful stench and one heard the despairing moaning of the sick.'

But even the deportations did not break the spirit of the teachers and there were only a few defections.

For a few months, Quisling kept up the pretence that the Front had a future. With the schools bereft of teachers, the country's entire educational system looked like collapsing. He was forced to give in and reopen the schools.

Like a petulant child whose favourite toy has been taken away, he assembled a group of teachers and stormed: 'You have destroyed everything.' A little later, the prisoners from Kirkenes returned home, greeted as heroes.

But Vidkun Quisling did not allow himself the luxury of sulking for long. Instead, he turned his attention to the Norwegian Jews.

The Jews of Norway, never a large community, had settled comfortably enough in Norwegian cities after fleeing from the dark pogroms of Russia and Poland. By April 1940, at the time of the German invasion, the Jewish population was still only around 1,500 including some 350 political refugees from the Nazis.

Against this pathetically vulnerable minority, who asked only to be left in peace, the Germans moved with savagery and speed. Richard Petrow, in his book *The Bitter Years*, which covers the period of occupation in Denmark and Norway, records:

Within days of the invasion, German troops slashed out at visible signs of Jewish life. In Trondheim, German soldiers smashed into the synagogue, where they replaced Stars of David with Swastikas, demolished all holy objects, and pockmarked the interior walls with bullet holes after using the synagogue's large religious lamps for target practice.

Terboven, a spiteful anti-Semite, lashed Quisling into greater activity. Until the arrival of the Germans, the Nasjonal Samling party had not openly avowed anti-Semitism; getting its cohorts to change their minds was not that easy. If the rank and file had scruples, the police had none. Arrests of Jewish shopkeepers were stepped up, along with the confiscation of their businesses. The letter J was stamped on all identity papers held by Jews.

There was a rash of arbitrary arrests on the flimsiest of political charges. The Nasjonal Samling police were helped out with enthusiasm by a strong and ruthless Gestapo. It was not just a question of unpleasant imprisonment in Grini. There was large-scale deportation for Scandinavian prisoners to, among other places, Auschwitz in Poland, Bergen-Belsen near Hanover, and Ravensbrueck, the women's camp north of Berlin.

Of the 760 Norwegian Jews deported to Auschwitz, only twenty-four survived the war.

But among the Jews of Scandinavia were those who did not perish at Auschwitz or elsewhere. The Danes received advance intelligence of what was in store for them.

Resistance was mobilised for action.

11

On the morning of Friday 30 September 1943, the Jews of Copenhagen were a puzzled people. It was the day before Rosh Hashana, the Jewish New Year, and the 150-strong congregation gathered at the town's synagogue stood before the Holy Ark.

Rabbi Marcus Melchior was telling them bluntly: 'There will be no service this morning. Last night I received word that the Germans plan to raid Jewish homes throughout Copenhagen. They intend to arrest all Danish Jews for shipment to concentration camps. They know that tomorrow is Rosh Hashana and our families will be at home.'

He pressed on urgently: 'We must take immediate action. You must leave the synagogue now and contact all relatives, friends and neighbours whom you know are Jewish. They must pass on the word.

'You must also speak to all your Christian friends and tell them to warn the Jews. You must do this immediately, within the next few minutes, so that within two or three hours everyone will know what is happening. By nightfall we must all be in hiding.'

It was scarcely believable. Hitler, it had been widely supposed, was prepared to be kind almost indefinitely to his *Musterprotektorat*, his model protectorate.

It had seemed that the tenets of National Socialist philosophy allowed for the Danes being pure Nordics, descended from the stock that had inhabited the Danish islands before the Stone Age. The racial theorists of the Third Reich had been pleased to note that the Kimbric peninsula, Jutland, was the birthplace of the Teutons and the Gottons; the Danes, it was patent, were blood brothers of the Germans. Toleration was obviously called for, and this would even be extended to the Danish Jews. If Germany pursued so enlightened an attitude, it was suggested, then there was likely to be little trouble from possible resistance groups.

By no means everyone within Hitler's Germany was so tolerant. To the SS of Heinrich Himmler, Jews were Jews, wherever they might happen to be. How was it that 8,000 of them were allowed to live in peace in Denmark? Here was the ultimate in heresies.

Cecil von Renthe-Fink, the German plenipotentiary, was, above all, a diplomat. There was sense, he believed, in treading warily with the Jews. If they became incensed, if there was an attack on their civil rights, then there would plainly be violent upheaval. Why was it necessary to prejudice what appeared to be good relations between the two countries? Of course, there were the so-called 'Jewish experts' who insisted on bombarding him with memoranda from Berlin about the Jews. Renthe-Fink was prepared to meet them some of the way: he suggested that Jewish firms in Denmark be deprived of their allocations of coal and fuel from Germany.

Surely, in the name of common sense, such a measure would be sufficient. It was considered nothing of the sort. Berlin responded to Renthe-Fink's delicate approach by sending to Denmark one of Himmler's most assiduous disciples, Dr Werner Best. As a key man within the Gestapo, Best had impeccable credentials.

As early as 1935, the Prussian Supreme Court of Administration, which was answerable to Himmler, then deputy chief of the Prussian State Police, had ruled that the orders and actions of the Gestapo were not subject to judicial review. The courts were barred from interfering in any way with the activities of the Gestapo – a rule which received more than an approving nod at the time from Dr Best. Indeed, he had put Himmler's case well: 'As long as the police carry out the will of the leadership, it is acting legally.' Such a lack of scruple, it was considered, would stand him in good stead when it came to dealing with the hitherto feather-bedded Danish Jews.

But Best was not just a textbook Nazi. He had a fund of pragmatism and soon was telling his stupefied masters in Berlin that Renthe-Fink was right: Denmark was supplying Germany vast quantities of foodstuffs, far beyond the agreed quotas. From Danish factories there poured a seemingly endless stream of marine diesel engines, parts, aircraft and armoured vehicles. Ideology was all very well; the Reich had need of such hardware. Talk of the Fuehrer's plan to make Europe free of Jews did not allow for such practical considerations. Besides, this was 1942. A bitter and bloody war was being fought in the Soviet Union; the very future of the Reich was being determined. All reason suggested that the Danish Jews should be left alone.

For Foreign Minister Von Ribbentrop such ideas were abhorrent. The proposition that these Jews, unlike those of Poland, Slovakia and the Ukraine, were to remain inviolate could not be tolerated.

Plainly, both Renthe-Fink *and* Best needed a further lesson. An even grimmer mouthpiece of the Gestapo was despatched to Denmark. SS-Standartenfuehrer Rudolf Mildner was of far sterner stuff. Not only was he a proven anti-Semite, but he had done sinister work at Auschwitz, where he had introduced some novel methods of torture. Mildner was hastily snatched from Poland and despatched to Scandinavia.

The result served only to sting Von Ribbentrop and Himmler into fresh fury. Mildner reported: 'The fact has to be faced that hatred of anti-Semitism in Denmark is endemic. There is an atmosphere of racial and religious tolerance that cannot be denied. The deportation of the Jews will be politically unacceptable.'

The argument raged for nearly a year. Eventually, Hitler's patience snapped. Werner Best was summoned to Berlin. The Fuehrer stormed: 'The idea that Danish Jews should walk around free is loathsome. I demand action.' He went on to point out that, aside from the Jewish question, the Germans had been facing growing resistance from the Danes. There was now an admirable pretext for moving against the Jews.

Danish resistance, previously slumbering, grew steadily bolder. At first, Denmark had enjoyed the fruits of booming exports to Germany. But the occupying power had steadily drained the country dry. The Danes, legendary for eating abundantly and well, had suddenly been faced with serious shortages. They were in mutinous mood.

Even more serious for Germany, they were beginning to sense a change in the tide. The fortunes of the Reich had turned. There had been catastrophic defeats at Stalingrad and El Alamein. In the summer of 1943, Sicily was invaded by the Allies and Mussolini had been toppled from power. All Hitler's instincts were for retaliation.

To Best, Hitler added menacingly: 'If conditions get any worse, I will entrust the government to the military commander.'

Best returned to Denmark pale and shaken. He had good reasons. If Hitler turned over the initiative to the Wehrmacht and its commander, General der Infanterie von Hanneken, the Gestapo would plainly be in disgrace.

And that is what happened. Best was relieved of his job as plenipotentiary and replaced by the Wehrmacht commander. He clung desperately to his position within the Gestapo. He would seek salvation in action.

The pretext for moving against the resistance was ready to hand. Workers' groups, protesting at the food shortages, launched a rash of strikes in the Copenhagen and Odense shipyards. The initial response of the Germans could not have been more insulting to Danish pride – members of the Schalburg Corps, Danish pro-Nazis who had volunteered to fight in the east, were ordered home to turn against their own people. At first, the strikes had been contained and manageable; now they spread like a virus throughout the city. The inevitable violence was dramatic.

When a German officer opened fire on the strikers, the crowd turned on him in fury and beat him to death.

There were mass arrests of known or suspected dissidents. Best called a meeting of Danish newspaper editors and stormed: 'In this ridiculous little country, the press has inoculated the people with the idea that Germany is weak . . . From now on, every editor will be responsible with his head for seeing that the people are no longer poisoned.'

The editors reacted by forming one of the most effective underground newspaper organisations to be found in any occupied country. Like other Danes, they were smarting from a proclamation issued by Hanneken and, at his insistence, broadcast incessantly over Danish radio:

'The latest events have shown that the Danish government is no longer capable of maintaining law and order in Denmark. The disturbances provoked by foreign agents are aimed directly at the Wehrmacht. Therefore in accordance with the articles Nos 42–56 of the Hague Convention of the laws and customs of war on land, I declare a military state of emergency in the whole of Denmark.'

Then followed a shoal of decrees. Crowds and gatherings were restricted to no more than five people, with a rigid curfew and a total ban on the use of mail services or the telephone. Inducements to strikes 'which would cause disadvantages to the Wehrmacht' were punishable by death.

The call to resistance placed the Jews in a hideous dilemma. There was widespread approval for protests against the occupation and the more obvious tyrannies. On the other hand, the Danish Jews reasoned that up till now they had led a charmed life. The Germans, hideously decisive in other countries, had been slow to move against them in Denmark. But for how much longer?

On 8 September 1943, Werner Best gave the answer. He dashed off a telegram to Berlin suggesting that the present state of emergency now amply justified the deportation of the Danish Jews. Sooner or later, the Jews would be sucked into the mainstream of resistance; diplomacy had patently failed.

Hitler was delighted; he promptly reinstated Best as plenipotentiary. A greatly angered Hanneken was instructed to take orders from Best. To Ribbentrop was given the task of ensuring that all Best's needs for the coming operation were met. The Reich's Foreigh Minister sent for Reichsfuehrer Himmler, and Best was telegraphed: 'The Reich Foreign Minister asks you to put forward concrete proposals with regard to the deportation of Jews decided upon, in order to determine how many policemen and how many SS should be detailed to the implementation of the operation in question.'

For Best, there could now be no turning back. On 11 September, he communicated his needs to Berlin. All were granted. Furthermore, Best was told that the men in charge of the coming raid would be SS-Standartenfuehrer Rudolf Mildner and SS-Gruppenfuehrer Guenther Pancke.

Best set about informing his lieutenants. Among them was his head of shipping operations, Georg Ferdinand Duckwitz. For the Jews, the choice of Duckwitz turned out to be highly significant. He had enjoyed a comfortable life in Denmark. He and his wife had gone there from Germany back in 1928, after he graduated from law school. He had secured a post with a Copenhagen coffee firm, followed by a job at the German Embassy as the head of shipping. Duckwitz liked the Danes and certainly had no stomach for delivering them into the hands of the SS.

The Duckwitzs had many friends in Danish political circles, notably in the Social Democratic Party; he was not to forget them in the wake of Werner Best's latest plans.

As for Best, he had not entirely swallowed his misgivings. In a gloomy mood he confided to Duckwitz that pressure from Berlin was rapidly becoming intolerable.

First, there had been Hitler's demands; then had come a request from Ribbentrop to submit plans for an operation that meant nothing less than shipping as many Danish Jews as possible to the concentration camps.

Duckwitz exploded: 'If you consent to this, then you are a disgrace to the German Embassy here.'

Best shrugged: 'I'm personally sympathetic to the treatment of Jews, but it is necessary to obey orders.'

It was too much for Duckwitz; he promptly turned his back on Best and began laying his own plans. The first move was to fly to Berlin and find out exactly what Ribbentrop was planning.

Of that there was little doubt. Ribbentrop had entrusted to Himmler all 'technical questions' involving the arrest and transportation of the Danish Jews to Theresienstadt concentration camp; all necessary troops, trucks and transport ships would be supplied.

It was now that Georg Ferdinand Duckwitz risked his life on behalf of the Danish Jews.

He picked an evening when he knew that his contacts in the Social Democrat party would be together at a meeting; it turned out to be just twenty-four hours before the raid was due.

Although fully aware that the shadow of the Gestapo loomed menacingly, Duckwitz calmly left his apartment and made for the meeting at 22 Roemer Street. Without ceremony, he marched straight into the building's main conference room and went over to Hans Hedtoft, the Social Democrat party chief. He told Hedtoft: 'Within a few hours ships will anchor in Copenhagen Harbour. Those of your poor Jewish countrymen who get caught will be dragged forcibly on board and transported. No one knows what will happen to them.'

Hedtoft barely had time to reply before Duckwitz melted away.

Clearly, there was more than hearsay evidence of German intentions. But to his dismay, Hedtoft came up against a wall of disbelief. Might not the whole thing, people reasoned, be an elaborate Gestapo plot to flush out Jews? Besides, Werner Best had informed the Jews countless times that no such action was contemplated; the Danish government had received his assurances. Hedtoft was pressed to reveal his source, but he could not bring himself to point the finger at Duckwitz.

With his warnings rejected, Hedtoft decided to act on his own. There could now be only one question: how could he warn the Danish Jews?

Time was not on his side. As early as mid-September, members of the Jewish Community Centre had complained to Best that their office had been raided by Germans in mufti: records of members' names and addresses had been seized.

Best seemed both penitent and embarrassed. He confessed: 'I'm aware of what happened. But in fact it is only a minor action' (*eine recht kleine aktion*). Best went on to explain that the quest had been merely a routine affair to root out saboteurs. There was no connection with 'the Jewish question'.

To Duckwitz, Best later told a different story. This was indeed the prelude to a planned raid. Duckwitz, as head of shipping, would have a crucial role to play and he would be kept informed. Even so, Best continued to be nagged by doubts. But there was little that he could do now to stem the plans of Ribbentrop and Himmler.

He made one more try. Could not, he suggested, the Jews be rounded up *after* the state of emergency in Denmark had been lifted? It would surely be possible for an edict to be presented whereby the Jews would be instructed to report for 'work' at the Wehrmacht offices. They could then be arrested and deported.

The suggestion reached the desk of SS-Sturmbannfuehrer Adolf Eichmann, who in January of the previous year had been assigned the task of the mass deportation of Jews to the extermination camps of the east. Eichmann was, in fact, the architect of the entire genocide operation. And he had no time for Best's pussyfooting. A special contingent of SS commandos under his direction was poised for work in Copenhagen.

Its mission was clearcut: to prepare for the transportation to Germany of 8,000 Jews. There would be no question of those Jews being lured into a trap; they would be arrested in a carefully planned 'lightning raid' on 1 October.

Hints of the dangers reached Rabbi Marcus Melchior. The rabbi pondered recent happenings, the state of military emergency, the seizing of the membership lists of the Jewish Community Centre.

No delay could be justified; he forthwith warned his congregation. They were stunned, disbelieving, even hostile. A few hours before, the very idea of ranting in his own synagogue, surrounded by the sacred scrolls of the Torah, the silver candelabra and the prayer books, would have been unthinkable. But now here he was shouting: 'You must do what I tell you.'

The traditional authority of the rabbi had its effect.

News of the planned German raid coursed through the Jewish community. Those who had been at the synagogue were soon telling everyone they knew of the vital need to go into hiding. Many risked the telephone, but, conscious that the Gestapo could well be listening in, word-of-mouth intelligence spread rapidly. Jews told not only other Jews, but Christians they felt they could trust.

No haphazard warnings, however well intentioned, would be enough. Melchior targeted his intelligence through known sympathisers who were able because of their jobs to move around Copenhagen without arousing suspicion.

Christian and Jewish policemen, postmen, taxi drivers, shopkeepers, doctors, teachers and students spread the word during their normal working day. One of Melchior's most able lieutenants was ambulance driver Jorgen Knudsen; the rabbi reasoned that the sight of an ambulance parked outside houses and blocks of flats would not be likely to cause comment. Knudsen promptly agreed to take the day off and, armed with a list of prominent Jews, drove round to spread the word. Those Jews who panicked, he instructed to play at being patients. Swiftly, he ferried them to the local hospital, where a friend, Dr Karl Henry Koster, was willing to hide them.

Jens Lillilund, who at the time of the Danish invasion had expressed his contempt for the Germans by spitting at them and who had been arrested and later released for a singularly fruitless act of resistance, had broadened his activities. He wandered the streets at night, slashing the tyres of cars belonging to the Germans. After that, it was remarkably easy to become a full-time saboteur, blowing up Danish factories in production for the Germans.

Such activities were personally satisfying and even effective, but they paled into significance with this new threat. Lillilund was not Jewish and did not feel that he had any exclusive loyalty towards the Jews. But they were being threatened by the Germans, and that was more than sufficient reason to help them. He saw no need, however, to alter his normally impulsive style. Very well, the Jews would be warned. But *which* Jews?

The family doctor, Max Rosenthal, was to hand. A telephone call would be madness; Lillilund burst in on the morning surgery.

Rosenthal snapped: 'What the hell is the matter with you? You know better than to break in like this. I've a room full of patients.'

Lillilund retorted: 'If I don't talk to you there won't be any patients. This is very definitely an emergency.'

Dr Rosenthal was to hold no more surgeries for a very long time to come. Within the hour he and his family were in hiding in Lillilund's own home.

Mogens Staffeldt was most people's idea of a bookseller. He was short, mild-mannered, unworldly. Not for one moment would he have dreamt of aiming his bicycle at German troops, let alone spitting at them. Neither was he the type who would willingly spend cold winter nights priming fuses for explosives aimed at enemy factory buildings.

For choice, he would have preferred to ignore the Germans. Unfortunately, they had other ideas. When they moved into Dagmarhaus, the building where his bookshop was located, he was forced to find new premises. In high dudgeon, he moved across the road and prepared to start his business all over again.

But he was not allowed to. The curb on his activities, however, came not from the Germans but from his old friend Jens Lillilund.

Within days, the bookish Staffeldt, torn away from his beloved catalogues and shelves of stock, had become a dedicated resistant. Just how he allowed himself to be persuaded was always a perpetual mystery to him. The bookshop became a secret headquarters for the underground; the cellar was given over to printing illegal resistance newspapers containing accounts of German atrocities against the Jews in other European counties.

Then came the word from Lillilund of the intended German roundup.

Staffeldt promptly told his clerks that he would be away for a while. He mounted his bicycle and rode throughout Copenhagen to pass the warning to a score of Jewish families. Soon he had built up a network of Jewish informers whose job was to spread the intelligence still further.

To his considerable astonishment, Mogens Staffeldt actually began to enjoy his new life of intrigue. Soon word was abroad that his bookshop was a collecting point for Jewish refugees. He welcomed them all without question. His new-found enthusiasm began to worry Lillilund.

He protested: 'The risk is enormous. There are a lot of Germans in this building, and sooner or later they'll see something.'

Staffeldt argued: 'But they are excellent customers and spend money. When the place is free of them I'll indicate it by putting a copy of Kaj Munk's poems in the window. It will mean that the coast is clear. The absence of the book will mean that it is dangerous for Jews to enter the store.'

It was a piece of melodrama straight out of the movies. Jens Lillilund remained uneasy; the Jews kept on coming.

Some ninety per cent of Danish Jews lived in Copenhagen; it was a statistic that made the work of the underground that much easier. The Jews were found hiding places everywhere – in the homes of their relatives, Christian friends and even total strangers. They were harboured in Protestant churches and Catholic cloisters. They found refuge in hotels, summer huts, cellars and warehouses.

Shortly before midnight on 29 September 1943, the Germans struck. Two German transport vessels, including the large freighter *Wartheland*, anchored in Copenhagen harbour. Then two days later, right on schedule, came the Eichmann commandos. All telephone communications throughout the country were severed. Into the offices of the Ritzau news agency flooded German troops; the tele-printers were swiftly disabled. The dragnet was under way. But most of the knocks on the front doors of Jewish homes went unanswered.

Inevitably, there were tragedies involving families for whom the warnings had come too late. They were dragged away to the waiting ships. One hundred and fifty German troops threw a cordon around an old people's home next to a synagogue. The residents, aged from sixty to ninety were dragged from their beds, including a paralysed elderly woman who had been bedridden for eleven years. Bound to a stretcher, she was carried to the synagogue, and later questioned about sabotage operations. The elderly were forced to watch the synagogue being looted of its treasures. German soldiers urinated in the sanctuary.

By the standards of the Nazis, the raid could only be rated a dismal failure. A total of 202 Jews had been arrested – far short of the number that could be accommodated in the transport ships. Throughout the country the number of seizures stood at 284 men, women and children. The bulk of the Jewish population had escaped.

For Werner Best, embarrassment was complete. In a mood of misguided optimism, he had sent a premature telegram to Hitler: 'It was my duty to clean Denmark of her Jews and this has been achieved. Denmark is *Judenrein* – [free of Jews] and completely purged.'

Adolf Eichmann, the ravings of Hitler and Himmler still ringing in his ears, arrived in Copenhagen three days later. The full blast of his fury was vented on Best and Mildner. Eichmann declared later: 'That small country caused us more problems than anywhere else.'

The transport vessels departed with their meagre cargo. Eichmann, with more pressing business and more promising quarry in the east, departed with the instruction that raids were to go on. After all, he argued, the Jews could not remain in hiding for ever.

But where were they to go next? The doors of neutral Sweden remained tight shut.

As it turned out, one man was to be the key figure in helping to prise them open. Only then could the exodus of the Jews begin.

12

Danish scientist and Nobel prizewinner Niels Bohr was, by common consent, the world's leading authority on nuclear physics after Albert Einstein. And in 1943 Bohr was wanted urgently in the United States for developing the atomic bomb.

Late in September, he was spirited by the Allies from Denmark to Sweden, where he was swiftly contacted by Professor Lord Cherwell, Winston Churchill's personal consultant on scientific matters. Cherwell outlined an elaborate scheme. It involved Bohr flying to London as the first stop on his way to America, where he would begin work immediately.

To the astonished Cherwell, Bohr announced that he wanted nothing to do with the plan – at least, at first. Instead he demanded an urgent meeting with Sweden's Foreign Minister, Christian Guenther.

He got it. His demand was uncompromising: 'Unless you offer refuge to all Danish Jews who are able to reach Sweden I have no intention of leaving the country.'

The explanation for Bohr's ultimatum lay in an earlier meeting held in Copenhagen with Hans Hedtoft in which the German plans for rounding up the Danish Jews had been revealed. Guenther, however, appeared lukewarm. Bohr had no intention of leaving matters there. His next request was a meeting with the Swedish king. This time, the response was far more positive; King Gustav came across with his offer the very next day. Sweden *would* accept the Danish Jews.

Allied agents in Stockholm breathed again; Bohr would now be available for his essential work in America. But the Danish scientist had by no means concluded his mission. The Jews, he insisted, must be informed at once of Sweden's offer, otherwise plans for escape could not be formulated.

The Allies sweated. If this awkward scientist was not spirited out of the country soon, there was the real possibility that he might be kidnapped or murdered by German agents. But Bohr held the trump card, and Cherwell and his cohorts knew it.

Within days, the Swedish press was carrying the offer of refuge on its front pages. Swedish radio relayed the vital message to Denmark; Bohr was soon on his way to London.

He left behind a burning question: how were those Jews trapped in Denmark to be spirited to Sweden, literally under the noses of the Germans?

Clearly, the only possible way was by boat. It was an obvious route for the Germans to plug; several days before the 1 October raid they had ordered that all Danish boats were to be confined to harbour. The exception to the new edict was fishing vessels: an obvious loophole the owners were not slow to exploit.

Several hundred Jews in hiding rushed to coastal towns such as Elsinore, Snekkersten and Dragør. There, they hoped, would be fishermen willing to make the dangerous journey across the sound to Sweden.

People living around the towns did not hesitate to put up the Jews in hotels, farms, private houses and even garages. Nevertheless, the flight was hasty and chaotic and the Germans took full advantage of this obvious weakness. Most of the Jews caught by the Germans were arrested before the escape boats could be properly organised.

The one-time reluctant resistant Mogens Staffeldt was soon cheerfully accepting that his bookshop had become far more than merely a precarious refuge and meeting place for itinerant Danish Jews. The shop was the collection point from which they would make for other hiding places near the docks. Jens Lillilund was now undisputed boss of the Holger Danske resistance organisation, which took its name from a legendary Danish hero who rose from his sleep whenever his country was threatened. At first, Holger Danske had engaged in active sabotage against the enemy. But from now on, everything would be concentrated on the safe transport of the Jews.

Lillilund, meeting in the bookshop with his fellow resistants, did not mince words. There had, he stressed, been too many individual escape attempts in fishing boats, which had only resulted in capture by the Gestapo. The time had come to organise the business properly. Fishermen prepared to do the job must be pinned down to a fixed price. The existing Fishermen's Association would be given the job of nominating those of their members who were considered absolutely trustworthy; freelancers and freebooters would be out. That Lillilund was capable of such organisation was proved beyond doubt after the operation was over, when it was discovered that Holger Danske had under its control as many as a dozen fishing vessels, which had carried around 1,000 Jews to Sweden by the end of October.

Behind each sailing lay appalling risks. There could be arrest, deportation, imprisonment and even execution. Even successful escapes had their moments of terror.

One Jewish woman related:

We were taken by taxi to the beach near a little fishing harbour. Each of the four passengers and the organiser were then hidden under a bush by the shore. The plan was that at a certain time we were to crawl along the beach to the harbour, where there was a watchtower manned by Germans. We lay a whole day waiting for darkness. Up on the road we could hear cars drive by and we shivered with fright . . . At seven o'clock in the evening, a strange sight revealed itself. From the bushes along the beach human forms crawled on their stomachs. We discovered that these were other passengers of whose presence we had been completely unaware. After a while we reached the fishing boat without mishap and were herded into the hold, like herrings in a barrel.

Frequently, there was not enough space below; passengers were wrapped in fishing nets and sacks on deck. The whipping-up of the wind brought seasickness, and the refugees were forced on deck to retch, away from the stench of the hold. Possible searchlights from a German patrol boat were a recurring nightmare. Then the engine was stopped and the Jews stood silently around the wheel-house, whose weak light could well have given them away. A small boat would be blown off course by the gale and, in the light of early dawn, there was no way of gauging their position.

The Jewish woman's account went on:

Would we ever be saved? At seven in the morning, land was sighted. But what land? The boat approached the coast; we hoped that liberty was at hand. We were *really* in Swedish terri-torial waters. The Danish flag was raised and people threw their arms around one another and cried for joy. We were saved at last. The harbour we had sailed into was full of Swedish warships on whose decks sailors waved and shouted 'Valkommen'.

For Rabbi Melchior, bereft of any knowledge of boats, the escape to Sweden was an astounding experience.

It began promisingly enough. Arrangements were made by the Reverend Hans Kildelby, Lutheran pastor at Orselv, forty miles from Copenhagen, for a young fisher-man to ferry the six members of the Melchior family. Although it was pitch-black when the party set out from the island of Falster, everyone was cheerful enough. After all, the journey would take a mere six hours.

Anxiety mounted, though, when the six hours became eight and eventually stretched to ten. And then came alarm, when the rabbi spotted land. It was the Danish town of Gedser, near the German mainland.

Melchior turned on the young fisherman, yelling for an explanation. It emerged that the man had lost his way, was

111

terrified of running into German patrol boats and had wasted twelve hours cruising in a circle.

For the first time in his life, Rabbi Marcus Melchior hit a fellow human being.

The fisherman was left on the floor of the boat to nurse a swollen jaw. As for the rabbi, he never was able to explain how he had managed to grab the rudder and turn the boat around. He held it on course for six hours until he reached Swedish waters.

On the day that Germany invaded Denmark, Erling Kiaer's main reaction was one of intense irritation; the roar of aircraft had disturbed his sleep. Not that the arrival of the Germans came as any surprise; in Kiaer's view his government had been singularly spineless in standing up to the Nazi menace. He shrugged and went back to sleep again.

Later that afternoon, the young bookbinder, in common with many of his fellow townsmen in Elsinore, bicycled to the centre to find out what was going on. The number of Danish lives lost amounted to precisely thirteen and, in the face of that, the government had caved in. Kiaer settled down in some disgust to tolerating the enemy and getting on with his life.

It appeared remarkably easy to keep out of trouble; the secret was never to discuss politics. Then came the day when the Germans disturbed Kiaer's sleep for the second time. The disturbance now was not from aircraft, but from sporadic bursts of gunfire in the streets around his apartment. Soon the explanation was spreading through the neighbourhood. A number of Danish girls known to be sleeping with Germans had been dragged from their homes and paraded through the streets with their heads shaved.

Fraternisation had led to punishment for some of the German troops, who in turn had decided on a little revenge

112

of their own. A number of them had gone on the rampage and fired at random into Danish homes.

Such an incident chipped away at Kiaer's conscience. If the war was to be brought to the streets, should he not be playing his part? Was his self-imposed isolation from resistance any longer acceptable?

Soon he was discussing his conscience with three friends, all of whom had previously been more than content to keep out of trouble with the Germans. Thomod Larsen was a solid police officer whose routine work was still necessary, Germans or no Germans. Ove Bruhn beavered away contentedly as a book-keeper, while Dr Jorgen Gesfelt had more than enough patients to keep him busy in the fishing village of Snekkersten.

The policeman obviously had to be handled carefully; Kiaer, feeling his way, suggested to Larsen that possibly he could extend his work a little. He was in an ideal position, after all, to gain access to confidential reports, possibly about refugees and underground groups. Part of his job was to be a good listener; now was the time to eavesdrop on both Gestapo and Wehrmacht.

Bruhn had talents for organisation that would prove useful. A doctor was frequently needed to administer sedatives to the children of refugees smuggled onto the boats; Dr Gesfelt's main attraction, of course, was that he practised in a fishing village.

The nucleus of the group was complete. The search was on for the most innocuous cover name; the Elsinore Sewing Club was born.

The world knows Elsinore above all for Kronberg Castle, setting for Shakespeare's *Hamlet*. But for hundreds of Danish Jews in 1943, Elsinore was the springboard to freedom: base of one of Denmark's most effective underground units.

As a crossing place, the main advantage of Elsinore is that at this point the sound separating Denmark and

Sweden is only two and a half miles wide. But it is narrow, and was therefore easy for the patrolling Germans. To make matters worse, there were not enough Danish fishermen sufficiently daring to cope with the volume of passengers.

At first, there was an attempt to use trains; there was an important ferry crossing at Elsinore for German rail traffic. On the trip from Sweden, the trains were piled high with iron ore and other key war materials. But on the journey out they were often empty.

Although the trucks were kept locked, there was enough of a wait at Elsinore before they were loaded on to the ferries: time for the Danes to open them and sneak Jewish refugees aboard. Unfortunately, Danish security was lax, the Gestapo moved in to guard the empty trains. Once again, the fishermen came into their own.

There were inevitably delays, dangers and tragedies. The Germans made a number of successful swoops; tragedy struck at the town of Gilleleje where arrangements had been made to take one hundred Jews to a large schooner in the harbour. Kiaer and another colleague, journalist Borge Ronne, set out on foot to check final details at a farm which was to be the rallying point for the escapees.

For Kiaer, the going was particularly hard; he was weighed down with four thousand pounds needed to pay the fishermen, sewn into his coat lining.

At long last, the two men were knocking at the door of their resistance contact at the farm. There was no answer. The same thought struck both: had the Gestapo got there first? Or had there been a breakdown in communications and they were not expected?

The door was opened a cautious few inches. In the gloom, Kiaer and Ronne made out a face chalk-white with fear.

The man gasped: 'The Gestapo have called. I think they've rumbled the entire set-up.' The door was slammed shut.

It was far too late to warn the escapees who were already on their way. As two of the key resistants, it was essential for Kiaer and Ronne to remain at liberty. Within seconds, the pair had vaulted the garden wall, leapt several hedges and were hurtling towards the open fields. Kiaer was only too conscious of the weight of the money stitched to his coat.

Fortunately, both men knew the area well enough to avoid the roads. For several hours, they moved gingerly through fields of mud and dirt. Nowhere was there any sign of Germans. They decided to chance returning to the farm. There they were greeted by badly scared refugees who had been brought from Snekkersten in a convoy of trucks and cars.

Kiaer was terse: 'You'll have to go back to Snekkersten. There can be no question of a sailing tonight. It's far too risky.'

The drivers of the trucks and cars caught the mood of fear and refused to budge. Kiaer began ripping at the lining of his coat, desperately handing out money to make the drivers change their minds. The bribe worked, but by now many of the refugees were on the edge of panic. A mother and her daughter resolutely refused to make the return journey.

Kiaer explained patiently: 'If the area really is thick with Gestapo, it'll only be a matter of time before they surround the farm. You've got to move.'

The persuasion worked with everyone – except the mother and daughter. There was no choice but to leave them behind. The drivers doused their headlights and set out with the remaining refugees on the return journey. Later, Kiaer learnt that the Gestapo had arrived soon after. Mother and daughter were both taken.

It was a hard blow, but the Elsinore Sewing Club continued its work, extending it to ferrying out saboteurs, Danes wanted for political crimes, and English and American airmen shot down over Denmark while on bombing missions to Germany.

Erling Kiaer carved his own legend in resistance folklore as the 'Danish Pimpernel', perpetually elusive and bearing a charmed life. He also had a considerable sense of style. To the rest of the club, he announced: 'We can't depend solely on the fishermen. We need our own boat full time.'

The very idea was dismissed as ridiculous. To procure a boat independent of the professional fishermen was no easy task and virtually impossible to keep secret from the Germans. But the next day Kiaer had his boat.

'Where did it come from?' someone asked.

Kiaer responded happily: 'I stole it.'

That same evening he made his first trip to Sweden, celebrating his success with a gastronomic dinner at Helsingborg's Grand Hotel. He returned to Denmark and made three more successful crossings.

A handy donation from a wealthy Jewish doctor provided the down payment on a new boat. With contributions from the local townspeople, a second, larger one was secured. The original purloined vessel was returned to its astonished owner, who had not even realised it was missing.

News of the steady exodus of the Jews was greeted with cold fury by Heinrich Himmler. His sacred SS and Gestapo were beginning to look foolish. The local Gestapo was reinforced; the Germans went out looking for informers.

They were successful. Thomod Larsen, on the beach at Snekkersten awaiting the arrival of a fishing boat, was shot down in cold blood by a waiting German patrol. They had obviously been tipped off. But Larsen managed to convince his captors that he was a police officer on normal duty. An ambulance rushed him to hospital in Elsinore. Members of the Sewing Club took over; he was smuggled to Copenhagen, and from there, still gravely ill from his wounds, to Sweden.

Gestapo officers tumbled into Borge Ronne's apartment. His brother answered the door, giving the journalist a chance to escape over the rooftops. The following day he went into hiding in the home of another Sewing Club member. Several days later he was smuggled to Sweden.

All the key members of the Elsinore Sewing Club survived the war, including the 'Danish Pimpernel' himself. But no matter how sweet revenge may have been, it did not save the Elsinore Sewing Club. It was forced into extinction, destroyed by betrayal.

Two of the informers were eventually unmasked – O. I. Madesen, a police colleague of Larsen, and a naturalised Dane known as the 'Vienna boy'.

An offer of passage to Sweden was made to the unsuspecting Madesen. Halfway on the boat journey, the informer was throttled and his body thrown overboard.

The 'Vienna boy' lived a little longer. Furthermore, he did so in lavish style, thanks to his German masters. He was tucking into an elaborate dinner in his apartment when the men with machine-guns broke in.

Any regrets they may have felt for the ensuing violence were reserved strictly for the building's landlord. The killers left a note among the carnage. It read: 'Sorry for the holes in the wall.'

13

Mogens Staffeldt was enjoying himself. The successful exodus of the Danish Jews had boosted the courage of all the resistants. The time had come, they all felt, to attempt something more daring. Staffeldt's new ambition was to turn his bookshop into nothing less than an assignment centre for saboteurs trained in England and parachuted back into Denmark.

There were, Staffeldt pointed out to his no less enthusiastic colleagues, plenty of factories and railways just waiting to be blown up, to say nothing of the necessary liquidation of informers and traitors.

Inevitably, there was the day when the Gestapo came: three men dragged Mogens Staffeldt off to headquarters. Only the day before, twelve highly skilled saboteurs had left the shop for the south of Denmark, on a key mission of destruction near the German border.

The Gestapo men were all studied politeness, and they gave the impression of having all the time in the world. Furthermore, they did not seem to show any interest in sabotage activities at all.

One of them asked casually: 'Have you helped with the escape of Danish Jews?'

Staffeldt decided on a calculated risk. To admit it would do little harm now: all the Jews were away and presumably safe. It would make no difference whether he admitted it or not; plainly, the Gestapo would not let him go. His arrest was serious enough. All he could do was limit the damage. In any case, if he talked about the Jews, it might divert his questioners from the bookshop's function of providing a haven for saboteurs.

It was a forlorn hope. The next moment, he turned pale as one of the Germans said: 'By the way, we have caught your saboteurs. We would like the name of any others, together with your underground contacts.'

Obstinately, Staffeldt went on talking about the escaping Jews. Anything to keep his listeners busy; the main worry now was that they would take it into their heads to search the shop for arms.

But it was only delaying the process. The search was made, anyway. Staffeldt was no less astonished than his tormentors when nothing was found. Staffeldt later understood why. A fellow resistant, Christian Kieling, had got wind of his arrest and took the considerable risk of moving everything from the shop ahead of the Gestapo raid.

From Gestapo headquarters, Staffeldt was moved to Denmark's Vestre Prison. He escaped extreme torture; his captives contented themselves by losing their tempers and hitting him occasionally. He told them nothing.

The Germans, though, had their own ways of trying to get him talking. In the next cell was a close friend and fellow resistant, Svend Otto Nielsen, a mathematics teacher turned saboteur.

The Germans let Staffeldt hear Nielsen's screams under torture.

In attempting to escape, Nielsen had been shot no less than eight times. Life was a lot easier for his torturers after that.

He had broken his thigh-bone, and it was a simple matter to allow the limb to heal and then break it again and rub the fractured ends together. He was denied all medical attention; even the dignity of washing himself. Over the weeks and months, Nielsen's mattress hardened with cakes of blood, faeces and pus.

Staffeldt realised that, whatever the outcome, release would be out of the question, either for him or his friend. Talking would be hardly likely to relieve Nielsen's sufferings. He kept quiet. The Gestapo realised that they were getting nowhere with Staffeldt; he was forthwith despatched to the concentration camp at Horserod. His death sentence was never carried out. He and Jens Lillilund both survived the war.

And Svend Otto Nielsen? Suddenly, all torture ceased and the thigh-bone healed. Then came the day when Nielsen had recovered so well that he was able to enjoy the coffee and cigar which his suddenly amiable jailers brought him.

They next took him out of bed, sat him in a chair and carried him to the courtyard of the prison. Then they shot him.

Reichskommissar Josef Terboven had, by the end of the second year of the occupation of Norway, good reason to feel satisfied. The high spot of his achievement had been in June 1941, soon after the Germans invaded the Soviet Union. He had given orders for all Jews in Tromso and other towns in northern Norway to be rounded up and deported to the Reich. There had been hundreds of arrests around Kristiansand: twenty-four resistants and the leaders of Milorg, the organisation for Norwegian military resistance, had been executed.

Just what deportation meant for Jews leaving Oslo for Germany was illustrated by an eyewitness account from a Norwegian seaman:

The Jews ... were taken in lorries or, in the case of very sick people, in buses down to the harbour near Filipstad, in Oslo. The Germans and Norwegian Nazi guards prevented the deportees from taking leave of their friends. The Jews were immediately driven on board where they were given numbered discs. Embarkation went on from seven in the morning till one o'clock the following night. The Jews were taken in groups down into the two foremost holds where straw mattresses were spread on the floor. Space was extremely restricted, because the number of Jews was 200, more than had been expected. The youngest was a little boy of six or seven and the oldest was over 80.

In the morning, the *SS Kiel* sailed. The sea was rough and

conditions in the holds which had already become very bad during the night grew far worse. There were very few prisoners who had not been seasick and the smell was indescribable. The extremely inadequate sanitary facilities were soon unusable. Only in exceptional circumstances was anyone allowed on deck ... One young Jew tried to take his own life by cutting an artery with the lid of a tin can; another one tried to jump overboard. A woman gave birth to a child down in the hold and was allowed after trying to kill the child to move up into midships. The food was the most meagre imaginable. . . . The guards were very severe, and the slightest movement or the least word brought batons and fists into play.

In order to get permission to go on deck or to the lavatory, a prisoner would first have to kneel down and kiss the boots of the guard. Those who were seasick were hosed with water from the deck. The hose was also used to clean the holds. The straw mattresses and clothing became soaked and never dried throughout the voyage.

The ship cast anchor outside Copenhagen, and the woman with the baby together with a very sick old man and the young Jew who tried to commit suicide were taken away in a police boat – 'to hospital', it was said. On arrival in a German port, the Jewish prisoners were allowed to take with them only a few of their miserable possessions. The rest was thrown overboard or burnt.

Home-grown fascist movements fed on fertile ground with the advent of Nazi subjugation.

As for the Belgians, it was their lot during World War Two to suffer Leon Degrelle.

There had, admittedly, been a time when the Belgians seemed only too pleased to accommodate the strikingly handsome, fiercely nationalistic son of a prosperous Catholic brewer, who appeared to be equally mesmerised by Benito Mussolini and Adolf Hitler.

In the 1930s, making full use of an invaluable platform supplied by his directorship of a barely solvent publishing house called Christus Rex, the property of the Action Catholique de la Jeunesse Belge, Degrelle launched what he came to regard almost as a sacred mission. From a tiny office, he bombarded Belgium with pamphlets roundly denouncing corruption in high places – above all, politicians who were also financial manipulators. The country's powerful Catholic party cringed beneath the barrage of abuse and denunciation, and had to act; it forbade its parliamentary representatives from holding salaried directorships while they were members of Parliament.

It was not enough. Degrelle, far from deaf to the hoarse demagogy of the German and Italian dictators with their mass meetings and parades, bands and banners, desperately wanted a party of his own. From Christus Rex evolved a protest political group high on ideals but vague in aims. In a manifesto, called *Message of Rex*, Degrelle declared loftily: 'Rex is the realm of total souls . . . complete lack of selfishness and individualism; a cause which transcends the individual, demanding all, promising nothing.'

From Adolf Hitler, the new dictator of Germany, was to come unstinted admiration: 'If I had a son, I would want him to be like Degrelle.' Mussolini, however, provided a commodity far more valuable than praise: funds for the coffers of the severely stretched Rexists. All heady stuff. It was especially gratifying when the party, on an avowedly anti-Communist, anti-Socialist, anti-Semitic and anti-bourgeois programme, made a sensational showing at the 1936 polls.

A party which two years before had not even existed now swept into Parliament with twenty-one seats in the Lower House and eight in the Senate. People began talking about Degrelle as the coming man. The king sounded him out on his willingness to accept a cabinet post. It was arrogantly thrust aside: 'I desire power, complete power, not just a ministerial job for myself or one of my lieutenants.' Within three years, the dream had turned to dust.

Degrelle's courting of Flemish nationalists demanding autonomy, and a covert meeting with Hitler's propaganda minister Dr Josef Goebbels, chipped away at the popularity of the Rexists. In April 1939, when the movement again faced the electors, its slump was every bit as dramatic as its rise. Seventeen of its twenty-one seats melted away. The share of the poll fell from 271,491 in 1936 to 103,636. By the outbreak of World War Two, it looked as if the Rexists were a spent force.

The German advance towards Belgium not only changed all that, it quite probably saved the life of Leon Degrelle.

Inevitably, it triggered a panic over the activities of those likely to be sympathetic to the new conquerors. Degrelle was arrested and interned by the French at Vernet but eventually released by the Germans.

Revenge was to taste sweet indeed. After his return to Belgium, Degrelle had his former guards brought to trial. The officer who had been in charge was sentenced to fifteen years' hard labour.

Degrelle now gave himself wholeheartedly to Hitler. On a barnstorming tour of the country, he urged his audiences: 'Do not be afraid to shout Heil Hitler.'

The Rexist paper, *Pay Reel*, stormed at the clergy: 'Their passionate sermons, their continual interference in political matters, their insults to Hitler and Germany . . . the abuse of their clerical rights for provocative and aggressive ends, the atmosphere of rebellion which many priests and monks seem intent on spreading, all this is, quite frankly, unbearable.'

Any manifestations of resistance were dealt with harshly. On 30 April 1942, posters sprouted all over Brussels. They read:

On April 16, at nine o'clock in the evening, in a hall at the Grand Place, where Brussels Flemish SS-men were gathered, a bomb exploded under the platform. A few persons were injured, and considerable damage was done to to the hall. The criminals are certainly Communists. Ten Communist prisoners, some of them already under sentence for other crimes, have therefore been deported to the East. The population of Brussels is asked to help clear up this crime. If the criminals are not discovered by noon on May 5, an additional batch of Communists will be sent to the East.

The alternative often meant incarceration in Belgium's Breendonck concentration camp, where many of the guards were Rexist or Flemish men decked out in German uniforms. These men received special rates of pay, with superior food rations, free lodging, free food and – possibly the most attractive inducement of all – free fuel.

No such privileges were granted to those ordinary Belgians striving desperately to hold on to their pride and lead as normal a life as possible. Roger Motz, an exiled member of the Belgian Parliament, wrote in *Belgian Unvanquished*:

Poverty, hunger and the humiliation of foreign domination have cast a shadow of dismal gloom over the whole Belgian people. . . . As for the quality of the bread which is sold to the population – it is absolutely revolting. The bread contains about 30–50 per cent foreign matter; it is black and sticky; it is impossible to cut it with a knife and it can only be eaten in shapeless lumps. Needless to say it is completely indigestible and its nutritive value is practically non-existent. But for whole weeks there is none to be had, and the newspapers in Brussels frequently publish announcements advising the public not to get unduly upset on account of the total lack of flour, but of course it is the Germans who by their extensive requisitioning have disorganised the distribution of commodities. This is particularly so in the case of butcher's meat. The requisitions of the German army as far as slaughtered livestock is concerned have been so heavy that they have absorbed the whole national output. Recently the Nazis commandeered 8 million pounds of raisins for their wounded on the Russian front. . . . The population has kept alive mainly on bread, potatoes, milk.

People seldom received the full amount of their theoretical rations. Roger Motz commented dryly: '. . . It may be said that the only article which is plentiful in the system of food control in Belgium is the coupons. The products which they represent are to all intents and purposes almost non-existent.'

The Germans were swift to hit back at the black market with the ordinance: 'Anyone who counterfeits ration tickets will be condemned to death or, in less serious cases, to hard labour. An unsuccessful attempt will be punished in exactly the same way as a successful one.'

Anne Somerhausen, a Belgian woman who kept a diary throughout the occupation, wrote:

People read it, shrug, look more carefully at the ration tickets they buy – pay higher prices for them. . . . Blessed black market! On Saturdays and Sundays, before dawn, labourers and office workers pile into trains going to the provinces, tramp about the countryside in search of black market potatoes, wheat, butter and eggs and return at night bowed under suitcases and knapsacks in the blacked-out trains, tired but happy. They have black market food to sell at high prices to richer families, to war profiteers, even to Germans. They will feed themselves on the difference between farm and city black market prices.

They are however subject to nightmares of risk, for control officials inspect trains, stations, and street cars and fall upon these petty tradesmen. Black trading is not an easy calling. Yet, as I see it, it is the only one likely to save the little people of Belgium from German-imposed malnutrition.

The erosion of food supplies was far from being the only stranglehold exercised by the Germans. Even the simplest journeys within the country became virtually impossible. About 45,000 Belgian railways trucks were seized by the conquerors and sent as far as Italy and Romania; almost the whole of Belgium's stock of lorries had vanished. Private cars, even for doctors, had become merely a memory. But for those few fortunate enough still to have them, it was possible to get petrol – from the more enterprising Germans who were prepared to sell military stocks at rarefied prices.

And resistance? In Belgium, it seemed to many that the underground had, for a time at least, been cowed.

Elsewhere, too, there seemed little prospect of relief or release.

14

Gauleiter Gustav Simon's brutally direct methods of reversing recent Luxembourg history continued remorselessly. The Grand Duchy, he proclaimed, had always been German and, furthermore, would remain so.

True, Luxembourg had in 1815 formed part of the old Germanic Confederation; it was equally true, though, that in 1939 it had been declared neutral territory by the Treaty of London. Furthermore, at the Treaty of Versailles in 1919, Luxembourg, victim of an earlier German invasion in World War One, had been pronounced free of all German ties.

Such facts were both embarrassing and inconvenient; Simon decided, quite literally, to blast them out of existence.

The Monument du Souvenir, a proud, soaring spire in the centre of the capital, had been erected in memory of 3,000 Luxembourg volunteers killed during World War One. On 10 October 1940, the memorial was blown up by the Nazis.

Protests were ruthlessly put down by arrests and Gestapo beatings. There were any amount of German immigrants, their numbers stiffened by Luxembourg sympathisers, who, under the banner of Die Volksdeutsche Bewegung (the German People's Movement), were also more than willing to beat up anyone daring to demonstrate Belgian or French sympathies or unfurl the red, white and blue flag of Luxembourg.

Simon was set on a head-on attack on Luxembourg national pride. On 30 August 1942, the Gauleiter solemnly proclaimed the reunion of Luxembourg to the Reich as part of the 'Moselgau' (Moselle district).

In a public address he stated: 'The German Reich as a State has received you within its sphere of sovereignty. Thereby you accept all the duties entailed by Reich citizenship; at the same time you receive all the rights bound up with it. In this solemn hour I greet you as Reich citizens of Adolf Hitler's Greater German Reich.'

Compulsory military service was introduced; into the ranks of the Wehrmacht were sucked able-bodied men between the ages of eighteen and forty. As for racial and religious persecution, attacks on Luxembourg Jews were sadly predictable. There was confiscation of wealth, expulsion and deportation. But Simon reserved a special hatred for the Roman Catholics, the religious majority of the old Grand Duchy. For them he had special plans.

His SS descended on the ancient Benedictine monastery of Clervaux, timing their swoop with celebrations on 15 January 1942 for the feast of St Maurus, the patron saint.

Orders were terse: the monks were to leave within the hour. The Gestapo permitted the consecrated hosts in the tabernacle to be consumed. Each monk was allowed to take with him just two habits and a few devotional articles. The exodus was filmed by German newsreel cameramen for showing in Luxembourg cinemas.

The *Catholic Herald* newspaper, published in London, a few months later, reported:

After a minute and shameful search of each individual had been conducted, the monks left the monastic enclosure singing the Miserere and the Magnificat as a last farewell to the Blessed Mother. . . . With the temperature at minus 20 degrees Celsius the monks were forced to cover part of the way on foot; then they were taken across the Luxembourg-Belgian frontier in trains. There they were abandoned on the main highway after being given express command not to return to their own country.

Amid the terrible cold there were individual tragedies.

Josef Terboven and SS-Obergruppenfuehrer Wilhelm Rediess
are met by Vidkun Quisling at Oslo Airport. (Courtesy
Historical Research Unit.)

Vidkun Quisling inspects men of the naval branch of the
Hird. (Courtesy Historical Research Unit.)

Joseph Terboven on a tour of inspection in Norway. (Courtesy Historical Research Unit.)

Memorial service held in Copenhagen on 17 December 1943 for members of the Danish Free Corps killed on the eastern front. Right: SS-Gruppenfuehrer Dr Werner Best. (Courtesy Historical Research Unit.)

French Chasseurs Alpins wearing their traditional blue berets. (Courtesy Historical Research Unit.)

Members of the Jeunesse Europe Nouvelle, a branch of the Milice, on parade in Grenoble. (Courtesy Historical Research Unit.)

Hanns Rauter (left) and Anton Mussert inspect Waffen-SS unit in Holland. (Courtesy Historical Research Unit.)

A unit of the French Milice on parade in Vichy, June 1944.
(Courtesy Historical Research Unit.)

Generalmajor Dietrich von Choltitz, Commandant of Paris.
(Courtesy Historical Research Unit.)

SS-Obersturmbannfuehrer Leon Degrelle and his adjutant
Lucien Lippert return in triumph from the eastern front.
(Courtesy Historical Research Unit.)

Maréchal Pétain at his trial. (Courtesy Historical Research Unit.)

Felix Plottier of the Haute-Savoie Maquis. (Courtesy Felix Plottier.)

Forty-six-year-old French monk Joachim Bredoux, already seriously ill with a raging fever, died in Clervaux town. The local people defiantly gave him a spectacular funeral.

As for the monastery, Simon swiftly converted it into military barracks, ripping out the interior and destroying all religious insignia. The well of the church was then divided to take in a large swimming pool and gymnasium.

As an added insult, captured Jews had their bank accounts seized; 100,000 Reichsmarks of the money was used for the conversion of other monasteries into barracks.

The crucifix was forthwith banned from all courtrooms and public buildings. Similar treatment for the red, white and blue of the Luxembourg tricolour proved more difficult. The *Luxembourg Bulletin*, published be emigrés in the United States, reported, 'All over the country Luxembourgers empty eggs so that they can fill them with red, white and blue colours. At a given moment, they throw them at the walls; the Luxembourg colours appear in many patterns.'

At the small town of Rumelange, there was considerable entertainment value in the sight of a German Gefreiter baulked by a 150-foot factory chimney topped by the banned Luxembourg flag. The sergeant was detailed to remove it. A conscientious soul, he dutifully began scaling the chimney's iron rungs. But the individuals who had raised the flag had removed the rungs nearest the top. There was nothing else for it; the Gefreiter, to the delight of the crowd, was forced down. The flag was later despatched with several hundred rounds of machine-gun fire; the Luxembourgers reckoned they had won a sort of victory.

Among little Luxembourg's larger neighbours, however, moments for light relief were sparse.

In the Netherlands, Obergruppenfuehrer und General der

Polizei Hanns Rauter worked away as industriously as ever.

The veteran Freikorps warrior from Austria had never actually been noted for subtlety. The ideological baggage of National Socialism obviously required some lip service, but secretly Rauter regarded it all with contempt. He was a man who liked to think on his feet.

When the Dutch showed a distressing reluctance to listen to the rigidly controlled radio stations Hilversum 1 and 2 but preferred instead to bolt windows and doors and tune into the BBC and Radio Orange from London, Rauter's solution was simple. He confiscated radio sets by the hundred; the SS swooped on houses and blocks of flats. The haul was more than 800,000 sets. After that, having a radio became both illegal and dangerous throughout the Netherlands.

Under the relentless, efficient *Arbeitseinsatz* system, able-bodied men and women were mustered for work in the factories of the Reich. Those likely to be affected sped into hiding. Rauter made it his business to root them out; again, the methods were characteristic.

From as early as March 1941, everyone above the age of fifteen had been required to carry a personal identity card at all times – a regulation even applying to swimmers, who were expected to tuck their documentation into their costumes.

There was little taste for these measures; the Dutch evolved ingenious schemes for dodging them. But Rauter was ready. Orders were given for the existing ration card to be redesigned. It would be issued only to those who applied personally; without it, there would be no way of getting food or clothes.

Those stubborn enough to remain unregistered from July 1943 onwards became the victims of Rauter's man-hunts. Whole villages or sections of cities were cordoned off for house-by-house dragnets. Those who fell into the net – Jews, ex-servicemen, escapees from forced labour, members of the underground – were deported.

130

The three largest organisations of the resistance – Armed Squads, Order Service and Council of Resistance – made plans to combine. The joint aim would be to deal with Hanns Rauter personally. But the effectiveness of Nazi oppression meant such plans were slow.

By contrast, in France resistance was already at white heat.

15

It seemed to many Parisians that the tone of the BBC broadcasts from London in the first October of occupation was disappointingly bland.

There was a reminder to French citizens that Armistice Day was approaching; everyone should be ready to demonstrate on this traditional holiday commemorating victory of France and the Allies over the Kaiser's Germany in World War One.

The broadcast suggested that this should be a peaceful affair. Patriots should gather at the Arc de Triomphe and merely lay flowers on the Tomb of the Unknown Soldier. A shade more aggressive, perhaps, might be the act of putting wreaths midway down the Champs Élysées at the foot of the statue of Georges Clemenceau, the 'Tiger of France', who, from the brink of defeat in that earlier war, had whipped the country to victory.

To Roger Langeron, the police prefect of the capital, this advice from London seemed unrealistic. He doubted if such conciliatory tactics would satisfy the Parisians. Demonstrations – and quite noisy ones at that – were highly likely on 11 November.

It was not just the appeal of the date. Already, Langeron had received reports from his men that students were especially incensed by a meeting between Henri Philippe Pétain and Adolf Hitler.

Hitler had flattered Pétain as a head of state. There had been elaborate courtesies for the old man: the salutes of three generals in full dress and the presenting of arms by a company of the Wehrmacht as he crossed the demarcation line into the Occupied Zone. Baron Alexander von

Doernberg, Germany's head of protocol, had done the Vichy leader proud. The strong handshake from the Fuehrer had been recorded by film and press cameras. After it, Pétain appealed for 'the acceptance of collaboration'.

But the new generation of students did not venerate an old man; it had its own hero in General Charles de Gaulle, who, ever since the armistice, had denounced all *rapprochement* in his own broadcasts from London.

And now Langeron was learning that an increasing number of de Gaulle stickers, handbills, pamphlets and suggested slogans (ideal for graffiti) were finding their way into the capital. It was not long before they were appearing on the Boulevard St Michel and all the streets surrounding the ancient university of the Sorbonne.

Potentially more serious, attacks were being made on German vehicles by dropping incendiary gas bottles from rooftops.

The Germans caught the mood. On 13 October German wall posters in Paris adopted an ominous new tone. From now on, anyone harbouring English soldiers would be shot. Parisians were informed that they must report to the German Kommandantur before 20 October with any information on sheltered English military personnel. If information was withheld after that date, then the penalty was also the firing squad.

Against this background, some form of rebellion looked increasingly likely. Then a single action by the Germans made it inevitable.

On 10 November, the Paris press carried the communiqué: 'Public administration offices and private establishments will work normally on 11 November in Paris and in the department of the Seine. Commemorative ceremonies will not take place. No public demonstration will be tolerated.'

For the students it was more than enough.

Early on the morning of the Armistice anniversary, a Citroën truck rumbled into the Place de la Concorde and turned into the Champs Élysées, making for Clemenceau's statue. Solemnly, the occupants of the truck unpacked its contents. These were not wreaths, which would have represented death and the past. Instead, there was a gigantic yard-long banner wrapped in a blue, white and red ribbon and bearing the legend in thick capitals 'Le Général de Gaulle'.

The police moved in to take away this prize piece of heresy. But not before it had been spotted by a number of Parisians, who gleefully spread the news. Soon the statue was steeply banked with flowers.

Within hours the Tomb of the Unknown Soldier had also attracted the crowds. Despite the order from his German masters, Langeron held off his men for as long as he could. The demonstrations, after all, were peaceful; if the Germans were prepared to turn a blind eye, little harm would be done.

It was a vain hope. German troops began patrolling the Champs Élysées; in the meantime, students from lycée and university poured out of the metro and up the Étoile.

The banner had been provocation enough; the tricolour ribbon was something else entirely. As it was unfurled, the first shots sliced into the students jammed into the Place de l'Étoile and the Arc de Triomphe. Then the troops went in, their batons flying. The screams of anger and terror were drowned by the shrill sirens of cars and trucks charging the mob. Other students attempted to rescue their fallen comrades; they were run down. The scene switched to further down the hill from the Étoile, where Paris witnessed an impressive meeting of the generations. The students there had the support of war veterans. All, massed together at the corner of the Avenue Georges V and the Champs Élysées, were chanting, '*Vive la France! A bas Pétain! A bas Hitler! Vive de Gaulle!*' Then came the singing of 'La Marseillaise'.

The Germans were not prepared to let it alone. Crack SS troops concealed in a nearby cinema were joined by convoys of military bunched in the side streets. As they hurled towards the mob, machine-gun crews peeled away to set up positions. At the sight of the crews, students and veterans scattered, and shots mingled with the screams. The Germans chased their quarry well into the night, arresting whoever they could. In fact, their haul was sparse; around 120 were seized, among them 90 lycée students and 14 university students. Many were eventually released.

But young engineer Jacques Bonsergent was not so fortunate.

The day before the protests, Bonsergent's main preoccupation was not students, resistance, or even the Germans. Of infinitely more importance was the wedding of his closest friend, Robert Abadie. Sunday 10 November had been set aside for a little celebration: Bonsergent was to join the young couple and four other friends for a convivial evening.

When it was over, the companions lurched cheerfully down the rue St-Lazare towards the metro. The fact that Paris was in darkness and that there was an air-raid alert bothered them not at all.

That darkness was to prove particularly unfortunate; also in the rue St-Lazare that night, and belligerently drunk as distinct from merely merry, was a group of Wehrmacht troops.

At the sight of the revellers, a German waded in. One of the Frenchmen retaliated with a shove, sending the German flying. Furious at his injured dignity, the Wehrmacht man came out, fists flaying. In no time at all, there was a free-for-all on the darkened Paris streets, the blows and shouts punctuated by the screams of the women. For no particular reason, the arriving reinforcements pitched into Jacques Bonsergent, ignoring the rest. He was forthwith marched to the nearest military post.

Bonsergent's friends, when they eventually regrouped, were not unduly worried. It was bad luck for poor Jacques, certainly, but it was unlikely that much harm would befall him. It would mean a few months in the prison of Cherche Midi at most.

Bonsergent took the same view. From his cell, he calmly wrote to his older brother Gabriel, requesting that his employer be told what had happened and pleading for a razor, toothbrush and a change of clothing.

The next day the students of Paris marched. The German military command was in a mood to do something dramatic. To hand was a young Frenchman who had struck a German soldier.

There was now no holding the German court martial. Bonsergent, not sensing danger, took full responsibility for the event of the previous night. He refused to name any of his companions. On 5 December, he was condemned to death.

Bonsergent's defence counsel was reassuring. It was, he told his client, a mere formality. The Fuehrer would undoubtedly show leniency; indeed, the Germans had taken a fairly lenient view of the events of 11 November and there had been few serious recriminations.

But Hitler was not so easily placated. Another unrelated event was to seal Bonsergent's fate.

Hitler had previously conceived what he regarded as a magnanimous gesture towards the French. The Fuehrer had ordered that the ashes of Napoleon's son, l'Aiglon, should be returned to Paris from their resting place in the Capuchin Chapel in Vienna. The ceremony, with its heavy Teutonic trappings, was largely shunned by the people of Paris, who proved remarkably unimpressed by Hitler's gesture. Pétain shunned the ceremony for a different reason: he believed that his attendance and that of his entourage might be a cunning trap. The Maréchal had other problems as well. He had become highly suspicious of the activities of the vice-premier, Pierre Laval, whom he suspected of attempting a *coup d'état* within the Vichy government. Pétain demanded and received Laval's resignation, although Laval was later reinstated.

Here were unforgivable affronts to the power of Germany and the authority of Adolf Hitler. Clearly, these stubborn French were getting out of hand and must be taught a lesson.

Bonsergent's appeal for mercy was turned down. Jacques wrote to his brother Gabriel on 22 December:

They have just told me that my plea for pardon has been refused. I am to be executed tomorrow morning . . . I will die the victim of a mistake.

. . . I am accused of having struck some German soldiers on the tenth of November . . .

Above all, don't cry too much for me. I might have been killed at the front.

Votre petit
Jacques

The long drive to the rifle range at Vincennes was preceded by confession, heard by the German priest who stayed with the condemned man all night.

Bonsergent told the Abbé Stock: 'I would have preferred to die in battle.' At the moment of death he refused the blindfold. The Abbé later declared: 'He died, brave, pious and determined . . .'

The death sentence appeared in the local newspaper – 'condemned to death by military tribunal of the army of occupation in Paris and shot on 23 December 1940.'

A sympathetic German censor could not bring himself to refuse publication but was content merely to plead that it should be placed in a 'discreet' part of the paper. Gabriel Bonsergent countered bitterly: 'Did you shoot my brother discreetly?'

The student defiance had left German and Vichy authorities badly rattled. Radio broadcasts from London had enthusiastically fed reports to resistance groups on the spot. The bulletins were picked up by clandestine listeners in other parts of France and occupied Europe.

The lesson was now clear: in occupied France the hated German conquerors could expect to face the most determined resistance of all.

And as far as Paris went, the intellectual revolution,

137

typified by the students massing at the statue of Clemenceau and the Tomb of the Unknown Soldier, was just beginning.

16

With his striking fair good looks and clear blue eyes, it might have been thought that thirty-year-old gifted linguist Boris Vilde could be regarded proudly by the Nazis. Any sculptor seeking a model for 'a pure blond Aryan' need have gone no further.

The Germans might well have been further attracted to Vilde on learning that this bright, fair-skinned native of St Petersburg had previously served a sentence for anti-Soviet activity and had eventually decamped to Berlin.

His credentials for National Socialism seemed impeccable. He was a language expert on the staff of the Musée de l'Homme (the Museum of Man), which is situated on the broad esplanade of the Trocadero in Paris, and devoted to anthropology. A collaborator at the very centre of French academic circles who shared the Nazis' racial creed would have proved an ally indeed.

But Vilde was not for the Nazis. In fact, he might not have been for the resistance, either, if it had not been for tiny, dynamic Yvonne Oddon, chief librarian of the Musée de l'Homme.

Vilde had long been intrigued by Yvonne – intrigued, above all, by the stream of strangers who kept asking for her because she was giving them 'English lessons'. To the best of Vilde's knowledge, Yvonne had never done any teaching in her life.

What she was, as Vilde soon discovered, was an excellent hater of Germans. It had all begun with her friend Agnes Humbert, an historian working at one of the museum's offshoots, the Musée des Arts et Traditions

Populaires in the Palais Chaillot. Agnes's experiences there in the wake of the Nazi occupation were sickening.

First, there was the rape of the library. Books by Jewish scholars were literally torn from the shelves and destroyed. Their place was taken by crude tracts on National Socialism, together with anti-Semitic diatribes. The staff could probably have lived with those. But Agnes Humbert could not stomach her museum director's subservience to the Germans, or the constant parade of society ladies with their obvious worship of Pétain. And there were the German soldiers, who swarmed over the museum, attracted by nauseatingly fawning posters announcing that there would be no charges for Germans.

Agnes Humbert had taken a whirlwind of fury to Yvonne Oddon.

Launching an underground newspaper, to be called *Résistance*, seemed a reasonable start to the two women. There were other young academics prepared to launch a stream of propaganda tracts lambasting the Germans and Vichy with equal enthusiasm.

Vilde had long known of the existence of a mimeograph machine in the cellar of the Musée de l'Homme. Even before the occupation, it had put out diatribes against the far right in France. It had all seemed a bit of a game then, great fun calling yourselves the Vigilante Committee of the Anti-Fascist Intellectuals. In those days there had not been the Gestapo or the threat of the firing squad. It was different now.

Vilde made further enquiries about Yvonne Oddon. What he learned explained the English lessons and squared with her mysterious telephone calls and meetings, and her frequent absences.

There came the day when he asked the girl casually: 'Would you give me English lessons?'

Yvonne smiled broadly and held out her hands.

For hours, they discussed how it might be possible to contact General de Gaulle's Free French in London. The trickle of leaflets and pamphlets denouncing collaborators and the Germans was destined to become an avalanche. From the talks, it was but a step to sounding out those on the staff of the Musée de l'Homme and other possibly sympathetic institutions.

One of Vilde's first actions was to seek out his close friend Anatole Lewitzky, chief of the European Asiatic Department of the Musée de l'Homme. Lewitzky, like Vilde, was Russian-born. When his family fled the Bolshevik revolution, he had made for Paris. For White Russians in those days it had been a question of scratching any living. In true tradition, he had become a cab driver. Almost killing himself with exhaustion, he drove by night and completed his university studies by day. It paid off: he gained his degrees with honours, completed his military service and became a French citizen. Like Vilde and Oddon, he hated the Germans and was an ideal recruit to a resistance movement that as yet could do little to nourish its dreams.

Indeed, it seemed to the trio as if they alone constituted the intellectual resistance. They were badly in need of friends.

René Creston, a colleague at the museum, proved among the most active. One of his earliest moves was to strike out for Brittany with the task of contacting London. Creston, it turned out, had valuable contacts at the German submarine base of St-Nazaire. Here was the chance to show London that the tiny group in the Paris museum possessed some muscle. Plans and maps of the port and base were drawn up, particularly of a water-locks system which would be agreeably vulnerable to British bombers. The documents went to London.

Vilde realised the full significance of Yvonne's parade of 'English students'. They served as excellent potential couriers for contacting the resistance on the ground: those agents willing to undergo all the risks of taking the St-Nazaire documents with them to England.

The little group which Vilde built up recruited more

141

agents, including a fisherman in Brittany able to sail the Channel.

Almost imperceptibly, the mood of the Musée de l'Homme group changed. Resistance ceased to be an intellectual abstraction; the chiefs were no longer simply known as Boris Vildé and Anatole Lewitzky. They were respectively codenamed Maurice and Chazalle. The men and women of Musée de l'Homme, scholars in arms, were going to war with a vengeance.

In London, the Musée de l'Homme network began to attract the attention – and the considerable respect – of General de Gaulle's movement for infiltrating agents into France. This was the Bureau Central de Renseignements et d'Action, the BCRA. During the late autumn of 1940, not the least of de Gaulle's problems was to snatch one of his most promising agents from under the shadow of the Gestapo. André Weil-Curiel, codenamed Dubois, had been on a key mission: to infiltrate occupied France, take the measure of Gaullist support and see how many patriots he might recruit.

The mission was a total failure. It was time to pull out. But how? Traversing the Channel was highly dangerous. A journey across Spain would depend on reliable contacts. At this point, it was time to turn to the Musée de l'Homme.

Boris Vildé's choice of a resistant able to arrange Weil-Curiel's departure fell on Albert Gaveau, a resourceful aviation mechanic.

It was true that Gaveau was an odd character, a loner without friends. Unlike most of the resistants, he seemed detached from politics, even from patriotism. That was not necessarily a drawback; emotional idealists could be a nuisance. And Weil-Curiel could not deny the man's courage; he was plainly willing to take risks. After numerous false starts on his journey to England, Weil-Curiel found himself shunted to Toulouse. There Gaveau told him confidently that their problems were almost over; he had wind of a departure for London the day after next from Nantes, which is east of St-Nazaire and on the Loire. It would be necessary to meet up with another resistance group next morning in Tours, which lies to the east.

Weil-Curiel, with a mixture of elation and anxiety, began his packing. Gaveau might be a strange individual, but there was no doubting his efficiency. He made all resistance work appear to be simply a matter of pushing buttons. Gaveau explained that they were making for the demarcation line between occupied and unoccupied France. The farm which was their goal was in the Unoccupied Zone. There were other farms and buildings on the way which were situated on the German side. It was a matter of moving quietly and quickly from farm to farm. There would be no problem in crossing the line. A car would be waiting.

Weil-Curiel asked sceptically: 'What about guards?'

The other man was brisk: 'There won't be any.'

And so it proved. Gaveau seemed unflappable, even when, at the meeting at the farm, he revealed calmly that the car had broken down and had to be collected from the nearest garage. Weil-Curiel found such detachment difficult; it seemed to him that every delay made disaster more likely.

But, sure enough, the car was ready; evidently all that had been lost was a little time. Gaveau climbed into the front seat next to the young driver. Weil-Curiel got into the back, idly glancing at the driving mirror.

What he saw made his bowels turn to water. The low black Citroën of the kind used by the police slid to a halt immediately behind. But Weil-Curiel relaxed when he saw the occupants were a man and a woman.

Not that relief lasted very long. There was another Citroën in front now. Out tumbled the German police. Weil-Curiel was bundled into one car, Gaveau into the other. As they streaked towards Tours, Weil-Curiel stole a glance behind him.

The road was empty. Only later did it strike him as curious that there was no sign of the car from which he had been abducted.

From Tours, the Germans took Weil-Curiel to Paris – more specifically, to Gestapo headquarters in the rue de Saussaies. Its reputation was only too well known. It was said that the cooks, whose quarters were on the second floor, often complained that they were disturbed by the screams of the victims being interrogated on the fifth floor.

But there were to be no tortures that day, at least not for Weil-Curiel. SS-Hauptsturmfuehrer Doehring was all smooth courtesy. He explained: 'I am completing the file on the affair of the Musée de l'Homme. You could be of considerable help by telling me of your relationships with these people.'

Weil-Curiel kept his nerve. Blandly, he told the Hauptsturmfuehrer that, of course, he knew some of these people. As far as he was aware, Lewitzky and Agnes Humbert had directed their activities primarily against the government of Vichy.

It was a shrewd reply. Weil-Curiel knew that the SS had its own twisted code of conduct: it had no love for traitors. Doehring nodded as if in sympathy. Then he snapped: 'Come with me.'

Doehring led his prisoner to the glass door of an office, beckoning him to look through. Weil-Curiel mentally composed himself and peered in.

The office's sole occupant was Boris Vilde.

Doehring laughed confidently: 'That is the ringleader of the bandits of the Musée de l'Homme. The ring is broken. Soon we will have the rest.'

The next to be picked up was Agnes Humbert. Once they had seized Vilde, the link with Agnes was not difficult to establish; indeed, her fingerprints had been all over the stencils for *Résistance*. She was taken to the Cherche Midi prison.

Vilde had been seized while walking unsuspectingly across the Place Pigalle. Another member of the group, a Socialist Jew named Leon-Maurice Nordmann, who had been furnished with false papers by the ever willing Albert Gaveau, had been picked up before Weil-Curiel.

144

Nordmann and Gaveau were aboard a train leaving Paris when Gaveau slipped away to the toilet. As the train slid to a halt at Versailles station, the Germans broke into Nordmann's compartment and hustled him away. They did not think to check the toilet; as the train pulled out of Versailles, Gaveau leapt to safety.

René Creston, the agent with the St-Nazaire contacts, was picked up later but released. Even though his work had been crucial, there was little solid evidence against him and, sticking to a previous plan, Oddon and Lewitzky disparaged him to Doehring as an ineffectual pawn of resistance and of no importance whatever.

The Nazis contented themselves with hounding Creston out of his job at the museum and out of Paris. His role was long over: several copies of the St-Nazaire papers had reached London and the Allies were able to lay their plans for eventually destroying the harbour.

The Nazis decided they would have some sport with Nordmann, their prize Jewish prisoner. He had been arrested previously, charged with producing a clandestine newspaper. The penalty, much to his relief, was a mere two years in jail. For a Jew, it had been an incredibly lenient sentence. But with the seizure of the other leading figures of the Musée de l'Homme, Nordmann was arrested on a new charge and brought to trial.

He knew only one verdict was possible.

As they awaited trial, one question was uppermost in the minds of all the accused: just who had betrayed the resistants of the Musée de l'Homme? The truth, as it turned out, was to come from an unexpected source. The trial judge, Hauptmann Ernst Roskothen, a German lawyer who spoke fluent French and detested the job he had to do, saw no reason to protect a traitor. He confided to the defence attorney: 'The newspapers shouldn't be calling this trial the Vilde affair. It should be called the Gaveau affair.'

It was Gaveau who had arranged the ambush of Weil-Curiel at the demarcation line, and vanished so con-

145

veniently afterwards. And Gaveau had disappeared again, of course, by speeding to the train toilet when the Germans came for Nordmann. There had been other instances of his diligent service to Hauptsturmfuehrer Doehring of the Paris Gestapo; all were to help seal the fate of the brave patriots of the Musée de l'Homme.

The courage of the seven men who in the winter of 1942 were taken to their deaths at Fort Mont Valerien just outside Paris was sublime. They chatted and joked as they were tied to the execution posts.

For the condemned men there was one last agonising decision. Since there were only four posts, who would go first and who last? Boris Vilde volunteered to be the last to die, along with Anatole Lewitzky. Another of the resistants, Pierre Walter, codenamed 'Didier', had also stood trial and been condemned to die with the others.

All the men scorned blindfolds and broke proudly into 'La Marseillaise' above the crash of the bullets.

The death sentence on all of the women involved were later commuted to prison sentences, and they were deported. Most survived the war.

André Weil-Curiel, agent of General de Gaulle, was another of the lucky ones. For some reason, Hauptsturmfuehrer Doehring had taken a fancy to him; possibly the German had the idea of nurturing him as a double agent. In any event, he came up with a strange proposition: would Weil-Curiel be willing to travel to the Unoccupied Zone and return every fortnight with a review of what the local press was saying? Naturally, the distressing little matter of his involvement with the Musée de l'Homme could be forgotten. Furthermore, there would be a salary and expenses.

It was a handy way of getting out of Paris. Weil-Curiel took a chance and agreed.

Once in the Unoccupied Zone, Weil-Curiel set about asking questions. But not about local newspapers. Did anyone know the quickest way to Spain? In the meantime, it would seem rather churlish not to let his benefactor

Doehring have something. Diligently he filed reports of innocuous information.

Then came the day when Doehring's seemingly attentive acolyte was seen no more in Paris; he was on his way across the Pyrenees to London.

His mission had ended. And so had the resistance cell of the Musée de l'Homme.

17

From his modest suite of offices and bedrooms on the third floor of the Hôtel du Parc in Vichy, Maréchal Henri Philippe Pétain presided over the destiny of Unoccupied France. Its boundaries were not marked by fences, barbed wire or brutal slabs of concrete; the seemingly haphazard division would be marked at one place by a road and at another by a stream. There was nothing remotely haphazard, though, about the patrols of Germans and the vicious guard dogs on the northern side. Between one zone and another lay a hundred yards of no-man's-land, forming a hazardous trip for anyone brave enough or foolhardy enough to cross the line illicitly.

For those living in Vichy France but having a family or friends in the Occupied Zone, life was a mixture of fear and frustration. In the early days, means of communication were limited and letters illegal. Inevitably, ways were found of circumventing the letter ban. Plain one-sided postcards, known as 'Cartes Interzones', subject to the close attention of the Nazi censor, were allowed; it did not take long to realise that these could be made to serve as a letter simply by sending a number at a time and numbering them. On delivery they could be read in sequence.

But there were times when even more ingenuity was called for. The restaurant-car attendants on the Paris-Vichy express became adept at removing a panel in the dining saloon, popping a bundle of letters inside, and replacing the panel. At Vichy, the panel would once again be unscrewed and letters removed.

Equally, there was no shortage of helpers for those anxious to make the trip to the Occupied Zone. These

148

were *passeurs*, willing, either for money or nothing, to operate on the Franco-Spanish frontier. Most of the help was extended to military personnel or to Jews fleeing from the ever present threat of deportation, torture and death.

The *passeurs* were skilled at gauging the intervals between German patrols. Some were fishermen who carried their passengers across rivers or provided ropes strung across banks. As the threat of the resistance increased, the Germans became more wary and stepped up their patrols. Many an illicit traveller knew what it was like to crouch fearfully in the mud while dogs growled and snarled above. Their German masters would turn up and the dogs would be allowed their fun. Then would come the beating, followed by a spell in jail.

But few disputed that the most dangerous German patrols were to be found in the railway stations. Illicit travellers – those lacking the coveted *Ausweis* – knew there was no prospect of escape as they huddled in the crowded carriages. The Germans did not look at a suspect's face – at least, not at first. Their concern was with dirty and mud-caked shoes, the telltale sign of the demarcation-line traveller.

Then would come the demand: *Your papers....* Inevitably, troops or police would take their time, deliberately prolonging the comparison between photograph and bearer. With the removal of a suspect, those left behind on the train, packed so tightly together, sensed each other's slackening of tension. But, of course, the Germans would come back.

Your papers.... The nightmare would then start all over again.

The war began almost gently in the pleasant market town of Bonneville, which nestles below the mountains of Andy and Le Bugey with the Plateau de Cenise between. This part of eastern France, in the department of Haute-Savoie, close to Switzerland, came within the writ of Vichy.

Indeed, in June 1940 there was fighting and there was occupation: the Italians had moved in to secure their small toehold on this corner of France.

Felix Plottier, who had done his national service with the mountain troops of the 27th Battalion Chasseurs Alpins and who was eventually to play a key role in local maquis resistance, today runs the family business in Bonneville. He explains: 'We fought the Italians for something like fourteen days, but nobody's heart was really in it. After all, this had been the old kingdom of Savoy and there were a number of families who, while being good French patriots, were nevertheless of Italian origin. Few of the soldiers sent by Mussolini were dedicated Fascists. They must have wondered what they were doing.'

Certainly, no other parts of occupied Europe were favoured with such an obliging Italian officer as the one in Bonneville who wanted to take over the local school as barracks for his men. Recalls Plottier: 'We told him he couldn't have it because of the children, and would he put up with an old château that had once been a prison? He was quite happy.'

This, at least, was not a murderous war – not against Alpine troops who spoke perfect French and knew the mountains better than many Savoyards. The people of the region were not yet living under the threat of lightning arrests, torture and mass deportation.

Felix Plottier's English wife, Joan, explains: 'Resistance to the Italians probably didn't go beyond a little childish baiting. When they visited a café and hung up their distinctive plumed hats, it was a favourite sport to sneak up and cut off the feathers. It made the Italians cross but not much else.'

Opposition was of the sullen kind. When the Italians took it into their heads to march through Bonneville with a blaring military band, they would suddenly find the streets unaccountably empty, the shutters of shops and houses firmly bolted.

Silence was one of the less sharp weapons of resistance.

But in faraway Paris, repression had grown steadily harsher with the years of occupation, and the change of mood was contagious. Even Bonneville was not immune; all too soon, the demand for militant resistance was expressed, quite literally, in countless knocks on the front door of Felix Plottier himself.

It would only be a slight exaggeration to say that Capitaine Henri Frenay had been a soldier virtually from the moment of conception. He came from a family the length of whose military tradition no one could quite remember. His mother had worshipped Maréchal Pétain just this side of idolatry; his bedside stories had been an eternal retelling of the glory of French arms. In the hot August of 1939, he had stood proudly on the Maginot line.

That elaborate string of forts designed to protect the central part of northern France had been considered impregnable. This was the same Maginot line that was bypassed and enveloped, its defences forced to fall back in rout.

Stunned into disbelief by the disaster, Frenay recalled in his memoirs:

We, the defenders of the Maginot line, had received the incredible order to retreat. Nothing had prepared us for such a move, neither our individual equipment nor our permanent armoured emplacements, least of all our garrison's standing order to hold the line at all costs.

After the debacle, Maréchal Pétain was called to the highest post in France, while Henri Frenay was destined to become one of the most celebrated heroes of the resistance, architect of the militant Combat movement, which was ultimately absorbed into a single Armée Secrète (Secret Army).

The Armée Secrète flowered during the winter of 1942. As seemed only just, this coincided with a sharp downturn in the fortunes of Adolf Hitler. Rommel, the 'Desert Fox' and darling of the German people, had escaped encirclement at the Battle of El Alamein and been forced to abandon Benghazi. At the same time as he was carrying out the evacuation of Egypt, Operation Torch was under way at the other end of North Africa with the landing of American forces. The anti-British Jean Darlan, Minister of Marine in the Vichy government and Vice Premier in 1941, had unexpectedly returned to North Africa two days before the invasion. Allied forces found themselves with an unforeseen opponent but, after fierce fighting, Darlan was persuaded to tell the French commanders to surrender.

Hitler now had the pretext he had long wanted. On 11 November, four days after Darlan's capitulation, the troops of Generalfeldmarschall Gerd von Rundstedt, in full battle array, crossed the demarcation line and occupied the whole of France. The French army was demobilised shortly afterwards.

The reinstated Pierre Laval, even more of a lackey of the Germans now, proceeded in Paris to rub salt in the wounds by instituting the STO, Service du Travail Obligatoire. This was a forced-labour conscription in which young Frenchmen would be obliged to work in German industry in return for the repatriation of French prisoners of war.

For potential victims of the STO this was to prove altogether too much.

Henri Frenay, however, relaxing with comrades on a snowy 31 December, found Laval's decree the best of all New Year presents. His evening celebration was interrupted by the arrival of a colleague, Marcel Pecl. Sections of Paris, he declared, were on the brink of revolt. Young Parisians had fled the capital ahead of conscription. They had made their way south and, armed with revolvers they were not afraid to use, were bent on resistance.

Michel Brault, chief of intelligence for Combat, commented thoughtfully: 'They've taken to the maquis.'

The word means scrub-wooded upland. At least, that was so at the dawn of 1943. Now it signified a new style of resistance – armed camps in the woods, ready for action.

18

The creation of the maquis was just the sort of adrenalin that the French resistance needed. In just one year the mood of the country changed miraculously.

But back in 1941 morale had plunged with the leaves of autumn. The onset of winter had been a spectre to dread, not just because of dwindling food supplies, but because of the chronic shortage of fuel for domestic heating. The resistance then seemed a lonely, abandoned force; German jamming of BBC broadcasts had become more sophisticated. Moreover, links with England were fragile.

There had been crumbs of comfort. The RAF had been able to bombard both Berlin and the still formidable Luftwaffe. British aircraft, it was said, were pounding the cities of northern Germany. But in the Soviet Union the stupefying victories of the Wehrmacht had become monotonous. True, the German armies had to be content with a glimpse of the towers of the Kremlin rather than conquest of Moscow. But still a self-confident Hitler could proclaim: 'The enemy on the eastern front will be crushed before the onset of winter.'

The despairing French, huddled in their now fraying prewar clothes, shivered in queues for shops and tramcars. Henri Frenay, recalling those days, wrote: 'I had the impression that for 90 per cent of the French people this was somebody else's war and that they believed Russia had already been beaten. Soon it would be England's turn.'

With the onset of 1943, the first cracks appeared in the Nazi facade of success: there was defeat at Stalingrad, followed by collapse at the Kursk salient, a hundred miles north of Kharkov.

A new mood swept through totally subjugated France: not least was the determination to frustrate the detested Service du Travail Obligatoire. Countless young people had been neither collaborators nor resistants. Above all, they had wanted a quiet life; that was now something the STO threatened to deny them. Previously, there had been an attitude that it was only worth attacking when attacked. All that had changed. The leaders of the resistance spelled out the new philosophy in the starkest terms: strike the Germans wherever and whenever possible.

But where to start?

An early choice of battlefield was the city of Montluçon, northwest of Vichy. Here on 27 November 1942, workers had been snatched from their homes and forced on to trains by police. Soon intelligence reached the resistance that another roundup was planned for the coming January.

Flying squads of painters, armed with pots of liquid tar, swarmed all over the town, daubing strike slogans and incitements to rebellion on the walls, particularly at the large Dunlop tyre factory.

But the organisers felt that one single act of defiance would be more effective than merely swabbing walls. Workers were told to turn up at the railway station at 1 p.m. for a protest meeting. The result was more successful than anyone had dared to hope. A crowd of around 6,000, consisting of young men and women who had already been conscripted, confronted the police in charge of herding the Reich's fresh labour force on to the trains.

At first, all was calm, but the solid police lines soon infuriated the crowd. Fights and scuffles broke out. The armed police force, the Garde Mobile, struck out with rifle butts, only to have their weapons seized by the demonstrators. Into the main station concourse they poured, singing 'La Marseillaise' and 'L'Internationale'. There were cries of *Vive de Gaulle! Vive L'Union Soviétique! A bas Laval!*

There were elements of comedy. As a number of young

men already herded on to the train jumped clear, the badly rattled stationmaster signalled for it to move. The engine pulled out alone; the demonstrators had uncoupled the locomotive.

Even when the train was recoupled and on its way, there was further trouble. Railway workers, bristling with wrenches and sledgehammers, had already mangled the track. The police, smarting under the jeers and shouts of triumph, withdrew. They were replaced by armed-to-the-teeth Wehrmacht troops, but the resistance was not giving up. They delayed the departure of the train until midnight; by then most of the intended victims of STO had melted away.

For the Germans, the operation was humiliating: out of 180 requisitioned young people, only around twenty made the journey to the Reich. A good number of those who escaped made for the strongholds of the maquis.

As the German fortunes changed in the east, so the Nazi grip tightened. The creation of maquisard cells intensified. In the south, strongholds were established in such places as the steep-hilled department of Corrèze, a prewar centre of Communist and Socialist dissent that seemed a natural habitat for hardened resistants. The steep, thickly wooded countryside became a crucible into which was poured a fair microcosm of dissenting France. Here came Jews on the run from Paris, Spanish fugitives fleeing the rule of General Franco, teenagers from half the departments of France and even deserters from the Wehrmacht.

In the north and east, expanses of wood and mountain soon cradled cadres of the maquis. In particular, two plateaux – the Vercors, in the southeastern Alps, and Les Glières, above Annecy in Haute Savoie – became settings for tragic clashes of arms in the unfolding saga of France's shadow army.

In Bonneville, Felix Plottier became virtually sole organiser of resistance under Colonel Vallette d'Osia, a notorious iron-nerved commander.

Plottier had formed the nucleus of a resistance cell as early as 1941. He declares: 'In those days probably only one per cent of local people were in favour of active resistance against the Germans. By the end of the war it was more like ninety-five per cent – but a lot happened in between.'

Not least in importance was the disarming of the French army. Plottier says: 'There were suddenly a lot of men without jobs and nothing to do. I wanted men who would make promising commanders. Unfortunately, leadership potential was not enough – resistants had to be for de Gaulle and against Pétain. That often created problems. There were, for example, men against the Germans but very much for Pétain. The conflict of loyalties was enormous.'

For Joan Plottier, some of the difficulties had to do with eager volunteers for the maquis with hair-raising disregard for even the most elementary security. She remembers: 'They used to turn up, little more than boys, banging at our front door or the family shop, brandishing identity papers and asking: "Where is Felix Plottier? We want to join the maquis." They even used to appear from behind trees in the garden.'

For the Plottiers, it meant living in perpetual fear that without warning either Germans or police would swoop down and seize those artless STO dodgers.

Madame Plottier had already made up her mind how she would receive unwelcome visitors. She explains: 'I worked out that I would be cosily in bed, keeping warm with aluminium hot-water bottles into which I planned to shove incriminating papers.'

From the same house, members of the maquis would be smuggled to refuges in the mountains in a variety of guises – anything from farm hands to priests. Madame Plottier says: 'The dressing up was accompanied by a lot of laughter. They were like kids at a party and they only stopped laughing when they got outside.'

In Bonneville, statues and monuments were ripped down and melted for the war effort, along with the brass ornaments that every household was supposed to surrender. The Plottiers handed over the tyres of their treasured red and black Simca coupé. But not the car itself. They buried that under faggots of wood in a nearby barn and forced themselves to forget about it.

There was, after all, a greater priority. In a France now wholly occupied, resistance and the maquis had a new enemy to rival the Gestapo. What was more, it was home-grown.

On his restoration to power in April 1942 after his bitter dispute with Maréchal Pétain, Pierre Laval lost little time in stepping up the repressive profile of the Vichy regime.

During a visit to France, Fritz Sauckel, Hitler's shifty slit-eyed Reichsplenipoteniarie of Labour, whose orders at the war's end would result in the movement of five million people from occupied Europe to Germany, all but insisted on the establishment of STO. His immediate demand was for 350,000 French workers. 'You provide them, or we'll take them,' he snapped.

Laval, sensitive to German threats, went on in 1943 to create the French militia (Milice Française), under the tutelage of his German masters.

As the Praetorian Guard of the Vichy regime, it began life as the Service d'Orde Légionnaire, an organisation with more than a few of the trimmings of Heinrich Himmler's SS, including the unequivocal oath: 'I swear to fight against democracy, against Gaullist dissidents, and against the Jewish leprosy.'

This was ominous enough, but it was not until the 31 January 1943 issue of *Journal Official* that the true character of the organisation really emerged. The journal carried a new law, signed by Laval, establishing the Milice Française.

Article 2 of the statutes declared: 'The French Milice is composed of volunteers morally ready and physically capable, not only of supporting the new state by their action, but also of cooperating in the maintenance of order.' Article 3 went on to require that members of the Milice be French by birth, not Jewish, not belong to any secret society and be volunteers.

Control of the Milice was to shift from Pierre Laval to Joseph Darnand, Secretary of State for the Interior. It was rubber-stamped by Pétain himself as 'the advance guard for the maintenance of order inside French territory in cooperation with the police'.

On the Milice were lavished all the trappings, ceremonies and insignia so beloved of the Nazi stormtroopers. There was a uniform already to hand: the khaki shirt and black tie of the Service d'Ordre Légionnaire. To these were added dark blue trousers and jacket and the beret of the Chasseurs Alpins. Then came army shoes, leggings, and a wide military belt from which a gun holster was suspended. At the start, the holster was stuffed with paper; Vichy was not permitted to supply arms. However, that was one deficiency that the Germans were more than pleased to remedy.

From now on, the resistance had to become reconciled to new brutal enemies on French soil. Neither the maquis nor the other groups was equipped to fight it alone. In his memoirs, Henri Frenay wrote: 'We were as ill-armed as we were ill-financed. The key to the arms question was in London. . . .'

London, indeed, was to fuel the resistance movements. And not just for France.

19

The Hardanger Plateau, northwest of Vemork and deep in the mountains of southern Norway, is a desolate place.

Hosts of migrant reindeer alone survive in this cheerless wilderness of cruel winter blizzards. Anyone unwise enough to venture there with features exposed runs the risk of laceration by stinging hail. Even if a man is prepared for this assault he can still perish; sudden squalls can snatch him off his feet and dash him bodily against the ice.

To the planners of the Special Operations Executive (SOE) in London, however, the friendless Hardanger Plateau was regarded as an ally. From there, it was proposed to launch one of the most daring resistance coups of the war. The reward for success would be a prize unrivalled: the destruction of a key element in the Third Reich's effort to produce a German atomic bomb.

But, first, for the Norwegian resistance there was to be disillusion and tragedy.

In the spring of 1942, the Norwegian coastal steamer *Galtesund* was appropriated by a group of Norwegians, who successfully reached Scotland. Their exploit was applauded enthusiastically by Special Operations Executive, the British powerhouse for subversive activity in Nazi-occupied Europe. But SOE's main interest centred on one particular escapee – Einar Skinnarland.

The fact that Skinnarland was a hydroelectric engineer had a lot to do with it. Furthermore, interrogation revealed that he was also a remarkable skier, an amateur radio operator and, by no mean consideration, in the pink of health.

His job was at the Norsk Hydro heavy-water factory at Vemork. The place was being used by the Germans to produce heavy water, an element in the production of atomic energy.

Lieutenant Commander Eric Walsh, head of the Norwegian section of British Intelligence, told Skinnarland: 'We've had our eye on this place for some time. We need an agent to operate inside Vemork itself.'

Both Walsh and Skinnarland were only too aware that there was little time. The Norwegian had told neither family nor friends that he was going to Britain and had merely mentioned a skiing holiday. Such a cover, obviously, could not last indefinitely.

Organisation within SOE moved fast. After instruction on the intricacies of the radio set he would take back to Norway, Skinnarland was rushed through basic parachute training. Then came exhaustive briefing sessions with Leif Tronstad, a major with particular responsibility for Norwegian espionage operations. The two men studied the layout of the Vemork plant in detail.

A mere three weeks after his arrival in England, Einar Skinnarland was back in Norway – dropped from an RAF bomber in the early morning of 29 March 1942.

He arrived ravenously hungry. What more natural, therefore, than to ski straight home and enjoy a breakfast cooked by his mother? He told her that his holiday had been most enjoyable. His friends were puzzled that he looked a little pale for a man who had presumably had a vacation of bruising athleticism.

Fortunately, no one pressed the point. Skinnarland went back to work.

As soon as he could, he was radioing back to London. His information was devastating: orders had been received from Berlin to pack and ship to Germany the plant's entire stock of heavy water.

The War Cabinet turned to Lord Louis Mountbatten,

Chief of Combined Operations and the overseer of special forces, which included the commandos. Mountbatten and SOE decided to pool their talents; SOE would provide the manpower for the first operation.

This involved a four-man advance party dropping near Vemork. This party would prepare a landing area for a following volunteer assault force. That force would home in by glider near Vemork and then shoot its way into the plant, which it would proceed to destroy. The bleak expanse of Hardanger was earmarked as the landing place, despite SOE uneasiness at the prospect of giant boulders and deep-cut fissures being hosts to flimsy gliders.

There was no time for debate; the news from Norway was getting steadily worse. In September 1941, production at the Norsk Hydro plant had been stepped up, and it continued to rise. Dr Jomar Brun, the plant's chief engineer, who had escaped to London, added disturbing evidence of German progress towards making an atomic bomb.

For operations behind enemy lines, the Norwegians were able to draw on considerable home-grown talent. It consisted of Company Linge, the volunteer group of special action troops, rigorously trained in hand-to-hand combat, signalling, sabotage techniques, map reading, advanced weapon handling, silent killing and survival.

The attack on the heavy-water plant could not have come at a better time, for Company Linge was demoralised and unhappy. Its original leader, Captain Linge, had been killed in a previous action, and it had been given little to do since. From the ranks of Company Linge, the SOE chose a four-man advance party, codenamed Swallow.

The advance party, led by tall, lanky Lieutenant Jens Poulsson, parachuted into Norway at around midnight on 18 October 1942. Right from the start, the mission faced disaster. A glance at the map revealed that the four had landed a hundred miles off target; the trip to Vemork would have to be undertaken over some of the toughest terrain in southern Norway.

At first, the men took considerable consolation from the weather. True, there was a layer of fresh snow, but the sun shone through it cheerfully enough. However, at an altitude of 4,000 feet, it proved a vastly different story.

Here temperatures plunged to zero. The men, struggling under heavy equipment, buffeted by high winds and chilled by cruel cold, pushed ahead towards Vemork. Failure was out of the question. Unless they all got through, the succeeding phase of the operation would collapse; much of the equipment that the men carried was needed to light a landing zone for the assault gliders.

Even on arrival, Skinnarland, who had been forewarned of the Swallow mission, could offer little encouragement. The local German commander had recently reinforced the guard at Norsk Hydro; resistance would be strong.

London was also worried. Something was plainly wrong with Knut Haugland, the unit's radio operator. The men of SOE had long developed a sixth sense which alerted them to possible false messages. It was not unknown for a German radio specialist to substitute for captured agents and take over a sending key. Acting on a hunch, the SOE began sending Haugland prearranged check messages. To the further puzzlement of London, all were answered correctly. Had the Germans completely penetrated the mission? It seemed unlikely. The truth, when London eventually learnt it, was distressingly prosaic. The bitter cold had stiffened Haugland's fingers and changed his normal touch.

His reports scarcely augured well for the mission. Toughened protection for the Hydro of course meant increased firepower for the Germans. They could reinforce the guard of the Hydro at whim; there was no question of London lavishing limitless resources. Combined Operations, however, had no intention of aborting the venture.

Out went the go-ahead signal for the actual assault, codenamed Freshman. Thirty-four specially trained

163

sapper volunteers, under the command of a British lieutenant, would leave within ten days.

The two Halifax bombers, each towing an Airspeed
AS51 Horsa Mk 1 glider, roared above Wick Airfield in
Scotland on 19 November. There had been some uneasiness over the wisdom of attempting the mission at all; the
glider pilots had never made night take-offs with fully
loaded gliders. Maps for the flight were not of the best,
but it was reckoned that this deficiency could be more
than made up by the highly skilled navigators. The use of
Horsas by no means pleased everybody; their windscreens
had only two small clear vision panels, and it was feared
that buffeting would break the towropes.

The initial meteorological report had been excellent,
but after reaching the Norwegian coast on correct bearings, the aircraft flew into a blizzard. To make matters
worse, the telephone links between each glider and the
towing aircraft did not work.

In addition, one of the Halifax's Rebecca radio units
failed to make contact with the Eureka ground beacon. It
was also later revealed that the briefing given to the Halifax
pilots had been inadequate. Even allowing for the thick
cloud curtain, the pilot on one bomber had insufficient
knowledge of the Norwegian coast to prevent him coming
in too low over the area of Egersund, southeast of
Stavanger.

It proved fatal. Fuel was getting disastrously low; no
more time could be spent scouring for the landing zone.
It was then that the towrope snapped; the glider, by now
smothered in snow, plunged into a mountain. For a few
seconds, it looked as if the Halifax would escape. The
pilot cleared the peak but smashed headlong into the next
range. All the crew were killed; they had barely reached
ten miles inland.

The other unit appeared to be faring rather better. The
10,000-foot altitude seemed safe enough, and progress
towards the dropping zone seemed good. But where precisely was the zone? In vain, the pilot strained to pick up

the welcoming pricks of light which should have been set out by the Swallow party. There was no margin for extra time; more to the point, there would soon be no fuel. The pilot of the Halifax prepared to turn for home.

Then it happened. The towline connecting glider and bomber broke apart. The Halifax began its slow descent to the sea.

The wreckage that had crashed near Egersund was found the following morning by German troops. From the position of the two wrecked aircraft, and the distance between them, it was evident that the bomber pilot had released the glider at the last minute in a bid to save his own aircraft. It had proved fruitless. All six crewmen of the Halifax were dead by the time the Germans arrived. Fourteen soldiers who had been in the glider survived the crash.

That they were on a sabotage mission was only too evident when explosives, small arms and radio transmitters were found among the wreckage.

What happened next was the direct outcome of events on 18 October 1942 when Adolf Hitler had issued what was termed a *Fuehrerbefehl* – a top-secret edict that spelt death for the Operation Freshman survivors from the moment that their gliders crashed in the snow-covered Norwegian countryside.

In the *Fuehrerbefehl*, Hitler accused Germany's opponents of using methods that did not conform with the Geneva Convention. Commandos were singled out for special mention; their behaviour was described as 'especially brutal and cunning'. Commandos, Hitler went on, were recruited partly from among hardened criminals who specialised in killing their prisoners. The order stipulated:

From now on all opponents captured by German troops in so-called commando operations in Europe or in Africa, even when it is outwardly a matter of soldiers in uniform or demolition parties with or without weapons, are to be exterminated to the last man in battle or while in flight. In these cases it is immaterial whether they are landed for their operations by ship or aircraft or descend by parachute. Even should these individuals, on their being discovered, make as if to surrender, all quarter is to be denied them on principle. . . .

Furthermore, it was decreed that such 'opponents' should not be held in military custody, but handed over to the Sicherheitsdienst, the intelligence arm of the SS. The implication was clear: no prisoners were to be shot until, under the tender mercies of the SD, they had divulged sufficient information about their mission.

As it turned out, the German battalion commander in Egersund's enthusiasm for the *Fuehrerbefehl* was absolute. Hot on Hitler's commando order had come his own decree: 'On account of the increased number of cases in which aircraft are used for landing saboteurs, who do serious damage, I order that personnel from sabotage aircraft shall be immediately shot by the first persons who come into contact with them.'

The Wehrmacht took this responsibility on its own shoulders. The fourteen survivors were rushed to Egersund and, after perfunctory interrogation, all shot.

The news was greeted with incredulity and fury by Reichskommissar Josef Terboven. Here was a group of saboteurs who threatened the country's security. No attempt had been made to probe their mission in detail. Nobody could be certain what their target was; a valuable source of information had been thrown away.

Obergruppenfuehrer Wilhelm Rediess, Chief of Police and SS in Norway, was equally furious but for different reasons: the Wehrmacht had by implication undermined his authority by taking the law into its own hands. Rediess fired off a teleprinter message to Berlin marked 'Urgent'. He was careful to keep it bland until the very last sentence:

On 20 November around three o'clock in the morning a British aircraft towing a glider crashed near Egersund; cause of the crash as yet unknown. As far as has been ascertained, towing aircraft's crew is military, including one Negro, all dead. There were 17 men in the glider, probably agents. Three of them dead, six gravely injured. Glider's crew was in possession of large quantities of Norwegian money. Unfortunately, the Wehrmacht executed the survivors so clarification is no longer possible.

As intended, the message caused consternation. General der Infanterie Nikolaus von Falkenhorst, the commander in chief in Norway, who was to be brought before a war crimes tribunal in 1945 for the murders, took steps to avoid the same happening again by ordering that in future the executions were to be delayed until the prisoners could be interrogated by the security police.

In the case of Operation Freshman, Feldwebel Kurt Hagedorn, in a statement to the court trying Falkenhorst, stated that troops had been awakened to capture English soldiers in the area covered by his battalion, which had its barracks at Slettebo. He was standing outside a barrack with a comrade when he saw the English soldiers being brought to the military hospital. They were carried under guard in the direction of the ammunition store. The Feldwebel stated:

At the same time I heard rifle fire. I went to the place from whence the shots had come and saw still more English soldiers at a distance of about a hundred metres bring brought to the shooting place. One English soldier was lying at the side of the road as he seemed to be hurt, and the others were standing up. Several German soldiers watched each English. Hauptmann Schrottberger, the battalion commander, was standing in front of the military hospital and gave orders as to which way the English had to go. "This way", and he pointed the direction out with his hand.

We went up the street and at the first ammunition store, I saw an English soldier being shot.

Wehrmacht troops, who had come from the ammunition store, lined up opposite the prisoner. An order was rapped out; the prisoner fell and was finished off with a pistol. The

167

body was carried to a hole by four Germans. Feldwebel Hagedorn witnessed some three English soldiers being mown down and tumbled into the same hole – shot, as he later learnt, for being 'saboteurs' by members of the Erschiessungskommando (firing squad).

Hagedorn was by no means the only witness of the event of that grim November afternoon. A Polish prisoner of war, Roman Zetelski, stated that ten of his comrades had been brought from the prisoner of war camp at Egersund to the barracks at Slettebo and sent to the place where fourteen dead soldiers lay. All were in English uniforms. The order went out to place in a truck the still warm bodies from which blood was flowing. The trucks were driven to a garage, where three more bodies, wrapped in sacks, were loaded. At a remote spot, the bodies were stripped naked and shovelled into a common grave.

Rediess, annoyed that he had been deprived of the custody of the dead bodies, had his pride salvaged by the discovery of the other British aircraft and glider. This time the Gestapo had its way. The British soldiers were subjected to a lengthy and brutal interrogation. Only when they revealed all they knew were they put out of their misery. They were executed in compliance with Hitler's commando order as amended and interpreted by General der Infanterie Falkenhorst, who pronounced himself pleased with the outcome. He proudly reported: 'The interrogation provided valuable admissions of the enemy's intentions.'

Jens Poulsson and his men, who waited for the gliders at the designated time, received what little information Combined Operations in London was able to pass on. He noted in his diary that it was 'a hard blow'. But to mourn the dead was a luxury no one could afford: his preoccupation now was keeping alive in the snow. As for food, it meant trapping the reindeer and devouring not only the animals, but also the contents of their stomachs.

This was to be a long winter, but the brutal truth was there: no matter what tragedies had been involved in Operation Freshman, the Vemork plant was still intact and still producing heavy water.

The men of Swallow would have to wait. London was planning its next assault, and all attention was on the Hardanger Plateau.

20

Lieutenant Joachim Ronneberg from Ålesund was an uncomplicated individual whose reason for fleeing Norway and arriving in Britain was, he disarmingly told interrogators, 'just to fight the Germans'.

For the men of SOE, who now had sole responsibility for bringing about the destruction of the Norsk Hydro, Ronneberg appeared to be the ideal leader. He had won his spurs as an officer instructor on other 'special actions'. He was itching for combat, and SOE was only too pleased to oblige him with its latest exploit, cloaked under the codename Gunnerside.

Ronneberg's initial order was to select five good skiers from the pool of talent within Company Linge and report for briefings in London. What Ronneberg learnt was scarcely encouraging. The element of surprise was clearly important in this sort of enterprise; that would be lacking because of what had happened to Freshman. The Germans would be armed to the teeth and waiting. Intelligence suggested that about a hundred guards would be on the alert, the majority of them Gestapo. Furthermore, that took no account of the unit stationed at Vemork itself.

By 15 December 1942, the 'most secret' order was ready. It instructed the Gunnerside force to 'attack the storage and producing plant at Vemork with high explosives so that present stocks and fluid in the course of productions are destroyed'.

Then followed another three weeks of training. A dummy plant duplicated the features of the real Norsk Hydro. Ronneberg was reassured by his team's progress; they could practically set explosive charges in the dark and identify the vital tanks and machinery purely by touch. Advance intelligence was so sophisticated that Ronneberg and his men knew where to locate a key which, if necessary, could be used to lock any prisoners in the plant's washroom.

Ahead of the 23 January deadline, Swallow force was alerted; the team moved from its building area near Cambridge to Scotland for the flight to Norway. Clerks at the SOE offices in London filed away last letters written to next of kin. They were all going on a highly dangerous mission; the possibility that they might not come back was very real. They boarded the RAF bomber carrying them over their dropping zone, each man clutching a small brown cyanide capsule. The instruction was to swallow it at the moment of capture.

All at once the grim spectre of the failure of Freshman rose to haunt the men of Gunnerside. The pilot could not make out the dropping zone, and spent two hours aimlessly cruising. Any prospect of flying above the Hardanger plateau was set at naught as German antiaircraft fire erupted in a vicious curtain of flame. Badly mauled and minus one engine, it limped back to Scotland.

The first attempt of Gunnerside had failed ignominiously; the next full moon was not until 15 February.

A different dropping zone was singled out for the second bid – Lake Skryken on the Hardanger plateau, thirty miles from the factory and chosen because it could be identified from the air, even without marker lights.

Steel rods of rain slashed into the faces of the six Norwegians as they again boarded the bomber, laden with demolition explosives, skis, provisions and white-camouflaged weapons and equipment. The dropping zone loomed up around midnight, the green signal lamp lighting up the fuselage hatch.

The clutch of parachutes separated. Six Norwegian soldiers and their drums of supplies drifted down to the smooth, level expanse of the frozen lake of the plateau a thousand feet below.

In a gale which lashed and screamed throughout the night, the party scrabbled around to salvage the parachute supply containers. These were dragged to a deserted hut on the shores of the lake. It was not until 4 a.m. that they finished burying their stores and a carpet of snow had obliterated all landing traces.

If they had cursed the weather previously, it was nothing to their feelings about the westerly wind which howled like a demented animal and drove them for two whole days into the welcome refuge of a hunting lodge.

The bad weather ultimately abated; its effects on the men remained. They had badly swollen neck glands; two of them looked like becoming seriously ill. When the party reached the original supply dump it was impossible to identify it. The snowdrifts had covered the marker stakes. Several hours of tiring work were wasted on the search for a single food container.

It took another forty-eight hours for the weather to be fine enough for Ronneberg to give the order for noon departure.

Fresh optimism swept the Gunnerside force. The vital task was to make contact with the men of Swallow, albeit six days behind schedule.

But Jens Poulsson felt little optimism. In such appalling weather, he reasoned, the men of Gunnerside must surely have perished.

Still, it seemed only reasonable that Sergeants Arne Kjelstrup and Claus Helberg should start the search for Ronneberg's unit on the slender chance that its members were still alive.

Ronneberg's men had skied southwestwards all night and all day, weighed down by their sixty-five-pound packs and the weight of two sledges heavy with two hundred-weight of supplies. At first, when they spotted the two bearded figures near Lake Kallungsja, fear gripped the men of Gunnerside. Might not these be Germans? But then Ronneberg heard wild yells of pleasure. Gunnerside and Swallow had at last linked up.

After they had reached the advance party's base hut at Sandvatn, some twenty miles from Rjukan, it was possible to pool joint rations and consider how to attack the plant at Vemork.

The hydrogen-electrolysis plant was built on a massive precipice. It was widely held to be impassable. On the other hand, aerial photographs had shown trees growing up the sides of the gorge. If trees could take root, then surely there was hope for men anxious to scale the rock-face. Lieutenant (later Captain) Knut Haukelid wrote in his account of the raid:

The Germans no doubt considered that Vemork was so well protected by nature that it would be difficult for attackers to reach it. The works lie like an eagle's eyrie high up on the mountainside. In front the way is completely barred by a deep and sheer ravine cut by the river Maan. . . . Across this crack, the Germans thought, no one could make his way. A narrow suspension bridge, about seventy-five feet long, crosses the ravine at this point, and this was kept under constant guard.

Latest intelligence pointed to fifteen Germans in the barrack hut between the turbine hall and the electrolysis building. Two more sentries, changing every couple of hours, guarded the suspension bridge. There were three patrols inside the factory compound. There were known to be four Norwegian night watchmen. Only one door giving out to a yard was left unlocked.

A formidable proposition indeed!

The final approach to the plant was timed for 8 p.m. on Saturday 27 February. The schedule called for an attack thirty minutes after the changing of the guard at midnight. The choice was deliberate. On Saturday night, the mood at the Hydro would be more relaxed; it was traditionally the one night of the week when discipline was not so stringent and more leave passes were given. Those unfortunate enough to remain on duty might well be less alert than usual.

With the knowledge that they were at last on the home

stretch, the Norwegians moved quickly out of their final rendezvous hut, weighed down with the explosive charges. Although they carried rifles on their backs, Ronneberg had ordered that the weapons were not to be loaded until the very last moment. The temptation to become trigger-happy too early might prove impossible to resist; if the garrison was alerted that would spell the end of the mission.

The first 600 yards down the mountainside were dauntingly steep, but the party barely noticed it because their attention was caught by the sight ahead. The seven-storey factory loomed like some medieval castle, hemmed in by precipes and rivers. The hum of the machinery was clearly audible across the ravine.

The saboteurs reached the clutch of houses near the northern end of the suspension bridge and abandoned the road which snaked on in a series of hairpin bends down to Rjukan town.

It was now approaching ten o'clock.

Everyone knew that shifts would be changing, and confirmation came when a couple of buses laden with workers rumbled towards the plant. The men followed the course of the road for several hundred yards until they reached a spot where a wide cutting had been made through the woods for the Vemork power line. Now they were making for the reassuring dark woods to the right. Each man peeled off his white camouflage dress and donned the uniform of a British soldier. It was reasoned that this would give the Germans no excuse to blame civilians for the raid and thus take reprisals.

Pockets were filled with ammunition and hand grenades. Guns were seized, together with sets of explosives, some rope and pairs of armourer's shears. The final descent down the face of the rock had begun.

Because of the thaw, even the smallest move sent shoals of loose snow crashing into the valley. But the air was full of the low hum of the turbines to mask the noise.

The men streaked across the ice and started to climb

on the other side. Once they had made it, the Gunnerside force took shelter behind a small building a few hundred yards from the plant. Now there was a chance to regain strength and review the plans for the actual assault.

The sentries changed on the stroke of midnight; it was now just thirty minutes to zero hour. A five-man covering party was to advance towards the factory to force the gate and the fence, if necessary.

The two sentries who had been relieved were in no hurry to depart. Long experience had taught Ronneberg patience; a precipitate move could ruin everything. Even when the sentries moved off, he did nothing. It was worth waiting until they were securely in bed and out of action.

After what he considered a reasonable time, Ronneberg ordered Sergeant Kjelstrup to advance towards the factory fence. The sergeant crouched low, clutching his armourer's shears in one hand and his rifle in the other. He raced forward, snipping a man-sized hole in the wire-mesh fence. Then he waved the rest of the party into the compound.

The attacking force fanned outwards to designated positions. Lieutenant Haukelid, touting his pistol and hand grenades, and Lieutenant Poulsson, gripping his Thompson sub-machine-gun, stationed themselves within twenty yards of the German barracks. Both men were able to enjoy the luxury of conversation; more than once, the steady hum of the generators was to be an ally. If German troops approached, there could be only one possible response: the wooden barracks would be holed with the steady assault of small-arms fire. Haukelid would lose no time in lobbing his grenades.

Meanwhile, the demolition teams had moved speedily in the direction of the demolition plant. Ronneberg and Sergeant Frederick Kayser tried at first to get in through one of the doors on the ground floor. It would not yield. Then the pair somehow became separated, but they pressed on, eventually crawling into the building over a web of tangled pipes and cables. Through a vent in the tunnel, they were able to catch the merest glimpse of the high-concentration room, where one man was working. Within minutes, the man was looking down a gun barrel and being pushed into a corner.

The prisoner watched, frozen with fear, as Ronneberg started laying the charges. The leader of Gunnerside had his attention distracted fleetingly by the sound of broken glass as two more of the party forced their way in. It seemed to everyone that the noise would betray them all, but the Germans had plainly heard nothing. Ronneberg pulled up his leather gloves, cursing the shards of glass that cut his hand, from which blood was trickling down.

His prisoner suddenly found his voice and pleaded urgently: 'Try not to short-circuit. If you do, there'll be an explosion.'

Frederick Kayser laughed harshly: 'Explosion! That's just what there's going to be.'

The fuses were set for two minutes. The reaction of the prisoner was so unexpected that Ronneberg and Kayser were briefly nonplussed. The man burst out: 'Where are my spectacles? I must have my spectacles.'

Ronneberg snapped: 'They're on your nose. Frederick, get him outside.'

The prisoner was told to run. The demolition team went on to complete the job of setting the explosive charges on the heavy-water tanks. Two-minute charges and a single thirty-second fuse were placed on each cell. There was thus a double backup system, ensuring that no cell would escape.

In all resistants there lurks something of the schoolboy, and now it was demonstrated. The Norwegian saboteurs had their own way of cocking a snook at the Germans; they scattered around the room unofficial calling cards deliberately calculated to confuse their enemies: authentic British parachute badges. When all was ready, Ronneberg ordered the fuses lit. The four-man-strong demolition team fled for cover; their Norwegian prisoner, curiosity overcoming fear, had suddenly rematerialised and was almost touchingly pleased to be dragged to safety. They only just made it before the charges went off with a dull rumble.

In his account of the raid, Ronneberg wrote that after the explosion he 'looked back down the line and listened. But except for the hum of machinery that we heard when we arrived, everything in the factory was quiet'.

Certainly, German reaction seemed remarkably muted. A lone, bareheaded Wehrmacht soldier was seen peering hesitantly out of the barracks. He reappeared, with a helmet thrust hastily on his head; he clutched a rifle and a flashlight which he circled uncertainly over the ground.

The action told him nothing. As he disappeared around the corner of the plant, Haukelid and Poulsson retreated from their posts, making for the previously earmarked assembly point. Ronneberg and the rest of the Gunnerside team were exultant. The job had been done; their task now was to look after themselves.

The explosion may have been muted, but the damage was all that could have been wished. The base had been knocked off every cell and the priceless fluid had flooded down the drains. Flying shrapnel had shattered the tubes of the cooling systems and the high-concentration room was awash with spraying jets of water. This particular water was of the ordinary type, but it had the effect of ruining the heavy variety.

Nor was this all. Eighteen cells had been completely drained of almost half a ton of heavy water. The Germans would have to face the fact that, even after the torn and twisted installation had been replaced, it would take weeks of full-power working before the contents of each cell were usable.

The Nazi uranium programme had been put out of action for months; the Germans could ill afford the delay.

It was time for the Gunnerside and Swallow forces to split up. If they considered that their movements had been fast on the way up, it was nothing to the speed of their retreat. The men hopped and slid down to the Maan river

177

and made their way across. The water had sharply risen by then; because of the thaw there was a good deal of water on the ice.

Knut Haukelid later wrote:

When we were down in the bottom of the valley, we heard the air-raid sirens. This was the Germans' signal for general mobilisation in the Rjukan area. They had at last collected their wits and found out what had happened. That did not matter much to us. To capture nine desperate, well-armed men in a dark wood at night would be difficult enough for people with local knowledge; for Wehrmacht men it should be quite impossible.

On the main roads, things began to get lively. Several cars, including a large vehicle with a gas generator in tow, scorched past. There was just time for the party to throw itself into a ditch. On the other side of the valley, away on the railway line, the lights of torches could be spotted. The German guards had discovered the line of the saboteurs' retreat.

Lieutenant Ronneberg led four members of his unit on a 400-mile trek to Sweden, a journey successfully accomplished within eighteen days.

Knowledge of the full extent of the damage inflicted by Gunnerside threw General der Infanterie Falkenhorst into a towering rage, which he vented on the unit's officers and men in the presence of a group of Norwegians – who considered it tactful to keep straight faces. When he had calmed down, the General conceded to a colleague: 'It's the best coup I've ever seen.' It was a remark that reached the delighted SOE planners in London.

Members of Norwegian resistance working outside their own country had dealt a crippling blow to the activities of the occupation forces within. The muscle in London was indispensable for fuelling the resources of the various 'secret armies'.

But there were no easy victories for the resistance.

There were also the traitors.

21

Slim, dark, grey-eyed Trix Terwendt experienced a sharp jab of pain as the final stages of her otherwise immaculate parachute jump into the Netherlands went badly awry.

A sudden snatch of wind knocked the former KLM hostess sideways; her jaw struck the ground with a violence that seemed to wrench her head from her body. The reception committee of Dutchmen were polite but formal. And, in the manner of resistants everywhere, one of their number grumbled: 'London doesn't understand our problems. We don't get all the backing we need. Communications are very bad.' Then he added with a touch of malice: 'Our chief will not be pleased that they sent a woman.'

If Trix had not been in pain from her fall she would probably have exploded, but she was too tired and there was too much to be done for argument. She shrugged and walked with her new friends across the field, away from the dropping zone.

The Allied information network in the Netherlands had long been infiltrated by the Abwehr (German Military Intelligence). It took two years for SOE to come anywhere near repairing the damage; by 1942, agents and radio sets were being poured into the area. But what was needed above all was the setting up of an escape line to Belgium organised by the Dutch from within.

And that, as it happened, was the speciality of the top-secret section of British Intelligence within M19, code-named LS9 (d). It was true that there had been a number of Dutch guides who had already brought would-be resistants to Belgian territory, but there were spies everywhere and it proved unwise to trust the guides too much.

Besides, the Germans – at any rate, for the moment – appeared to hold most of the trump cards. It was all due to the presence of a certain washing line dangling below a suburban block of flats in The Hague. It was to provide the Abwehr with one of its biggest coups.

The Abwehr radio-detection van, masterminded in a routine surveillance operation by Oberstleutnant Hermann Giskes, the senior intelligence officer responsible for the Netherlands, had long suspected the existence of one particular two-way set, being operated, as it turned out by, SOE wireless operator Hubertus Lauwers, codenamed Ebenezer.

The woman from whose flat Lauwers and an associate were working noticed the suspicious arrival of some plain-clothes men just a little too late. The only course of action was for her to throw the radio into a clump of bushes below. Unfortunately, it tangled with a washing line and was clearly visible. Both SOE men were seized.

A proposition was put to Lauwers: would he care to work for the Germans, operating his set to London? He was told: 'We are impressed by your expertise. We can find you plenty to do.'

Lauwers readily agreed. But not because he had decided to turn traitor. London, he assumed, would notice that he had deliberately omitted his vital security code.

Unfortunately, London did not. The absence of the security code went unnoticed. In desperation, Lauwers inserted the word CAUGHT into the coded message. London did not spot that either. All the information transmitted back to the Netherlands by SOE fell into the eager hands of the Abwehr.

A victim of this particular lapse in security by SOE Dutch section was Trix Terwendt, the agent with a special mission. Her task was to assemble a number of Dutch people prepared to shelter airmen on their way to Brussels. It was her intention, in fact, to create an escape line.

Advance information of Trix's mission was studied with the gravest attention by Oberstleutnant Giskes and SS-Sturmbannfuehrer Josef Schreyeder of the SD. Both men assured SOE in the most courteous of terms that all arrangements had been made to receive the new agent with containers of arms and a radio set.

At midnight on 14 February 1943, Trix donned her parachute harness and clutched her supply of Dutch currency and the papers which identified her as a hospital nurse. As she climbed into the Halifax, a group of Dutch and British intelligence officers stood saluting.

Promptly on her arrival came the message: 'We extend a welcome to a gallant woman comrade.'

Oberstleutnant Giskes of the Abwehr was enjoying himself.

Trix's instructions from SOE were to submit to the authority of her Dutch reception committee for twenty-four hours. Then she was to break contact before proceeding with her mission to establish the escape line.

Before leaving, Trix had been given the address of a man named Smit, who was to be found at the Bally shoe shop in The Hague. Smit had provided sanctuary for RAF evaders and his name had figured in M19 interrogation reports over the previous few weeks. The unsuspecting Trix could see no reason why this information should not be given to the Dutch reception committee.

Her escorts took Trix in driving rain to a wooden shed. One of them threw a blanket over her shoulders, explaining that the colour of her raincoat was light and conspicuous. Suddenly, the man who had been holding the blanket seized Trix's wrists, then yanked her hands behind her back.

She tried to fight down panic by laughing: 'Don't make

silly jokes. You think I'm frightened because I'm a woman?'

But even now she could not grasp what had happened. Possibly, she hoped, she had fallen into the hands of some Communist resistant louts who intended nothing beyond boisterous horseplay. There was no time to ponder over the puzzle; she was bundled roughly into a car, which sped to the Abwehr headquarters at Dreibergen.

On the way, she cursed that she could not swallow her poison pill, but her captors had wrenched handcuffs on her and she lay in the back of the car, trying to make sense of it all. Her tears were not those of fear: they were born of the knowledge that unwittingly she had sealed Smit's fate.

Her Dutch captors, judging by the way they talked, were clearly part of a highly efficient organisation that had thoroughly infiltrated SOE, most notably its wireless communication. One thing above all else was clear: she had been dropped straight into the hands of the enemy.

From his initial success at securing Lauwers, Oberstleutnant Giskes had gone on to capture more English wireless sets and organise a string of 'reception committees' for parachuted SOE agents. The deception had been given the codename of *Nordpol* (North Pole) and was also known as '*England Spiel*' (England Game).

From a purely technical view, Giskes was well pleased with his coup. But cooperation with the SD evoked his distaste. The rivalry between the Abwehr and all departments of Himmler's SS was notorious; the Reichsfuehrer was known to have been intriguing for years to remove Admiral Wilhelm Canaris, the Abwehr chief.

Giskes reflected that at least he would not have the distasteful task of interrogating a woman. That particular assignment had been appropriated by Sturmbannfuehrer Schreyeder.

The SS man was in an avuncular mood, greeting Trix

with the suspicion of a twinkle. He remarked: 'I see that Felix has landed safely in spite of the wind and rain. That's precisely the message I've sent to London.'

Trix really was frightened now: the Abwehr even had her SOE codename. . . .

Schreyeder maintained a silky courtesy throughout. It was almost as if the SD regarded her as one of themselves, that her arrest was an unfortunate necessity and it could only be a matter of time before things were put right.

Perhaps, Schreyeder suggested, they could all work together. It would be a lot more pleasant, he announced blandly, than a spell in a concentration camp.

Trix's interrogation stretched over four days and nights, with just one break for a bath and sleep. She was not tortured. It was scarcely necessary since her extreme tiredness was in itself a form of torture.

The moment she had dreaded most came when Schreyeder proclaimed: 'We would like you to go and find this man Smit in The Hague. After all, you gave us his contact address.'

Stung into fury, she riposted: 'I would weep for shame if I had to do that.'

The answer appeared to disconcert the SD man. For a few seconds, he stared at his prisoner with something like admiration. *After four days and nights.* . . . Then he was the cool professional again, summoning his subordinates and telling them to get the girl ready for transfer to the prison at Haaren. There, a horrified Trix learnt the extent of the damage *Nordpol* had done to SOE. The Germans possessed detailed knowledge of names and meeting places, even of the activities of the SOE training schools.

Trix Terwendt remained at Haaren in solitary confinement for six months. After that, the only relief was supplied by another female prisoner put in her cell. But the woman turned out to be an SD informer.

After that, Trix went to Ravensbrueck concentration camp, transferring to Mauthausen in January 1945. She reached Switzerland through the Red Cross at the end of the war.

Beatrice (Trix) Terwendt, alias Felix, was one of the few survivors from the *Nordpol* operation; she told her captors nothing.

Although the agent Smit was arrested and perished in a concentration camp, his escape line held. No justice came to the Dutch traitors who had lain in wait for Trix that night.

They escaped revenge. Others were not so fortunate.

By November 1943 the occupying forces in Denmark had conferred a dubious distinction on Jens Lillilund.

Only three years before, he had expressed his hatred of his country's enemies by literally spitting at their feet. But now, as head of the Holger Danske sabotage group, he was one of Denmark's most wanted men. One evening the warning had come: *Stay away from your apartment. The Germans are waiting.*

He and an agent whom the resistance knew only as John had returned to Copenhagen from a particularly tricky sabotage mission. And they had nowhere to sleep.

John suggested: 'There's Hedwig Delbo's apartment. She's an agent from Norway. It has been used more than once by our people.'

Lillilund was doubtful. 'Is she to be trusted?'

John was suitably reassuring, and the two men cycled out to the grubby, nondescript back street near the Trianglen traffic junction.

John pressed the bell of No. 4 in the drab brown hallway. A handsome blonde drew back the glass-panelled door a few inches, and John was asking: 'Mrs Delbo, can you put us up for the night?'

As if it was the most natural thing in the world, the woman led them into the apartment, down the narrow hallway and into a room that Lillilund noticed was cluttered with pieces of cloth, packets of pins, spools of thread, a sewing machine and women's garments.

John introduced Lillilund by his cover name: 'Hedwig Delbo, Mr Finsen.'

Plainly it was unnecessary. The woman raised an eyebrow in mild irony and said: '*Finsen?* The leader of Holger Danske?'

Despite himself, Lillilund shot a questioning glance at his companion. If Hedwig Delbo noticed, she gave no sign. She fed the two men, showed them beds and promised to wake them.

The two saboteurs were ready and dressed before eight o'clock and plainly anxious to be gone. But their hostess was in a chatty mood, urging breakfast. She pleaded: 'Let me get some milk from across the street.'

Her absence stretched to ten minutes; Lillilund felt a mounting anxiety. He snapped: 'We're moving. We're wasting time and it could be dangerous.'

Outside, they unlocked their bicycles and pushed them to the end of the street. It was only when they got to one of the bigger thoroughfares that they noticed the large black saloon parked in front of a newspaper shop. In Nazi-occupied Copenhagen, only the Germans or the police had large cars. No one else had any fuel.

Crouched over the handlebars and not daring to look round, they heard the whirr of the starter motor and the sound of tyres crunching asphalt. Lillilund was firmly in command: 'Don't look back. Go round the traffic island and sharp left down Osterbrogade.'

The presence of other people cycling to work was oddly comforting; the traffic lights favoured the two resistants, who were able to circle the traffic island without stopping. Within minutes, the car had caught up with them.

The two men put on a burst of speed, suddenly turning completely round and doubling back.

Behind them, they caught the sound of screeching tyres. There was just a chance they could lose them in the heavy cycle traffic. It was then that the occupants of the car began shooting. John's hand darted to his jacket, but Lillilund shouted: 'Don't waste time. You can't shoot from a bicycle. Let's get away.'

At the corner of Osterbrogade, he caught a final glimpse of John swerving off to the right. Lillilund kept on, steering straight through the traffic, making for Rosenvaengets Allé. It was there that he passed another black car, which swerved round and came up directly behind, and joined the chase.

All Lillilund's concentration was now on reaching the other side of Rosenvaengets Allé because he knew that past the apartment blocks and the large town houses was a short path which could take a cycle but would defeat a car.

As for John, his hand was still clasped inside his coat but he was not reaching for a weapon. He was desperately trying to staunch blood from the bullet wound in his chest. The men in the car kept on shooting. This time they got him in the leg, toppling him from the cycle. On the ground, he managed to find his weapon and, desperately fighting the rising nausea, shot straight at the car's windscreen, killing one of the Germans. Then he fainted.

The second car, thwarted in the attempt to find Lillilund at the top of Rosenvaengets Allé, sped back, screeching to a halt by the buckled bicycle. One of the Germans got out, scooped up John's pistol and brought its butt crashing down on the saboteur's head. Then John was picked up and thrown over the bonnet of the black saloon.

Within an hour, Lillilund had made contact with a number of Holger Danske members who were able to give him the grim news of John's capture.

He declared: 'Somewhere, there just has to be an informer. What do we do about this Mrs Delbo?'

It was necessary to concoct some plan that would clear or condemn the Norwegian dressmaker. By mid-morning some of the main details had been worked out. Lillilund rang Mrs Delbo and came straight to the point: 'This is

Mr Finsen. I suppose you know that John was taken this morning?'

Her reaction of horror seemed genuine enough. 'What are you going to do now?' she asked, with every sign of anxiety.

Lillilund urged: 'It's absolutely vital I get to Sweden tonight. If I stay here I might as well commit suicide. I must see you before I go.'

'Where are you now?'

He merely said that he would be at her apartment by three o'clock.

The two lovers who strolled down the grubby back street near the Trianglen junction appeared interested in no one but themselves. Occasionally, they stepped into various doorways to embrace passionately. They seemed to show no interest at all in the two black saloons, one at either end of the street, or in the handcart covered with Christmas trees outside No. 4. A man in a black leather trench coat left his vehicle and began talking to the street seller. The two lovers ignored that, too.

But, as agents of Holger Danske, they had both noticed the ugly snout of the sub-machine-gun which peeped through the Christmas trees.

Jens Lillilund did not keep his afternoon appointment with Hedwig Delbo.

At the hastily convened meeting later the same day, one of the saboteurs, suffering from a bad cold, blew his nose noisily and told his companions: 'I've stayed at this woman's apartment. It could have been any of us in John's shoes. I'll do it.'

It was then that they showed the man with the cold the pistols whose barrels were about a quarter of an inch in diameter and around a foot long. He took in the triggers of bent metal tubing and the handgrips which, when unclipped, became magazines for the 7.65 mm bullets. The main virtue of the weapon was that firing it made no more noise than a sharp slap on the wrist. It was British made, had never found its way into any armaments museum, and was created specifically for the assassination of traitors. As far as anyone knew, there were no more than 150 currently in Denmark.

Two afternoons later, a newspaper seller looked out of his shop on the corner of the street where Hedwig Delbo lived. On grey winter afternoons it was usually deserted, but now a group of young men were loitering in doorways. At around four o'clock, another man arrived. He seemed to have a bad cold and was blowing his nose vigorously.

The newspaper seller did not like what he saw. He went to the back of his shop and lifted the telephone.

The man who fingered the silent pistol was about to enter No. 4 when the police streamed into the street. He turned round and sprinted into the apartment building opposite. An old woman answered his tap on the ground floor.

He shoved past her and slammed the door, reaching for his knife to slash the telephone wires. Then he positioned himself in the front room to watch the police round up the Holger Danske men who had presented a sitting target. He was even able to see the outline of Hedwig Delbo in the window of her own apartment. She appeared totally oblivious of the commotion.

After the police had left, the man with the cold apologised profusely to the old woman, tossing her some money to have the telephone repaired. Then he sneaked away, crossed Copenhagen and rejoined his comrades.

He commented bitterly: 'A total blunder. We might as well have told them we were coming. We'll have to try again in a hurry.'

'No guards, this time.'

Even if there was to be a smaller cast for the new attempt, there was an additional risk, which involved stealing a Gestapo car. But Lillilund reckoned that, provided the car could be ditched quickly, it would be worth it; no police would dare stop an SS vehicle without good reason.

As the car sped towards the target's apartment, other members of Holger Danske telephoned the Rosenvaengets Allé police station, where their comrades were being held. Holger Danske had friends there. A few hours later, the officers on duty were remiss enough to leave a back door open. . . .

One of the resistants at the wheel of the stolen car looked anxiously at the would-be killer with the silent pistol. 'Your cold must be killing you. Your eyes are watering terribly. Are you sure that you are up to the job?'

The man made reassuring noises. In his mind's eye he saw Hedwig Delbo placidly sewing dresses, unaware of what was in store for her. It gave him no satisfaction. Sabotage was one thing, liquidation quite another.

There were three men in the car and they parked it a short distance away from where Mrs Delbo lived. All blackout curtains had been drawn for the night and there was a heavy silence. The killer allowed himself to blow his nose one last time. Then he pocketed his handkerchief and pulled out the silent pistol.

The rap at the door was answered instantly by a slightly nonplussed Mrs Delbo. She recovered quickly and invited him in.

Her back was to him now and he waited until she had opened the living room door and turned to face him. She pushed the back of a clenched fist to her mouth in a gesture of horror. What he had not reckoned on was the scream which masked the slap of the bullet. Mrs Delbo crumpled forward and the assassin readied the weapon for another shot. But the gun jammed. His temples were throbbing now and he realised that his heavy cold had turned to 'flu.

The killer staggered away.

But the job was not yet done. Even in death, Mrs Delbo would spell danger. It was necessary to tip off friends at the Rosenvaengets Allé police station. The killer took on the job himself. His reception was explosive. The police informant yelled: 'You *idiot*! That woman you think you killed is in the next room and singing your name to the Gestapo. Get out!'

The whole of Denmark was alerted. Hundreds of photographs of the man with the cold were circulated.

That Mrs Delbo had survived the attempt was in no doubt; now she appeared to have vanished off the face of the earth. Jens Lillilund and the entire Holger Danske sweated with anxiety, a form of purgatory they were forced to endure until the new year. Then Holger Danske received a call from a contact in the Copenhagen office of Thomas Cook.

Hedwig Delbo had surfaced at last. And she was leaving Cook's at six o'clock that evening for a Lufthansa flight to Norway.

There could be no question of any fresh attempt being made in the travel agency; that would blow the contact. A swift bullet from a passing car on the way to the airport seemed more sensible. It was rapidly set at naught when the resistance driver picked for the job had a flat tyre. He eventually reached the travel agency, only to be told: 'She left five minutes ago. It would have been highly dangerous if we had held on to her.'

News of the latest failure was flashed to SOE in London, who made it clear that the matter was now in the hands of the Norwegian resistance. It was a body blow to the pride of Holger Danske; there was a certain wry consolation though for Lillilund on learning that, after another attempt in Bergen, the woman had escaped yet again.

But it turned out that Hedwig Delbo somehow felt safer in Denmark than in her own country. She returned, but there was no trace of her until a telephone call to the bookshop of Mogens Staffeldt.

The informer, a fellow bookseller in Copenhagen who kept busy throughout the occupation with varied tasks, told Staffeldt: 'I think I've seen her. A Norwegian-speaking woman came into my shop for a book from our lending library. When I told her the book was out, I asked if I could send it. She looked nervous and said she would call again.'

Several days later, the woman had been back – calling herself Mrs Dam and giving a telephone number.

Holger Danske could scarcely have survived without friends in the Copenhagen telephone service. There was no listing for a Mrs Dam and finding an address from a mere number was difficult.

'Difficult but not impossible?' pleaded Jens Lillilund. The address, it was eventually revealed, was in the Sankel-marksgade area.

Mogens Staffeldt was instructed: 'Ring Mrs Dam and tell her you have the book.'

The two Danish policemen who spotted the car parked outside Mogens Staffeldt's bookshop were conscientious souls. The car, on inspection, had no petrol-ration stamp on the windscreen. What was it doing there? The driver, catching sight of them in the mirror, became nervous. 'We'd better go,' he muttered to his companion.

The woman who had given her name as Mrs Dam turned up a few minutes after the car had driven off.

There was still no proof that this was in fact the elusive Hedwig Delbo. For any man to attempt a lone killing would be madness; the Gestapo would be nearby. But Mrs Delbo was a genuine dressmaker – a call by a woman just might work.

The girl who had posed as one of the lovers in the earlier bid offered: 'I'll call on her and order a dress.'

By the evening she was back and reporting laconically: 'The dress will be ready by 9 March. By the way, the woman is Hedwig Delbo.'

The men who went with the girl now had little patience with the British-made pistol that had been custom-built for disposing of traitors. It had failed them once, and that was enough.

The killers were carrying old-fashioned automatics which would not jam. In Sankelmarksgade, the men entered the building first and climbed to the landing above the apartment.

At the door, the girl pushed the bell several times, and when the target appeared, announced: 'I'm back for my dress, Mrs Delbo.'

The use of the name was the only warning the traitor got.

The two men leapt down the stairs, shoved the girl aside and opened fire. The girl walked coolly down the stairs, leaving her male colleagues to make sure that this time Hedwig Delbo was indisputably dead.

The news of the execution reached the man in prison whom everyone knew only as John. The Germans had not been disposed to give him much medical treatment for the injuries he had suffered through Mrs Delbo's treachery.

They eventually shot him.

22

The dreaded cold northerly wind which each winter bites viciously across Geneva's Lake Léman can be felt just across the border in France, whistling along the mountains and high valleys of Haute-Savoie.

In the closing months of 1943, the most perilous years for the French resistance, this wind appeared to many to be a grim portent of fresh disasters.

One calamity seemed to eclipse them all.

The local Gestapo who pounced on the tall, tweedy Frenchman making his way across the Swiss border might have been forgiven for thinking that they had secured nothing more sinister than a local farmer ignoring the curfew. In fact, they had come close to slashing the very jugular of resistance in Haute-Savoie. The fortunes of the underground movement were primarily in the hands of Colonel Vallette d'Osia, commander of the 27th Battalion of the Chasseurs Alpins in Annecy, the mountain troops forced into disbandment in 1940.

At that time, Vallette d'Osia had urged his followers: 'The armistice is an illusion and one day we will be called upon to take up the struggle against the occupying forces.'

The chance came with the total occupation of France. But by then army dissidents were committed to underground opposition within the Organisation de Résistance de l'Armée (ORA). In Haute-Savoie, under Vallette d'Osia's leadership, by February 1943 it had become a formidable resistance cadre, receiving guns, explosives and medical supplies through parachute drop from England.

But within seven months, the Gestapo had snatched

Vallette d'Osia; the Germans soon realised that they had landed a sizeable fish.

In the sealed compartment of the train to Paris, d'Osia contemplated his two Gestapo guards and an indisputably grim future. He had already decided that he had no intention of testing his powers of endurance under torture in some Paris cellar. He felt a glimmer of hope soon after midnight, when his two guards fell asleep. They had slipped handcuffs on him, but none the less it was an inexplicable blunder that they should have allowed him to sit alone opposite them. The point seemed academic in a compartment with locked doors; he would have to take his chance with the window.

It was a considerable effort for a man built like a tank to get to his feet nimbly and silently, but somehow he managed it. To prise open the window would have been hard enough even with free hands. It was of the standard design in French trains, with two knobs set wide apart for pulling it down. To tug at both simultaneously while wearing handcuffs was out of the question. He pulled first at one and then the other, and there was an inevitable creak, which he felt sure would disturb the guards. Things were a bit easier then because it was possible to place both hands in the centre of the top end of the glass. It came about halfway down, leaving a gap in the top half just wide enough to pass through.

Vallette d'Osia catapulted through the window, after counting the seconds between telegraph poles. The train was passing along an embankment, which meant that he would have further to fall but possibly on to a softer surface. It seemed an age before he hit the ground, but he forced himself to stand up immediately, foregoing the luxury of even a breather.

It was as well. Behind him, the embankment erupted with gunfire and he heard the cry: 'Stop, a terrorist has escaped.' Even before the train came to a halt, he had melted away.

The news of his arrest had plunged the resistance of

Haute-Savoie into gloom and fear. An entire agonising week stretched out before news was received of a bedraggled, handcuffed figure appearing at a farmhouse near Dijon.

The apparition had told the startled farmer: 'I'm Vallette d'Osia and I've just jumped from a train.'

The reaction was hostile. The farmer was a true patriot and no collaborator, but he was a family man and he had heard plenty about Gestapo and Milice stooges. Colonel Vallette d'Osia of the Chasseurs Alpins was locked up unceremoniously until his identity was confirmed.

There was no question of returning to his position within the resistance or, indeed, remaining anywhere in Haute-Savoie. The hounds of the Gestapo would be baying for blood; the threat to others would be as real as if his capture had been successful. In late October 1943, Colonel Vallette d'Osia was flown to England by SOE.

He was by no means the only serious loss.

Felix Plottier, creator of the maquis in Haute-Savoie, acting initially under the order of Vallette d'Osia, had proved himself a formidable opponent of the Milice, the assiduous lackeys of the Nazis in occupied France.

As the dedicated evaders of forced labour made their way to Bonneville, the local Juge d'Instruction tetchily issued a warrant for the arrest of 'Felix Xavier Arthur Plottier, born 1 November 1908 in Bonneville, son of Maurice François Joseph and Marie Josephine de Freyre.'

Plottier was 'accused of attacking the external security of the State and forming a group of felons. Height: 1 metre 72, wavy chestnut hair brushed back, blue eyes, sturdily built, always bare-headed. Usually dressed in sports clothes, very athletic, loving the mountains. Could be in Annecy or Aix-les-Bains, where he has relatives, or trying to reach the Swiss frontier. This arrest warrant replaces that numbered S 43. If discovered, advise by telephone or telegram the head office of the Security Police situated in Vichy. . . .'

But Plottier, the zestfully unrepentant resistant, had fallen foul of the Vichy police long before. At the pinnacle of his own personal list of resistance heroes was Henri Frenay, architect of Mouvement pour la Libération Française (MLF), eventually to be known as Combat. This was also the name of the movement's newspaper, which proudly displayed a quotation by Clemenceau: 'In war as in peace, the last word belongs to those who never give up.'

Plottier willingly took on the task of distributing the newspaper in his own region. Inevitably, the local Milice were alerted; he became a marked man.

He recalls: 'From then on, it became impossible to sleep on some nights in our house on the hill outside Bonneville. We had an arrangement with my mother that if I was on the way home after work and the Milice was around she would hang out a towel on the tennis court. It was a coded warning. We slept elsewhere.'

Several times he toyed with the idea of escaping to England and aiding the resistance from there, but the risk was too great: so many of the escape lines had already been severed.

The alternative of remaining in France was, however, scarcely more attractive. Under the Vichy warrant for his arrest, on 28th October Plottier was sentenced in his absence by the special section of the appeal court to ten years' forced labour, 'for taking part in a plot and associating with felons'.

The choice of language was remarkably mild in the circumstances. After all, the warrant referred to the actions of a maquis leader with a twelve-hundred-strong resistant force which had its own camps and dropping zones at the plateau of Glières within the Borne Massif mountain range.

Haute-Savoie itself became too dangerous. The Swiss frontier at Geneva beckoned, a mere twelve miles away.

One night, the breath of the Gestapo warm on their necks, Felix and Joan Plottier crossed into Switzerland, hoping that their two young sons would be able to follow in safety later.

Surrounded by vassal states of Hitler's empire, the Swiss faced the ever present threat that they might be the next country to experience the dubious benefits of Nazi 'protection'. The fear was aggravated with the capitulation of Italy in 1943. All frontier posts that had previously been held by Italians were taken over by the Wehrmacht.

Smuggling arms into France from the Swiss side was still vital to the resistance. But the obstacles were formidable.

Plottier explains: 'These included a twelve foot fence which the Swiss had placed all along the frontier, rigidly guarded by Swiss-German troops. My job was to get arms into France, smuggling them to various points close to the Swiss-French border in the upper Rhône valley and elsewhere into France.'

There was only one way in which the supplies of pistol ammunition, reels of detonating fuse, binoculars, food-stuffs and morale-boosting leaflets could be spirited out: in boxes on men's backs, across the mountains north of Chamonix.

Felix Plottier was a brilliant skier with unrivalled knowledge of the mountains; that made the day when the Swiss caught him a considerable blow to the resistance. It was not the first time he had clashed with the authorities. In the May dawn, an armed patrol swooped down on the maquis group which, intent on shipping arms and supplies, was working closely with its Italian counterpart in the Aosta valley, close to the border between Switzerland and France.

The area of Champéry, where Plottier was arrested, had been proclaimed a military zone closed to civilians. His violation of this edict was bad enough; in addition, Plottier had, under an assumed name, rented a chalet for storing arms.

197

There followed months of interrogation in prison. Plottier recalled: 'There was no torture, no Gestapo methods. But there was no comfort, either. The jail authorities never tired of telling me that I wouldn't hope to get out in under twenty years for arms trafficking, possessing false identity papers and trespass in the military area of Champéry.'

But the Germans were on the run from France; Plottier's case never came to court and he was freed on payment of fifteen hundred Swiss frances – on condition he quit Switzerland.

By then, the knowledge of their inevitable defeat had fuelled a fresh ferocity in the Germans. They and Darnand's Milice flexed their muscles for fierce engagements in the mountains of Haute-Savoie and the Jura, in the central forests of the Corrèze and in the southwestern vineyards of the Dordogne.

It was a corner of Haute-Savoie, however, that was to be the backdrop for one of the greatest resistance tragedies.

23

Within the vast sprawling range of Borne Massif, which extends for more than twelve and a half miles within Haute-Savoie northwest of Annecy, lies the hollow of rolling grassland which is the plateau of the Glières.

Shaped like an elongated diamond, it stretches five miles northeast to southwest and is a mere one and a half miles across at its widest point. Forests girdle the mountains and the sheer rocks act as stern, uninviting sentinels.

It was natural that the resistance would be attracted by the inaccessibility of the Glières, which seemed virtually impregnable against any large-scale surprise attack. In addition, here was also an ideal dropping zone for parachutes and supplies. Captain Henri Romans-Petit, the successor to Colonel Vallette d'Osia, believed that no more than a hundred maquisards would be needed on the Glières. Such a number, it was reasoned, would be enough to guard the approaches, receive the containers of arms and transport them to storage dumps, ready for allocation to other resistance groups.

But Romans-Petit had reckoned without the staunch individualism of twenty-nine-year-old charismatic Lyons aristocrat Theodose Morel, known as Tom, a product of the St-Cyr military academy who had opted for service in the Chasseurs Alpins and been appointed to command the 27th Battalion at Annecy.

To Tom, the Glières represented a sacred stronghold of Free France and not just a dropping zone for Allied supplies. The leaders of the Haute-Savoie maquis expected mass drops of arms and food, which they saw as infinitely more practical considerations than a paragraph or two in the annals of military glory. In fact, Tom marshalled some 450 members of the maquis to the defence of the plateau under the slogan *Vivre Libre ou Mourir* (Live Free or Die).

On the evening of 29 January 1944, the maquis first came to the Glières. It was at the end of a week in which the mountains had been enveloped in heavy mists. The columns of men groped forward slowly in the snow and darkness; the paths which crisscrossed the plateau were a rink of ice. There was a moment of tragedy when a local fourteen-year-old boy, Noel Avettand, who had come to guide the maquisards, plunged to his death. To many who made that journey, the Glières seemed like the end of the world, a place whose sadness was somehow accentuated by the snow cloaking the landscape in a shroud.

It was, above all, a place where men would fight and die, where down in the dark, still valleys there lurked, not just the Germans, but the French collaborators, the Groupes Mobiles de Réserves with their dark blue and mustard-coloured uniforms, black helmets and black boots, their chests banded with the leather straps bearing their equipment.

The expected arms were dropped in mid-February. On the first night, four aircraft dropped fifty-four containers, to be followed by guns and munitions. The whole venture was unopposed; there was fresh confidence in the leadership of Tom Morel.

But the landings had been witnessed both by the Germans and the Milice; now they could pinpoint the position of the forces on the plateau.

Disaster, when it came to the maquis, was from an unexpected cause.

The waves of aircraft had barely departed before the Germans moved up attack troops to the plateau. At around the same time, Michel Fournier, deputy medical officer to the battalion, went down to Grand-Bornand village to pick up some badly needed medical supplies. Some bargaining between the Milice and the resistants had led to a precarious promise that there would be no interference with emissaries sent to collect such supplies.

Fournier did not return; Tom learnt that he had fallen into the hands of the GMR. There was, Morel realised, little point in appealing to the Vichy authorities on behalf of a fellow Frenchman. Some form of confrontation was inevitable; the impulsive leader of the Glières maquis was in the mood for it.

Morel despatched a special unit; it seized thirty of the GMR contingent with little difficulty. As a gesture, this doubtless relieved feelings, but was robbed of any point when it was learnt that Fournier had been hustled away to Annecy hours before. The maquis leader then made an offer: he would exchange the thirty prisoners for the safe return of Michel Fournier.

What seemed like a reasonable bargain was struck with the Milice. Morel released his prisoners; there was still no sign of the medical officer.

Plainly, it was no good conducting negotiations in the spirit of St-Cyr. A new attack was forthwith launched on the GMR command post at Entremont village.

Tom was determined that this would be no puny act of retaliation; the maquisards went in with rifles, grenades, Stens and Thompson sub-machine-guns, supplemented by two Hotchkiss heavy machine-guns and a single mortar. They succeeded in blasting their way into the GMR headquarters at the Hôtel de France in Entremont, seizing prisoners and swiftly disarming them.

The commander of the post, Major Lefebvre, suppressing his rage with difficulty, demanded the traditional right of an officer to keep his pistol to maintain his honour.

Morel asked coldly: 'What is your honour worth, since you refuse to keep your promises?'

The maquis leader then went on to demand the surrender of the entire garrison against the release of Michel Fournier. It brought the rejoinder: 'I have no intention of surrendering but I suggest you do, here and now. I will not negotiate with traitors.'

Now it was Morel's turn to feel mounting rage, and he saw no reason to suppress it. The use of the word 'traitors' by a representative of Vichy led him to lose his temper completely. He hurled insults at Lefebvre, who suddenly appeared bored with the discussion, abruptly turned his back and prepared to re-enter the hotel.

Then it happened. Totally without warning – beyond spitting out 'Salaud' – Lefebvre swung round and, pistol in hand, fired point-blank at Morel. With a look of mingled bewilderment and fear, the Chasseurs Alpins lieutenant, the hero of the Glières, clutched his stomach, gave a single cough and fell dead.

But within minutes Lefebvre was cut down by a single burst from a machine pistol fired by a maquisard who had accompanied Tom Morel with an improvised flag of truce.

What happened next was inexcusable in military terms but at least understandable in men who had lost a beloved leader. The maquis stumbled into the Hôtel de France, tearing to pieces all who stood in their way. Those members of the Milice who were not shot on the spot threw themselves out of upstairs windows in sheer terror. It was either that or be cut to ribbons with knives and bayonets. When the bloodlust had finally been slaked, the Hôtel de France resembled an abattoir.

It was then time for the resistance to count its own cost. Incredibly, in addition to Morel, the defenders of the Glières had lost just one man: Adjutant Georges Descours, a peacetime policeman from Annecy.

The dazed members of the maquis made the sad journey back to the plateau with the bodies of their two comrades and captured arms and supplies. As far as the foot of the mountain, the remains of Morel and Descours were transported by sledge. But after that, everything had to be unloaded and carried for the rest of the way.

With the stretcher parties leading, the difficult ascent up the steep, snow-choked paths began. Five-and-a-half hours later, at 9 a.m., the long and silent line of mourners was back on the Glières.

The bodies of Tom and his adjutant were taken to the community hospital, where, covered with the flags of Free France and on beds draped and canopied with red, white and blue silk taken from RAF parachutes used in arms drops, they lay in state until the funeral. A round-the-clock guard of honour was mustered; the men stood with heads bowed and with rifle or machine-gun at the reverse.

But the outward show of mourning had to be brief. The maquisards, even before the death of their leader, had been aware of just how precarious their position was.

Somehow they all sensed that the Germans would not keep them waiting long.

During the morning of 11 March, the Milice mounted in force up the western front of the plateau, but after an hour of bitter fighting were driven back. Then, flying out of the sun, a Messerschmitt fighter raked the chalets. Incendiary bullets and cannon shells churned up the snow and splintered the wooden walls, but no one was hit and the buildings suffered little damage.

A second German aircraft flew low on a photo reconnaissance mission. Its photographs revealed four fresh piles of logs which had clearly been stacked to light a further Allied parachute drop.

The maquis awaited the signal from London that would tell them when the aircraft were coming. Then, among the personal messages broadcast after the BBC's nine o'clock evening news that same night, they heard it. The newsreader intoned twice: '*Le petit homme aime le Byrrh, le petit homme aime les tessons de bouteille*' ('The little man likes the apéritif, the little man likes the broken bits of the bottle').

Maquisards were alerted by the throbbing roar of four-engined bombers. The drop was truly gigantic: almost ninety tons of arms and munitions, more than sufficient to arm 4,000 men. All at once, the defenders of the Glières ceased to be useful resisters, but became instead frantic foragers, hunting feverishly all over the plateau for arms that had been scattered in 400 places.

More than one maquisard reflected ruefully that the supplies might just as well never have been dropped, for they became trapped into the sticky embrace of the snow or fell into ravines. Day after day, scores of men scoured the fields, the woods and the snowbanks. It was almost a point of honour to retrieve the arms, thus preventing them from falling into German hands.

As for the Germans, they possessed infinite patience. They were content to wait and watch. There was more than enough time for the task they had planned.

General Julius Oberg, commander of a crack Alpine division, conferred with Luftwaffe commanders, Gestapo chiefs and members of the Milice. A force of some 15,000, together with two air squadrons, was at the Germans' disposal.

The order for a general assault was given on 25 March. Hell came to the maquisards on the Glières. Wave after wave of fire sliced into the plateau; trees suddenly became blazing torches and banks of snow melted away. Fifteen thousand Germans against 500 maquisards.

The Glières was now an entrenched camp, where men dug holes into which they vainly tried to snuggle. All too soon, Captain Maurice Anjot, the successor to Tom Morel and also an officer of the 27th Battalion of Chasseurs Alpins, learnt the strength of the opposition. There were training units throughout Haute-Savoie and operational headquarters had been set up at the Hôtel Imperial at Annecy. The mountain troops, white smocks over their grey field uniforms, advanced up the snowy slopes towards the pine trees held by just twenty maquisard to the east of the massif.

By early afternoon only one maquisard remained alive in the sector. He went on firing until his ammunition was spent. Then came the volley which put paid to him too.

The chiefs of the various sectors were cut off. Forced to abandon his command post, Captain Anjot, his officers, doctors and medical orderlies, together with some severely wounded men, huddled in a cave which, poignantly, lay in the shadow of the simple wooden cross that had been erected above the grave of Tom Morel. By twilight, the plateau was being held by this last core of defenders, and with the light fading from the summits of the mountains of Frêles and Auges came nightfall and silence.

With an attempt at cheerfulness, Anjot commented: 'We have at least saved our honour.'

But another maquisard was more prosaic: 'It's the end of the battalion of the Glières.'

And it was. The decision was made to cease fighting, with the injunction that each survivor should seek to join his original maquis. After a fifteen-hour march in the snow, Anjot and a little group reached the village of Naves.

The Germans were waiting.

In the barrage of machine-gun fire, Maurice Anjot was the first to fall.

Leaderless and dispirited, the remaining maquisards, suffering from cold, hunger and lack of sleep, kept up an endless march, dogged by the Germans and the Milice.

Those who were not mown down by execution squads were dragged, battered and beaten, to hotels and villas in Annecy which had been hastily converted into detention centres. Then they were hauled before token tribunals, condemned as 'terrorists' or 'bandits' and immediately shot.

Total repression had come, not just to Haute-Savoie, but to the hamlets and camps of yet another so-called impenetrable fortress: the proud, grim massif of the Vercors in the eastern Alps.

It has been said that no army corps of engineers could have designed and built a better redoubt for hit-and-run guerillas than God had done in this section of the Alps.

With its sheer walls thousands of feet tall, it dominated the plain of the Rhône and Isère rivers like some vast cathedral glimpsed in a distorted dream. On the map it resembles a huge arrowhead thirty miles long by twenty feet wide. Its limestone had proved more pliable than granite could ever be; the bitter weather had combed it into gorges and deep grottoes, locking it from the rest of France within rugged mountain peaks.

Such a position had hitherto discouraged the Germans, providing welcome cover for the camps of the maquisards. True, there had been punitive raids by enemy columns; villages and houses had been burnt following arrests. But the maquis had behaved strictly according to the textbook rules of guerilla warfare: lightning retaliation followed by withdrawal into the welcome protection of the Vercors passes.

Then came June 1944. The Allied armies were on the coast of Normandy, beginning the slow, agonising push to the frontiers of the Reich. No longer was the role of the resistance to be seen as defensive. The BBC, acting at the behest of General de Gaulle and the French National Committee in Algiers, issued the rallying call: the French underground was to rise and do battle.

But after a series of clashes which left neither side beaten, the Germans launched an attack of ruthless brilliance at the very heart of the Vercors.

The massif was alive with hope on 21 July. To the delighted ears of the maquisards came the roar of aircraft, from the south – the direction of Algiers, headquarters of the French government-in-exile. It seemed too good to be true: the long lines of gliders, forty in all, with airborne troops swooping down from the sky, released by the bombers who had towed them in. Liberation was in the skies!

Up went the ecstatic cry: 'It's the Yanks! It's the Yanks!'

But the black crosses on the wings had the immediate effect of turning the reaction to one of sheer panic: 'It's the Boche!'

And it was. In waves they came, troop-filled gliders in tow, supported by the Fokker-Wolfes and the Dorniers which streaked and roared ahead of the transports, unleashing their bombs and peppering everything with machine-gun fire.

The maquisards leapt too late to their machine-guns. One German glider was blasted out of the skies, but most of them were on the ground, their crews setting up heavy machine-guns on the airstrip. The SS fanned out, seizing the village of Vassieux and the neighbouring villages of Mure and Château.

The Germans took their time over leaving Vassieux; they had plenty to do there. Those few who survived had appalling stories to tell when it was all over. People were burnt alive in their homes. The SS perfected its own technique of hanging: two victims were suspended by the neck from opposite ends of the same rope, which was thrown over the branch of a tree. Only one of the victims could touch the ground with the tips of his toes. The two seesawed. Death for each was postponed as one man managed to get his toes to the ground. Eventually, the pressure on the neck would become unbearable and both victims too exhausted to survive.

More than 200 people, many of them elderly peasants, were slaughtered indiscriminately. Corpses were found castrated, breasts cut off, tongues removed. For hostages, it was not merely a question of swift death by firing squad: they were tortured first and then butchered. Death, when it came to maimed and broken men, was by machine-gun fire in public squares.

Members of the maquis were, in one sense, luckier than the civilian population. It was not so easy to pin them down. They were forced to keep moving, to seek the protection of countryside they knew well. Nevertheless, the Germans thoroughly and systematically combed out each plateau.

The maquis was forced to break off the fight and run for high ground in the fir forests, where the Germans, in ignorance of the terrain, did not dare follow. There they stayed until they heard the news of the landing of the French Army in the south and its march up the Route Napoléon towards Grenoble.

Only then could the heroic survivors of the Vercors join with their comrades in the campaigns of liberation.

24

Throughout the four years of Nazi occupation, the city of Paris endured its daily humiliation.

From the fall of Paris on 14 June 1940 to the day of its liberation, 3 August 1944, a Nazi band and a battalion of Wehrmacht circled the Arc de Triomphe. At the stroke of noon, the procession made its way down the Champs Élysée to the Place de la Concorde. Like some massive metronome, their footfalls tolled out to Paris and to all France the passage of another day of occupation. It began on the stroke of the drum major's baton, followed with heavy predictability by *Deutschland, Deutschland ueber Alles* and *Preussens Glorie* (Prussian Glory).

The symbols of oppression were everywhere; from the top of the Eiffel Tower flew the black hooked-cross banner of the swastika. Anyone who wanted to be reminded of the national flag of France had to visit the army museum in Les Invalides, where the banned tricolour was locked behind a glass case.

Even the most compliant of Parisians could not escape the black, white and red sentry boxes barring their way in the rue de Rivoli, around the Place de la Concorde in front of the Palais du Luxembourg.

In the Place de l'Opéra were black-lettered signs indicating such destinations as MILITAERBEFEHLHABER IN FRANKREICH, GENERAL DER LUFTWAFFE and HAUPTVERKEHRSDIREKTION PARIS.

It was true that the ration of each Parisian was two eggs, 3.2 ounces of cooking oil and 2 ounces of margarine. It was equally true that wine was in short supply, and at the pavement cafés it was only possible to get ersatz coffee made from acorns and chickpeas. Gas and electricity as public services might be only a memory, but the weather was good that final August of occupation and Edith Piaf was singing at the Moulin Rouge.

Above all, Paris had survived intact. While other cities had been torn apart, some divine providence had spared Notre Dame, Sainte Chapelle, the Louvre and Sacré Coeur.

But for how long?

Hundreds of miles away, deep within the gloomy drooping pine forests of Rastenburg in East Prussia, Adolf Hitler dreamt of death and destruction. From his FHQ (*Fuehrerhauptquartier*), the German dictator proclaimed his determination to reduce Paris to such a shambles that neither Gaullist nor Communist forces would stand to gain from liberation.

Hitler needed an able and ruthless lieutenant to implement his plans: he summoned to Rastenburg Generalmajor Dietrich von Choltitz, an officer from the western front with promising credentials. In the words of an OKW superior, Choltitz had 'never questioned an order, no matter how harsh'. Plainly he was his Fuehrer's man.

His track record boded ill for Paris. In May 1940, he had been one of those who had ordered the bombing of Rotterdam. At the siege of Sevastopol in the Crimea he had won promotion to general at the cost of an arm wound and devastating losses. But he had taken the city and annihilated it. In the retreat from the Russian front he had left behind only scorched earth. He was well aware of his tough reputation, saying: 'It is my lot to defend the rear of the German army. And each time I am ordered to destroy each city as I leave it.'

As might be expected, there were few things capable of shocking this dedicated soldier with the bearing of a provincial burgomaster; Hitler in August 1944 was the exception.

The Fuehrer, badly rattled by the nearly successful 20 July assassination plot in which a bomb had been placed inside his headquarters, launched into a tirade. He raged: 'Since the twentieth of July, Herr General, dozens of generals – yes, dozens – have bounced at the end of a rope because they wanted to prevent me, Adolf Hitler, from continuing my work.'

Hitler was now in a state of feverish excitement, saliva running from his mouth. Choltitz said: 'He was trembling all over and the desk on which he was leaning shook. He was bathed in perspiration and became more agitated.'

After what seemed an age, Hitler calmed down. He said to Choltitz: 'Now you're going to Paris. That city must be utterly destroyed. On the departure of the Wehrmacht, nothing must be left standing, no church, no artistic monument.'

A fresh thought seemed to strike Hitler. With a twisted grin he added: 'Even the water supply must be cut off so that the ruined city may be prey to epidemics.'

Choltitz stared in horror. Here were not the orders of a military commander but all the pent-up resentment of a raving maniac.

Nevertheless, Generalmajor Dietrich von Choltitz went to Paris.

A light wind swept across the Tuileries Gardens, whipping up the skirts of a pretty girl cyclist. The two men on the balcony of the Hôtel Meurice stared appreciatively at the exposed legs and thighs before the girl was lost to view.

The German turned to his mustachioed companion and said with deliberate casualness: 'It would be a pity to kill the pretty girls of Paris; and destroy their city.'

Raoul Nordling had been the Swedish consul-general in Paris for eighteen years; as a representative of a neutral country, he had the supreme advantage of having feet in both German and Allied camps. It was, he was the first to admit, a bizarre posture. But Paris was a bizarre place in these days.

Choltitz's remark gave the Swede a surge of hope. It

seemed to indicate that the German had not finally made up his mind to implement the appalling order of his Fuehrer. But Nordling was also only too well aware that the Commander of *Gross Paris* was being dangerously provoked.

On the grey, damp Saturday morning of 19 August, the Gaullist faction in the Paris Police Committee of Liberation had taken control of the prefecture. Paris was clearly in a mutinous mood; on the day before, there had been a call for a general uprising. And now, with the seizing of the prefecture, it had begun.

Fifty feet below the streets of the city, a vast air raid shelter, sealed off with steel doors and supplied with air from its own conditioning plant, served as the headquarters of the French Forces of the Interior, now the official name of the resistance movement.

Here were ten miles of underground corridors, built to give access to the water mains connecting with various parts of the city. The choice had proved ideal because only those few Germans whose job it was to supervise the water system even knew the place existed. Those who did had left Paris just before the uprising, leaving a young French colonel and his staff in undisputed possession. Throughout the ensuing battle, messengers made their way along the labyrinth of corridors, able to surface as far away as the Bois de Boulogne, where they could slip into cafés, shops and innocuous office blocks – the nerve centres of the various groups.

The ordinary Parisian had remained largely unaware of what was happening until he left home for work and encountered the traffic. It had gone haywire. Paris was one long traffic jam, and the situation got steadily worse during the day. There were no police to control it. German vehicles, many of them fleeing what they sensed was a capital threatened by invasion, were unable to move.

The organisers of the police strike let four days go by. Then three thousand of them, decked out in civilian clothes, returned to the prefecture. They battered on the gates, stormed the building and installed a new prefect. A few minutes later, from the flagstaff of the building fluttered the first tricolour from a public building in the capital for four years.

But as it turned out, the occupation of the prefecture did not go as smoothly as the insurrectionists had expected. Amid the mêlée, a German truck exploded when hit by an incendiary. German soldiers running for cover were struck by police marksmen. But there was no victory here; an explosive shell from a tank hit the iron gates of the prefecture and blew them open. A young law student, Edgar Pisani, who had been trying to work the switchboard, was lifted out of his chair and flung into the opposite corner of the room.

A German Tiger tank lumbered into the prefecture courtyard. The police defenders, crouching behind sandbags, were no match for such armour – and they knew it.

There was mass panic, with the defenders dashing in terror for the entrance to the metro station inside the prefecture.

One man now seized the initiative. Police Sergeant Armand Fournet, appalled at the sudden rush to escape, ran to the station entrance and blocked it. He waved a pistol and shouted: 'I'll shoot any man who tries to pass me. We must stand together, fight together. It is our only hope of survival.'

Incredibly, the panic-stricken mob halted. Fournet later recorded that he saw a collective look of shame; the men turned back to the courtyard and their posts.

Still the Germans kept up their fierce tank barrage. Policemen on the roof tossed Molotov cocktails towards the tanks – these comprised bottles containing sulphuric acid and several flasks of potassium chlorate.

Choltitz, on his hotel balcony, heard the bursts of gunfire. In a sudden fury, he vowed: 'I'll get them out of their prefecture. I'll bomb them out of it.'

Nordling, still at the commander's side, asked quietly:

'Do you realise what that means? Your near misses will fall on Notre Dame and Sainte Chapelle!'

Choltitz shrugged: 'What alternative do I have?'

The Swede realized that the present insurrection, if it continued, could sound the death knell of Paris, the city where he had spent most of his adult life and which he deeply loved. Already he had done his bit for the Allied cause, against all the rules of Swedish neutrality. He had successfully negotiated with Choltitz for the release of more than four thousand political prisoners.

Now he felt that he must do more: he would plead for the very life of Paris itself. He forthwith suggested a temporary ceasefire for the removal of the dead and wounded.

At first, the German greeted the idea with incredulity. The very suggestion of a ceasefire was a novelty; no such thing had been suggested to him before. This was not the way that the vanquished should talk to a victor; in Choltitz's book there should be total surrender.

A moment's reflection, however, showed him that a truce would release a number of troops tied down in a single action. Furthermore, once an attack was carried out on the prefecture, there could be no turning back.

Nordling waited anxiously for Choltitz to decide; he knew that the defenders of the prefecture could not hold out much longer. His hope was that a temporary ceasefire might ultimately be extended. He was playing desperately for time.

At last, the fat little general, his eyes slits of tiredness, turned to Nordling and said: 'Very well. If it can be shown for just one hour that the FFI officers can control their men, I will accept a temporary truce.'

A mere two hours after giving his undertaking to Nordling, the commander of *Gross Paris* received a terse order from Hitler: 'Prepare the Seine bridges for destruction. Paris must not fall in the hands of the enemy except as a field of ruins.'

It was an insane, purposeless order. Nothing could stop

the advance of the American and French forces. Besides, Choltitz needed the bridges for troop movements within the city. He decided to ignore the order.

But the calling of a ceasefire had taken no account of internal political ambitions. The Communists, thirsting for insurrection and determination to have Paris as their prize, refused to observe any truce.

For Breton seaman's son Henri Tanguy – cover name 'Colonel Rol' – it seemed the fulfilment of a dream. For sixteen years he had been a dedicated Communist, a thorn in the flesh of prewar French governments, and had been ejected frequently from factories for trade union and industrial agitation. He had fought in Spain; his cover name was that of a comrade fighting the forces of General Franco. Now Rol-Tanguy was longing to challenge the Gaullist faction head on.

At first, there were mere fissures in the seemingly solid rockface of the ceasefire. Then the fissures became cracks and the whole structure burst open.

Violence broke out all over Paris.

When it was spent, those involved recalled isolated incidents of horror amid the general carnage. Four truckloads of German troops were ambushed and then set alight with Molotov cocktails. The men staggered screaming through the streets, which soon reeked with the sourness of burnt flesh. Communist resistant André Tollet, who was among those who commandeered the Hôtel de Ville, recorded:

Four German tanks rumbled into the square and started shelling the building.

I saw a young woman, a bottle in her hand, run fearlessly up to the tanks and smash against the side. She ran away as the flames shot up but a German bullet sliced into her and she fell. But she had caused the other tanks to turn tail. She had saved the Hôtel de Ville.

General Jacques-Philippe de Hautecloque was a dour, lean individual whom General de Gaulle had named as

215

trainer and commander of an armoured division for the liberation of Paris. The man who called himself General Leclerc – the pseudonym was adopted to protect the family he had left behind at the time of France's surrender – was in charge of 16,000 men with 2,000 vehicles. All he needed was the signal to advance on the capital.

The Allies were split on the wisdom of sending large forces to liberate Paris at all. General Dwight D. Eisenhower, as Supreme Commander, told de Gaulle: 'I plan to pinch off Paris and let her hang there for future plucking.' Even blunter was Lieutenant-General George S. Patton, who declared: 'They started their goddamned insurrection. Now let them finish it.' Various representations from Paris reached the ears of the Allies: all the signs were that the Germans would not delay indefinitely their wholesale retaliation against the French capital. Eventually, Eisenhower relented: the French would go in.

Around dusk on Wednesday 23 August, Leclerc leaped from an aircraft on a field at Argentan, crying: *'Mouvement immédiat sur Paris!'* And at dawn the triumphant progress of the French 2nd Armoured Division began, as it roared out of its bivouac near Ecouché south of Argentan. A violent rainstorm lashed at the wild, winding country roads; the men, volunteers from every corner of the French Empire, had only one thought. They wanted to be in the French capital, which most of them – drawn from Indochina, Senegal, Tunisia, Morocco, French Equatorial and Central Africa – had never seen. Ahead of them was a bloody slog, in which the American-made Sherman tanks of 2nd Armoured were harried by Tiger tanks.

Paris prepared to celebrate. Its bells had been silent for the four long years of occupation. But now they rang out with the sheer joy of anticipated freedom. The first to peal was the south tower of Notre Dame, followed by Sacré Coeur in Montmartre. And then it seemed as if the whole of Paris was one vast chime.

In the Hôtel Meurice, at a candlelit dinner table,

Generalmajor Choltitz paused for a moment, shrugged, and went on with his meal.

One man in Paris, however, was deaf to church bells and celebration. The news that General Leclerc was on the way acted as a spur to Rol-Tanguy. He knew that time was running desperately short; if his Communist FFI was to be granted any role at all in the liberation, then he would have to move fast. General de Gaulle was also bound to make a grand entrance from his billet at the magnificent Château de Rambouillet. Rol-Tanguy installed himself in the Hôtel de Ville, symbol of Paris's political sovereignty. He reasoned that this was where de Gaulle would surely come. Rol-Tanguy was prepared to greet him as an heroic 'guest' but there would be no deference to him as leader or liberator.

Political manoeuvring aside, France was still at war and there was fighting ahead. The Germans were holding out at the Buttes-Chaumont tunnel, where a number of trains were parked, and the Prince-Eugene barracks of the Wehrmacht on the Place de la République. FFI units threw in everything they had, watching the dwindling of their meagre supplies of ammunition. The German guards at the Buttes-Chaumont were rapidly overcome; more than 125 prisoners were seized, along with arms and munitions.

Leclerc sent one column of men to Versailles, with orders to strike for the northwestern gate, the Porte de Sèvres. This column, in fact, was the smallest, but Leclerc was determined it would make the greatest noise and fool the Germans into assuming that Versailles constituted the main thrust.

The second column was then despatched some five miles to the southeast through the valley of the Chevreuse, entering Paris by Porte de Vanves. As for the main thrust, which he himself would use for his main entry into Paris, that would be entrusted to Colonel Pierre Billote, who would slip south, through Longjumeau and Fresnes, and break into Paris through the southern gateway of the Porte d'Orleans.

Late on the night of the twenty-fourth, the Communists of the FFI fought on desperately in their own bid to liberate the capital. But it was too late. Tough, red-headed tank commander Raymond Dronne swept across the city limits and made history as the first French soldier to come home to Paris.

It was a Paris, moreover, which had gone delirious with joy. A vast tide of humanity engulfed armoured vehicles inscribed with the Cross of Lorraine. Dronne was a handsome man, and he was looking forward to seeing his first Paris girls. As it turned out, there were so many seeking to embrace him, crush him and stroke his uniform that at the end of the day he could remember only one clearly: a heavy girl wearing the red skirt and black bodice of Alsace who had jumped on his jeep and smashed the glass of his lowered windscreen.

Generalmajor Choltitz was well aware that he was going down to defeat. But, he reasoned, any capitulation might as well be carried out in style. He made sure that his uniform was freshly pressed and his boots highly polished. He decided to have a last dinner in the Hôtel Meurice. By tomorrow, he might be dead; if life entailed surrendering to the FFI, to terrorists, then it was probably better so.

As for General de Gaulle, his political antenna was twitching vigorously. He was far too tried a hand to fall in with Rol-Tanguy's ploy and go to the Hôtel de Ville, where he was only too well aware that he would be received as a 'guest'.

He was no one's guest. He was the President of the Provisional Government of the Republic. Moreover, it was his tanks which had liberated Paris.

At the Gare Montparnasse, de Gaulle received the surrender document which Leclerc had previously signed with Choltitz. De Gaulle blazed with anger when he saw Rol-Tanguy's signature; the Communist had insisted on adding his name. From Gare Montparnasse, de Gaulle then drove to his old office at the Ministry of War, which he had left in 1940.

But neither de Gaulle nor the forces of Leclerc had finished with the Germans. By the time it was all over, a further 127 French – soldiers and civilians – were to die. The casualties for the Liberation of Paris amounted to 901 FFI and 582 civilians. A total of 2,788 Germans died.

It was the civilians who suffered most as a suicide squad of Germans clashed with liberators storming the Foreign Office. A volley of gunfire drove back the French. Then heavy fighting erupted around the back entrance to the building. The tanks were in the front line now, shelling the German positions and setting fire to the ministry. Flames from one of Leclerc's tanks licked into the crowd. Many bystanders were killed before the Germans were wiped out.

The victorious troops broke into Gestapo headquarters at the Hotel Majestic in the Étoile. After that, they were watched by a delirious crowd, who at long last saw the hated swastika torn from the Arc de Triomphe and replaced by the flag of France. Shortly after noon, the tricolour flew from the Eiffel Tower.

It was not a tricolour to satisfy the stickler for accuracy. It was fashioned from three ancient bed sheets stuck together. One was dyed pink, one a decidedly pallid blue, and the third was a washy grey.

But it was a tricolour, nonetheless. And at noon on 25 August 1944, that was all that mattered.

Earlier, Generalmajor Choltitz, at his desk at the Meurice, had long given up marking the large map of Paris with red crosses to show the penetration of Leclerc's forces. Soon, he reflected ruefully, he would be running out of pencil. It would be more pleasant to have one last glass of wine with his officers.

That done, he retired to a small room in the hotel and waited.

A few hours later, the Commander of *Gross Paris* faced Lieutenant Henri Karcher of the army of General de Gaulle. For such an historic event, the encounter was curiously banal. Karcher merely took Choltitz's gun as the symbol of his surrender, saying: 'Follow me!'

When Choltitz arrived at the prefecture as a prisoner, the close-shaven, well-scrubbed and perfectly uniformed German general stood to attention before a scruffy, unshaven Frenchman with mud-caked American GI boots and a travel-stained uniform. For a moment, it looked as if General Leclerc was the vanquished and Choltitz the victor.

The two men got down to discussing the surrender document, but their deliberations were interrupted by an angry Rol-Tanguy demanding admittance to watch the signing of the surrender of the city he had defended for six days. An embarrassed Leclerc agreed.

General Charles de Gaulle, who had left Paris in June 1940 as an obscure brigadier general, returned a hero on the afternoon of 25 August. He insisted on riding through the city, contemptuously defying snipers and stray bullets in an open French-made Hotchkiss car. Nothing would have induced him to have paraded in an American jeep.

The square on the Boulevard Montparnasse was alive with Parisians. To the chorus of 'De Gaulle! De Gaulle!' he stretched out his arms high and wide in a huge V-sign.

Behind the scenes, however, things were less happy. Although they understood the reasons for it, a number of de Gaulle's followers were uneasy over his refusal to go to the Hôtel de Ville. His hatred of Rol-Tanguy, it was felt, could be construed as a direct boycott of the resistance and all it stood for. Such a slap in the face would make the future governing of France much harder. In the end, de Gaulle allowed himself to be persuaded.

Most Parisians remained unaware of all this. In any case, even if they had known, it is doubtful they would have cared. On the streets and boulevards, they were too busy prancing about in German helmets. Members of General Leclerc's forces had their faces stained scarlet with lipstick.

At the Hôtel de Ville, de Gaulle was asked if he would go out on the balcony and proclaim the Republic. His response was in itself guaranteed to render his legend immortal.

There was an icy silence. Then in tones shot full with contempt, de Gaulle snapped: 'The Republic has never ceased to exist!'

Thousands were singing and embracing, sharing the joy of liberation with those who had made it possible. These experiences made up the memories that Parisians were to cherish down the years. The most sublime moment of all was when, dark and miserable for four long years of cruel repression, Paris suddenly lit up.

Arc lights threw the Eiffel Tower into sharp relief. The Palais de Chaillot, Les Invalides, Notre Dame, all suddenly leapt miraculously out of the night. The Sacré Coeur, above Montmartre, became a giant, shining translucent wedding cake. Those inside Notre Dame would for years recall the voice of de Gaulle intoning every verse of the Magnificat.

But Paris was also cruel and bitter and brimming with revenge. There was the woman, her face suffused with hatred, who spat full in the face of Generalmajor Choltitz with the scream of *Bâtard!* On the Place de Chatelet, French captors, forced their prisoners to witness the sight of young girls, their head shaved and their breasts bare, sporting signs reading: 'I WHORED FOR THE GERMANS'.

In the St-Antoine hospital, a wounded and unconscious German was slowly strangled, his Knight's Cross ripped from his neck. The few remaining snipers in the city who were caught never reached the POW cages: the crowd beat them to death. A special hatred was reserved for members of Choltitz's staff on their way to captivity. All along their path they faced a jeering, raging mob who tore the uniforms off their backs, clubbing and kicking them.

Old habits die hard. In the restaurants and hotels, suddenly doing roaring business, harassed waiters could perhaps be forgiven for still adding the mandatory Vichy sales tax to their bills. Indignantly, diners deducted the amount.

One man remained largely unmoved by the mood of celebration in Paris. General Charles de Gaulle muttered to a colleague: 'The struggle for the rest of France is just beginning.'

And not just for France. Far to the north in the Netherlands, resistance steadily became even more bitter.

Here tragedy was just beginning.

25

Throughout the years of Nazi oppression in the Netherlands, Hanns Albin Rauter exercised his awesome powers from the barrel of a gun.

It was not just that he was Generalkommissar; after all, there were four of those in the country. He was something infinitely more imposing: Generalkommissar fuer des Sicherheitswesen (Commissioner General for Public Safety).

Even this was not the end of the parade of titles; there was, of course, the even more powerful Hoehere SS und Polizeifuehrer Nordwest (Higher SS and Police Leader).

As such, Rauter spelt terror throughout the Netherlands. His rule, as cruel and merciless as his chief, Heinrich Himmler, could have wished, reached the very pinnacle of power in 1944 as the spectre of defeat for Nazi Germany rose menacingly after D-Day.

Rauter was by then no longer simply a policeman but chief executioner of the Netherlands, with squads of killers on permanent standby. Captured resistance workers were immediately put up against the wall. There were no fancy irrelevancies such as trials; dissidents were termed *Todeskandidaten* (death candidates), and there was no limit to the numbers that could be despatched summarily.

Furthermore, their executions took place in public; bodies were left rotting by the roadside. By late summer 1944, Rauter had fully earned the nickname 'Hangman of the Netherlands'.

He doubtless relished the title, but by that stage of the war he also had his worries. The allied armies were racing towards the Dutch border. The Netherlands would become once again a major theatre of war; it needed troops to defend it, not policemen.

His parade of ranks and titles came to the rescue. By June 1944, Rauter had already been appointed to the military rank of General der Waffen-SS, enabling him to report to Generalfeldmarschall Walther Model, commander of Army Group B, at his Headquarters at Oosterbeek. Rauter still controlled a number of Waffen-SS units and was determined to put them to good use.

The need was pressing; the Allies had landed at Arnhem. Rauter speedily left the Hague, and drove to a new headquarters at Apeldoorn, lying to the northeast. There was no question where the bulk of his forces should go; they were forthwith ordered to Arnhem, which lay to the south east of Apeldoorn. The Germans sustained heavy losses against British airborne troops, but after ten days of savage fighting the Allies withdrew. In the overall scheme of the war, it was a mere setback; but Rauter greeted it ecstatically as a key victory.

In terms of career prestige, the performance of his forces at Arnhem had done him nothing but good. Indeed, Kampfgruppe Rauter was raised to the status of a provisional corps and assigned a sector of the front along the Rhine and Waal rivers from Emmerich, just inside Germany, to Tiel, in the Netherlands, west of Arnhem.

In terms of numbers, Rauter possessed formidable military muscle. He tended it with consummate devotion, driving out daily to visit forward posts and inspect defences. His new responsibilities made him disenchanted with his old police work. However, Arthur Seyss-Inquart was still a figure with whom to reckon, and past responsibilities could not be disregarded. The Reichskommissar had moved to his own headquarters closer to the Fatherland and was now at Apeldoorn; he expected Rauter to drive there for a conference every Wednesday morning. The journey was made by Rauter from Corps Headquarters at Didam, a village ten miles east of Arnhem.

It was a routine that the Higher SS and Police Leader

followed faithfully. Then on Tuesday 4 March 1945, he changed his timetable.

That week, he was faced with two conferences at Apeldoorn. He was required at 25th Army headquarters as well as calling on Seyss-Inquart. He decided to allow himself rather more time and start out on Tuesday evening, breaking the journey at his usual hotel.

Orders were given to his driver to have the car ready for 10 p.m. It seemed an unimportant change of schedule. But for Hanns Rauter the consequences were to be dramatic.

The Netherlands had evolved its own form of maquis warfare; by September 1944 this meant the activities of the unified Dutch resistance under the banner of *Binnenlandse Strijdkrachten* (Dutch Interior Forces) under the overall command of Prince Bernhard. One of the areas in which it operated was District 6, comprising the Veluwe, an undulating forest region with extensive heathlands and large wooded tracks.

And at the core of the district, in the town of Apeldoorn, was a cell which, for resistance resources, was not at all badly served. The GC-Groep, favoured for the more risky operations, could boast a healthy supply of Sten guns, pistols and grenades.

GC-Groep had something else fiercely envied by other resistants – some genuine SS uniforms. It was generally agreed by jealous rivals that, when it came to the element of surprise, the GC-Groep had an unfair advantage.

Every group had its hero and District 6 proved no exception. Geert Gosens was a high-spirited young mechanic with, by common consent, rather more than his fair share of luck. There was the time when a posse of SD swooped on his house, where he had been hiding transport used by the resistance.

Gosens, who at the time of the raid had been asleep on the first floor, clambered to safety over the roof, clad only in underpants. The experience increased his adrenalin: the next day he came back with his Sten and opened fire on the Germans who were in the act of removing vehicles from the garage. He had the satisfaction of flattening the tyres and making good his escape yet again. Unfortunately, the vehicles were not recaptured.

The transport problem was acute for the resistance. On Tuesday 6 March, news reached BS that a single Wehrmacht truck was due to collect a sizeable quantity of pork for distribution to the Wehrmacht. It was to be picked up from a butcher in the nearby village of Epe the following morning.

The Apeldoorn BS Sabotage Commander forthwith instructed Gosens and his team to seize the meat.

For Gosens, the challenge was irresistible; the method he favoured conformed with everyone's popular idea of the model resistant.

Gosens reasoned that, since the group already possessed German uniforms, the problem was halfway solved. All that remained was to dress up the team and drive up in a truck before the genuine Germans were due and seize the meat.

That, of course, left the question: where was the right sort of truck to be found? To all questioners, Gosens shrugged with a grin: 'Steal it, of course.'

He set about picking a small team with the necessary loyalty and experience. The most important matter to be decided was where the ambush should happen. On the advice of one of the resistants, Wim Kok, in normal life a member of the Dutch Mounted Police, Gosens opted for the road to Arnhem.

It had the big attraction of being quiet and sparsely populated; it ran through woods offering ample cover. In addition, the team had a nearby campsite bolt hole. Their courage was fuelled by the fact that their resistance had previously ambushed and fired a German car, there-after taking the occupants prisoner. Success of that kind was apt to be infectious; there was general agreement that it was well worth trying again.

Shortly before 10 a.m. on the chosen day, the team set off on bicycles for the Arnhem road. Except for Kok, who elected to wear his everyday police uniform, the men were dressed as Germans. Sep Koettinger, an Austrian member of the Waffen-SS who had deserted to the Dutch, masqueraded as an SS-Oberscharfuehrer (Quartermaster Sergeant), while Gosens and his fellow Dutchman Henk de Weert were both dressed in the uniform of Rottenfuehrers (corporals). The other two, Dutchman Karel Pruis and another turncoat Austrian, Herman Kempfer, appeared to be SS private soldiers. All bristled with Stens except Gosens, who was content with his Walther pistol.

Concealed by a grass verge just beyond an inn called De Woeste Hoeve, the men lay in wait. Then out of the darkness came the sound of a heavy vehicle coming from the direction of Arnhem. The party climbed out of its ditch. Each man had his allotted task. Koettinger switched on his torch.

Seated next to the driver of the grey six-cylinder BMW convertible, Hanns Rauter tensed as he peered ahead, catching the flash of a white light and, in the glare of his own black-out shielded headlamps, two uniformed men signalled the car to halt.

Rauter's long stint as police chief had instilled in him a strong sense of suspicion and self-preservation. What was this? Only a short while ago he had decreed that nowhere in the Netherlands, at any time of day or night, were patrols to halt traffic in open country. Such patrols were instructed to operate only in built-up areas or on the outskirts of towns and villages.

Whatever was ahead, Rauter did not care for it. As he reached for his machine-gun, he yelled: '*Achtung*! . . . be ready . . . probably terrorists!'

Rauter's driver was ordered to plough on. To his orderly, Oberleutnant Exner, who toted a sub-machine-gun, Rauter barked:

227

'Defend the rear!'

It was then that the driver, through inexperience, committed a major blunder: he applied his brakes. As the car slowed, Rauter found himself looking directly into the eyes of one of the resistants and shouting: 'What's wrong, man? Don't you know who we are?'

Gosens realised the truth: not only had they all failed in their original plan to stop a lorry but had exposed themselves to some top Nazi brass.

Gosens pulled the trigger: Rauter slumped with the impact of the first blast. As if on some prearranged cue, De Weert and Pruis let loose with their Stens. For the next few seconds, the bullets raked the BMW in merciless fire. Oberleutnant Exner, facing rearwards with his weapon, died instantly. A bullet sliced into the driver's right ear and he slumped forward, dead. Rauter, himself bleeding profusely, took the weight of the dead driver, whose hand still clasped the hand-brake.

Through extraordinary good luck, Hanns Rauter was not dead. The first bullets, which had torn the car's windscreen apart, had smashed through the fingers of his right hand and sliced through the jawbone and through one of his lungs. In addition, a bullet from the rear had penetrated through the neck vertebrae; his body had slumped forward into the windscreen.

Rauter, struggling through the haze of unspeakable pain, managed to shove his dead driver aside and pull himself up by the windscreen frame. His only reward was an additional bullet through his left armpit and another which grazed his left arm.

A heavy curtain of silence descended on the stretch of road, fractured by the macabre horror of a death rattle from one of the dying. Then there was another sound: some sort of vehicle was approaching from the direction of Arnhem. The threat to the BS men was appalling: the magazines of their Stens were empty and there could be no question of pushing the BMW out of sight. The only course was to grab the bicycles and hide in the ditch on the west side of the road.

The Wehrmacht truck pulled up next to the bullet-ridden car. For a few agonising seconds, the hidden men heard its engine running. Then a door was slammed and the vehicle rumbled off at speed towards Apeldoorn.

The resistance group waited a few minutes before gingerly venturing out and approaching the BMW. The batteries of their torches were getting weak and they could see little. When they heard the sound of another car approaching, it seemed good sense to withdraw to that secret campsite a few miles to the east.

As for Rauter, he lay helpless with his injuries until around 6 a.m. Then he was discovered by troops with horse-drawn transport on the way to some training grounds. They wasted no time, storming into De Woeste Hoeve and commandeering the telephone in a desperate bid to reach the German authorities at Apeldoorn. Before long, an ambulance was streaking towards De Woeste Hoeve. Even though he had lost an enormous amount of blood and was desperately frozen with cold, Rauter, who still had some secret documentation with him, managed to hand it over before he was rushed to hospital for a life-saving blood transfusion.

The eighteen miles between Apeldoorn and Arnhem forthwith became the exclusive territory of the Sicherheitsdienst.

The sinister umbrella of the Nazi party, enveloping the all-powerful Gestapo, speedily despatched a two-man team to the area of the shooting, where the BMW remained with its two corpses.

The SD men were characteristically thorough; they made plaster moulds of all tyre tracks, mustered Dutch police representatives and ordered one of their photographers to record the aftermath of the incident as exhaustively as he could. The SD team was no less industrious when it came to investigating the possible role of the adjacent De Woeste Hoeve.

An incident room was established at the inn; inhabitants and neighbours were grilled mercilessly. All, predictably, professed total ignorance of events. Fortunately for them, they were allowed to go free. The SD apparatus, doubtless feeling the hot breath of Heinrich Himmler on its neck, had no time at that stage for idle acts of revenge: the actual would-be assassins of Generalkommissar Hanns Albin Rauter were considered the biggest game.

Despite the luck of those at the inn, what followed constituted the toughest reprisals of the entire occupation of the Netherlands – and some of the worst war crimes committed during the Nazi occupation of the west.

With Rauter out of action, it was inevitable that another leading member of the SD would take centre stage. The role fell on one of Himmler's keenest and most conscientious lieutenants. SS-Brigadefuehrer Dr Eberhardt Schoengarth, Rauter's deputy, set about his mission of revenge with relish.

Schoengarth had a meeting with Seyss-Inquart and came straight to the point: an attack on the highest official of the Netherlands called for 'the severest punishment'. Schoengarth was the man of the hour and he was determined to make the most of it. Himmler, he declared, had instructed him to shoot 500 prominent citizens taken as hostages.

Seyss-Inquart applauded the thinking of the SS man; in practice, he was in no position to protest. Schoengarth was now free to go shopping for hostages.

The various SD chiefs in the Netherlands were instructed to produce fodder for the firing squads. Some thirty *Todeskandidaten* in The Hague formed the nucleus of victims: it was far from being enough for Schoengarth, who declared: 'It doesn't matter if they are *Todeskandidaten* or not. Looters or curfew-breakers will do.'

De Woeste Hoeve was chosen as the site for many of the executions. A 150-strong team of Ordnungspolizei lined up prisoners in five groups of 20 and one of 16. Within half an hour, a long line of men lay by the side of the road. Next to the bodies a notice was set up: 'This is what we do with terrorists and saboteurs.'

Gosens and the other saboteurs who hid out and survived the purges learnt of these and other executions with horror; none had envisaged retaliation on so savage a scale. All they could do was hold up in their campsite fastness and wait for the wave of killings to cease. A total of 263 people were shot in reprisal for what the Germans still thought of as a planned assassination bid.

But any satisfaction the Germans may have felt for their acts of revenge was short-lived. For the end of the Nazi rule in the Netherlands was fast approaching.

On an evening in the summer, the Nationaal-Socialistische Beweging leader Anton Mussert had chaired a meeting of his chief functionaries at NSB headquarters in Utrecht. A bare two months earlier, after D-Day, Mussert had sworn that he would never be displaced: moreover, he had refused to prepare a contingency evacuation scheme for the wives and children of his members.

There had, however, been rapid progress by the Allies, since the British 21st Army Group had taken no time off to celebrate the liberation of Paris, but had steamrollered on to liberate northwestern France and by 4 September had taken Antwerp. Now Mussert, shorn of much of his arrogance, was at last prepared to discuss the very real possibility of evacuating women and children to Germany.

It was a reasonably calm gathering of Mussert supporters. The calm did not last long. False rumours had reached the Netherlands that the Allies were at Breda: well north of the Belgium border and on a direct line to Rotterdam. It was enough to throw thousands of NSB members into panic. On 5 September, which the Dutch were later to dub 'Mad Tuesday', Mussert supporters fled their homes, leaving everything behind. Their leaders, with the exception of Mussert, were the first to go; NSB mayors left their posts and Nazi officials fled from their uncleared desks. Yesterday's fanatical idealists, who had promised to fight to the last man, melted away. And so, incidentally, did scores of Germans. The wife of the Reichskommissar, Gertrud Seyss-Inquart, left the Hague for Salzburg in Austria with five suitcases.

In fact, it was not until 4 May 1945 that the Netherlands and Denmark were surrendered unconditionally to Field Marshal Sir Bernard Montgomery, five days before the final ratification in Berlin of Germany's unconditional surrender. In Hilversum, the radio repeated an endless warning: 'The Germans are still around', but it was largely ignored as total strangers talked, laughed and shook hands on the streets. Throughout the occupation the Germans had allowed only six stanzas of the Dutch national anthem, the 'Wilhelmus,' to be sung. Now the crowds chorused the anthem in full, with the forbidden first verse: 'Wilhelmus of Orange, I am of Dutch blood, true to the Fatherland until death.'

Southeast of Utrecht, General Johannes Blaskowitz, commanding German Army Group H in the west, surrendered his 120,000 men to the Canadian army. In Utrecht itself, the jubilant Dutch sprang aboard Allied armoured vehicles, while the resistance still grappled with snipers. The Prime Minister of the Netherlands, Professor Peter Gerbrandy, who was still in London, confirmed the signing of the capitulation, telling the Dutch people: 'The German Reich with its criminal elements . . . is beaten. Drink the cup of joy, but do not forget the suffering that is mixed in it.'

It was a needless plea; the memories of the suffering were only too great, and to this day the Dutch do not allow themselves to forget. Immediately after the liberation, a simple memorial was erected at De Woeste Hoeve to commemorate the victims of the reprisals of 8 March 1945. Those who had been executed were buried in a mass grave at the Heidehof General Cemetery at Ugchelen, southwest of Apeldoorn. Six weeks later, after the liberation, the bodies were exhumed for the gruesome task of identifying them from clothing and personal effects. A large number were interred at the National Cemetery of

Honour at Loenen, built by the Dutch War Graves Commission and inaugurated in 1949.

Perhaps the most telling reminder of all is a grim, stark statue of a man which stands on a plinth in a clearing at the end of a country road. Called 'Man before the firing squad', it is a reminder of the death of forty-nine inmates of Amersfoort concentration camp who had been included in the reprisals.

For the nation that grieved, the only balm was the machinery of justice which was now turned on the oppressors. Hanns Albin Rauter, still suffering from the effects of his injuries, came into the hands of the Dutch authorities to be tried for his four-and-a-half-year reign of terror. He protested to the court that he implored both Arthur Seyss-Inquart and Brigadefuehrer Schoengarth to refrain from reprisals following the assassination attempt. To the court it sounded either like a direct lie or a cowardly deathbed repentance. It made no difference. On 25 March 1949, he was executed.

Schoengarth, too, went to his death, as did Anton Mussert, arrested without a struggle by the resistance in Utrecht. After a trial, Mussert was shot by firing squad at Scheveningen, where so many resistance fighters had met their deaths.

But the German tenure in Holland had left a legacy; the purges of collaborators began.

Some countries salved their consciences by herding even their most minor traitors before firing squads; others escaped the net altogether.

In Belgium, it was generally agreed that Leon Degrelle possessed nothing less than the luck of the devil.

26

Faced with the collapse of all his dreams, Leon Degrelle had, nevertheless, remained intent on holding on to the last vestiges of power, not only within his own Rexist movement but as one of Heinrich Himmler's chosen within the elite field grey legions of the Waffen-SS.

In 1941, Degrelle joined a legion of Walloon volunteers to fight on the eastern front. Recruitment for the legion was brisk; there were some twelve hundred volunteers; Degrelle was one of the earliest. This, however, was not his first attempt to don a German uniform. In the months before Hitler's attack on Russia he had applied unsuccessfully to join the Wehrmacht. But his Nazi masters had felt he would be of greater value as a politician. As the conflict wore on and it became apparent that the Germans needed every fighting many they could get, his offer was eventually accepted.

The Walloon legion was flung into the cauldron of the Russian front. Although he had no military experience, it was generally agreed that Degrelle was a good soldier and his rise through the ranks was spectacular. Between December 1943 and February 1944, five Wehrmacht divisions and the Waffen-SS Viking Division, which included the Walloons, were encircled at Cherkassy in the Ukraine. Of the 56,000 beleaguered troops, 35,000 had punched their way out, covered by the tenacious men of Viking.

Of the 2,000 Walloons involved, just 632 survived. Lucien Lippert, the Brigade Commander, was killed; his place was taken by the newly promoted SS-Sturmbannfuehrer Leon Degrelle.

On his return to Belgium, Degrelle was determined to

make the most of what was hailed as the triumphant resistance at Cherkassy. A spectacular parade on 27 February 1944 was staged at the Sports Palace in Brussels and a portrait of Lippert was displayed prominently on the rostrum.

A few days later, a similar gathering was held in Charleroi. The German radio in Belgium, broadcasting in French, had a suitable enthusiastic report. It proclaimed:

Leon Degrelle, standing on a tank, passed through . . . at Charleroi, saluting the crowd with raised arm. The sight of the columns of the Legionnaires with the tricolour decorated with the Cherkassy badge, moved the huge crowd deeply. On the Place de l'Hôtel de Ville, decorations were awarded to 150 men who distinguished themselves on the eastern front. The band of the SS Leibstandarte Adolf Hitler played a slow march.

As a tribute to his own troops, Degrelle allowed himself a defiant peroration: 'We were a battalion and became a brigade. Tomorrow we will be a division.'

But any talk of tomorrow was pure illusion. In far better shape than the Waffen-SS, fuelled with Nazi ideology and precious little else, was the British guards armoured division, which stormed to victory from the beaches of Normandy to Cuxhaven on the Elbe estuary. When the Germans began their retreat to the Rhine, the guards division was the right flank formation of the British 2nd Army.

The division advanced from Douai, crossing the Belgium frontier on 3 September; by nightfall it had swept into the capital from the north and east.

Alexander Clifford of the *Daily Mail* wrote:

By the time we reached the suburbs of Brussels our hands were limp, our faces covered with lipstick, our car loaded with fruit and flowers, and our ears deafened with cheering. . . . It was an hour before we could move our vehicles. It was astounding that they did not crumple up beneath the weight of the Belgians, who used them as grandstands. Many of these people were in tears.

It was a rare and moving sight. If you got out of your car, in half a second you were overwhelmed and wildly kissed again and decorated with flowers and made to drink wine.

It was as if suddenly the Belgians lost all instincts of fear; from hastily abandoned German slit trenches they watched the British troops advance past the red glare of the Palais de Justice, which the Germans had put to the torch. The few pockets of resistance that remained were swiftly mopped up. Even the quick stutter of German machine-guns and the deep slam of the British tank weapons caused no panic or a sudden scuttle into homes and shelters.

In the Grand Place, on the steps of the Hôtel de Ville, the crowd burnt Hitler in effigy. All the relics of transport vehicles that could be found were dragged to numerous bonfires. At the former Gestapo headquarters, documents and files were also burnt by a delirious mob.

But there were those whose motives had little to do with the joy of liberation. Collaborators were covering their tracks.

Among them was Leon Degrelle. The sweepings of the Walloon, Flemish and French SS divisions had been hastily assembled as the pretentiously termed 'SS Army Corps West' to fight in the path of the Soviet advance into Pomerania.

It all proved useless. The Russians were unstoppable; most of the Flemish SS fell into Soviet hands, the French SS was a disintegrated flotsam on a sea of fleeing military and civilians. The Walloons fared rather better. Some remnants were evacuated by sea to Copenhagen, while others, Degrelle among them, made their way overland Schleswig-Holstein.

Imminent defeat, the annihilation of past hopes and dreams, the total collapse of the Third Reich – these things were now brutally obvious to most of those Rexists whose loyalty was strained to the uttermost.

But Degrelle insisted that all was by no means lost.

There was time for one last bold gamble. It rested on the say-so of just one man.

In the north of Germany, Heinrich Himmler roamed aimlessly round his headquarters, which were now at Ploen, on the borders of Denmark. Adolf Hitler had opted for a suicide pact with his wife Eva Braun. The Fuehrer's designated successor was Grossadmiral Karl Doenitz, who had no intention of employing Himmler in any capacity whatever.

Degrelle proposed a meeting at Malente, near Kiel. It turned out to be a grotesque pantomime; Degrelle was driving a Volkswagen powered by potato schnapps, and Himmler, looking faintly ludicrous in a crash helmet, was at the wheel of his own vehicle.

Degrelle came straight to the point, asking: 'What do you want of my Belgian SS? I am proposing that we either establish a northern redoubt in Norway or else disperse into some sort of Werewolf group.'

The Rexist leader had got wind of the underground civilian army which had been recruited and trained by the SS against the Allies, who were overrunning Germany. Surely such a group could be reinforced.

To Degrelle's consternation, Himmler appeared listless and uninterested. In an attempt to master his exasperation, Degrelle demanded of the Reichsfuehrer-SS: 'What *are* your plans?'

At that moment, the charade was interrupted by Allied aircraft sweeping down on Himmler's retinue. The party dived for the nearest ditches. Himmler was shocked, rebuking his staff by protesting: 'Discipline, gentlemen, discipline!' After the party had scrambled from the ditches, the two men bade each other farewell, Degrelle's question unanswered. Himmler was intent only on making his way through Allied fire to some imagined haven in Flensburg.

Still Degrelle refused to give up. How about sympathetic forces in Denmark? There were none willing to do business with him. All hope was now pinned on Vidkun Quisling, the bombastic Norwegian traitor, who was already shivering in the shadow of the firing squad. All Quisling was anxious to do now was present an image as his country's saviour.

Degrelle, the last hope gone, saw no reason to offer himself for slaughter. A private aircraft belonging to Hitler's Minister for War Production, Albert Speer, had been supplied to Quisling in case he should wish to escape to Spain. He showed no inclination to accept the offer; Leon Degrelle took his place.

Liberation was not simply a matter of wine-induced euphoria on the streets of Brussels: the newsreel and newspaper photographers followed sorrowing wives and mothers who laid their wreaths beneath the low drop gallows of Breendonck fort, situated between Brussels and Antwerp. Here many of their men had been slowly throttled to death. There were the rooms in which victims had been subjected to alternate blasts of fiery-hot and ice-cold air, and there were pulleys from which prisoners were slung.

The cameras recorded one particularly poignant moment: a black-garbed widow in the castle courtyard removing a sliver of wood from the stake against which her husband had stood before a firing squad.

And now special courts in Belgium were set up, manned by two civilian and three military judges. According to one set of records, some 100,000 persons were arrested, but only 87,000 were subsequently brought to trial; of these, around 10,000 were acquitted. Sentences of death were passed on 4,170 people, of which 230 were actually carried out.

As for Degrelle, he was eventually sentenced to death by a Belgian court in his absence. In 1946, he found his way to Argentina, later returning to Spain, where he managed to withstand all bids to extradite him to Belgium.

In the mid-1980s, the French-speaking channel of the Belgian television service ran him to earth in his luxurious

Madrid home. The decision to run three lengthy programmes on Degrelle and his wartime collaboration led to bitter protests from organisations of resistance fighters and survivors, particularly when it was learnt that the interviews had been filmed some years earlier but that the authorities had then judged it impossible to show them.

In more than an hour of detailed exchanges with Maurice de Wilde, a specialist on the record of wartime collaboration, Degrelle angrily refuted documentary evidence from SS headquarters in Berlin that he was willing, not only to raise volunteers to fight 'the Godless Communists in the east', but effectively hand over both the Walloon and Flemish regions in Belgium as a virtual German protectorate. Such an allegation, Degrelle insisted, was 'absolute rubbish'. He claimed that reference to the 'Reich' in those documents referred, not to a German Reich, but to 'a union of Western European peoples, each guarding its own proper identity – an idea which I always defended'.

Confronted by transcripts of his own speeches in which he referred to the French-speaking Walloons as 'part of the great Germanic community', Degrelle stated that until the early Middle Ages Wallonia was part of the German empire founded by Charlemagne. He also claimed that these historical references helped to win concessions for Wallonia from Hitler and Himmler. Indeed, Himmler had let Degrelle's 4,000 Walloon-SS volunteers have their own national flag and use the French language in military orders.

Over the years, Degrelle delighted in holding court to anyone who would listen, and readily granted interviews in his study crammed with books, video cassettes and memorabilia. When pressed, he was even ready to strut in his old SS uniform.

27

The twelve-year-old Third Reich of Adolf Hitler, envisaged to last for a thousand years, crumbled to death in
the last days of April and the start of May 1945.

On 30 April, the brain which conceived it rotted among
the ruins of the Berlin Chancellery. Hitler had presided
over the last of his noon situation conferences in his underground bunker fortress. The Fuehrer had listened without
emotion to news of heavy fighting in the Tiergarten and
the Potsdamer Platz, only a few blocks away from the
Chancellery. At about 3.20 p.m., he and Eva Braun withdrew to the Fuehrer's suite. Outside the door, the inhabitants of the bunker waited. Hitler shot himself with his
Walther 7.65 calibre pistol, probably biting into a poison
capsule at the same time. Eva Braun took poison.

On 4 May, the German High Command surrendered
all German forces in northwest Germany, Denmark and
the Netherlands to Britain's Field Marshal Montgomery.
The BBC Danish radio delivered the news to Denmark
at 8.35 the same evening.

Danish families greeted the news by placing lighted
candles on window sills. Danish intelligence agents, however, were more energetic. They were posted on the
Jutland-Danish border to pluck hundreds of suspected
traitors, Gestapo agents and SS officials from the columns
of retreating Germans and wandering refugees.

Within six weeks of the liberation, more than eleven
hundred arrests had been made at the border. The
number of those seized within Denmark totalled 20,000,
among them hundreds of 'field mattresses' – young women
who had slept with German soldiers. It was a sign of

the prevailing bitterness that the death penalty, whose introduction had been successfully resisted during the occupation, was restored for the worst cases of collaboration. Not only did Denmark reauthorise the death penalty, but it was made retroactive to the years of Nazi rule.

One of the most fortunate of the leading figures of the occupation was the German plenipotentiary, Dr Werner Best, whose death sentence was commuted to five years. Best was able to argue successfully that German officials in Berlin had initiated the action against the Jews and that, therefore, he could not in justice be held responsible for their fate.

The authorities made sure that those arrested, whatever their ultimate fate, suffered maximum humiliation. In the major Dutch cities, groups of suspected collaborators were driven through streets in open trucks, their hands raised high in abject surrender.

Some of the reprisals were so savage that the Danish branch of the War Resisters International Council, a pacifist organisation, urged the new Danish government to disband all resistance movements, so that alleged collaborators could be arraigned before properly constituted courts.

As for Norway, pious warnings were issued by the authorities against private settling of scores, but it was hard to slake the thirst for individual vengeance. As if fully aware of their likely fate, Reichskommissar Josef Terboven and Obergruppenfuehrer Rediess of the SS blew themselves up in a bunker located in the residence of the Crown Prince.

There remained Vidkun Quisling.

As the situation became progressively worse for the Germans, he steadily retreated from reality, nurturing futile dreams of eventually ruling an independent country which, with the help of a reconstituted Reich, would turn on Russia in a sort of 'Nordic defence'.

With the announcement of the German surrender in Denmark, he had contacted Terboven to see if further catastrophe could be avoided. Terboven had been blunt: 'The best thing for you is to get out of the country.' Then had come the offer of an aircraft to fly him to Spain, and there had been talk of a long-range U-boat making for South America.

It was a measure of just how deluded Quisling had become that he stoutly rejected both offers, optimistic that he could easily justify his wartime actions.

Quisling returned to his luxurious villa, clinging fatuously to the title of Minister President and entrusting his safety to his few remaining Hird bodyguards. He could scarcely credit the message he soon received from police headquarters: he must turn himself in on 9 May at 7 a.m. or be formally arrested.

He expostulated: 'I am being treated like an ordinary criminal.' The retreat into fantasy went even further. He attempted to plead on the telephone with Crown Prince Olav in London. The operator refused to connect the call.

Shortly after 6.15 a.m. on the day that the police had designated, Quisling, in greatcoat and soft felt hat, stepped out of the Mercedes Benz limousine which had been a gift from Hitler. It was the last comfort he was ever to know. Preliminary questioning over, he was locked into a bleak cell with a toilet bucket and a few sticks of furniture. Three months later, the trial began in the large assembly hall of Oslo's Freemasons' Lodge, which was doing duty as a courtroom.

If he had any remaining illusions of power or prestige, they were swiftly shattered. From the outset the mood of the court was hostile. Quisling complained to the judge that he had lost thirty-five pounds in weight, only to be told coldly: 'That is nothing to what some of our people lost when you put them in concentration camps.'

The charges were all-embracing: the prosecution was determined that Quisling should escape nothing. Allegations ranged from conspiracy to murder and complicity in the deportation of Jews, to theft of possessions from the royal palace and drunkenness and debauchery. His guilt

242

on the main charge of treason was incontestable, but there were those who felt considerable uneasiness at the hostility displayed towards him.

There was a widespread feeling that a fair hearing in such an atmosphere was impossible. There were even allegations that the prisoner had been subjected to a vigorous physical and psychological examination, including electrical probing of the brain. Quisling was pronounced sane and the trial continued. But the doubts persisted.

Quisling's eight-hour speech in his own defence was a rambling self-justification. He proclaimed: 'To me, politics is not a matter of party interests, professional job-seeking, or personal ambition and lust for power. It is a matter of self-sacrifice and practical action in the service of the historical development for the benefit of one's own country and to promote the realisation of God's kingdom on earth which Christ came to establish. If my activities have become treasonable, as they have been said to be, then I would pray to God that for the sake of Norway a large number of Norway's sons will become such traitors as I, but that they will not be thrown into jail.'

There were no signs of repentance. Indeed, he assured the court that, given the chance again, he would have taken the same course. Only the minor charges seemed to sting him into indignation.

He was acquitted of these, but sentenced to death for murder and treason. At 2 a.m. on 24 October, Quisling was rushed in a police car to Akershus Castle, shoved unceremoniously against a wall and despatched by a ten-man firing squad.

The death of the more prominent Nazis who had extended their influence over all the occupied countries of the west inevitably overshadowed the fate of lesser fry. Heinrich Himmler, for example, held his last staff conference at Flensburg on 5 May. At 2 p.m. on 23 May, he blundered into a British checkpoint at Bremervoerde. Six hours later he was identified, stripped and searched. As an army doctor's fingers groped in his mouth, he bit on the concealed poisoned capsule. Fifteen minutes later he was dead. A blanket was thrown over his corpse and two days later he was buried in an unmarked grave.

At the Nuremberg trial, Alfred Rosenberg, the 'party philosopher' who had headed the Nazi party's office of foreign affairs, was convicted of four charges; the judgement linked him closely to Hitler's invasion of Norway. It stated: '. . . Rosenberg arranged for Quisling to collaborate closely with the National Socialists and to receive political assistance from the Nazis.'

He was sentenced to death and hanged for war crimes at Nuremberg on 16 October 1946, along with Keitel, Ribbentrop and Seyss-Inquart, all of whom had had major roles in the Nazi invasion of the west.

Himmler, seemingly, was not the only Nazi war criminal to be consigned to the oblivion of an unmarked grave. Mystery surrounded the last day of Gustav Simon, Gauleiter of Hitler's 'Moselleland', who, early in 1945, left a shattered Luxembourg in a vain bid to reach Berlin for fresh instructions. Trapped in Westphalia, Simon hid under an assumed name in the British zone of occupation; by December a certificate issued in Paderborn recorded his death, but no accompanying details were released. There were unsubstantiated rumours that the certificate was a fake and that Simon had been smuggled back to Luxembourg and murdered by members of the Red Lion of Luxembourg resistance group.

As an act of revenge, it would have had a certain logic. During the occupation, members of the Red Lion had perished in front of firing squads in the concentration camp at Hinzert, after digging their own graves.

The tiny duchy had experienced the fallout from Hitler's last major initiative in the west: a bold counter-attack in December 1944 through the forests of the Ardennes, in the so-called Battle of the Bulge. Part of the territory involved comprised the northern half of Luxembourg.

Hitler's object was to recapture Antwerp; for the fruitless gamble, he snatched valuable units and tanks from the Russian front, together with the last remnants of the Luftwaffe and some 250,000 troops.

Under the full force of the onslaught, isolated villages in the Ardennes mountains were taken by surprise. There had been no time for evacuation; the Germans carried off men between fifteen and seventy for forced labour in the already shattered Reich. On a stretch of sixty miles along the German frontier to a depth of five miles there was wholesale eviction to create a no-man's-land for military operations.

The German initiative in the Ardennes was soon lost; Hitler's last dramatic gesture postponed the balm of full liberation for Luxembourg under the final year of the war.

28

In France, the search for collaborators took on all the ardour of a mission. The purge – known as *l'épuration* (purification) – lasted from September 1944 to the end of 1949.

Just over 2,000 death sentences were handed down, but women and minors were automatically exempted by General de Gaulle. These figures took no account of private vengeance or of collaborators summarily executed in the period immediately after liberation.

Many of these executions, of dubious or nonexistent legality, were carried out with a swift barbarity that would, in many cases, have done credit to the Milice and even the Gestapo.

It was to be years before the deep, festering wounds of *l'épuration* were to heal. And, even then, scars remained.

International attention focused on the two most famous collaborators of them all.

Maréchal Pétain was whisked away from Vichy by the Germans; while at the Hotel Matignon in Paris Pierre Laval, his luggage packed, luxuriated in a marble bath. It was his last indulgence and also his last day in France before he too was taken to Germany.

On 23 July 1945, Maréchal Pétain was arraigned on a charge of treason. Alone of the Vichy survivors, he requested to be allowed to return to France to stand trial: 'At my age, there is only one thing one still fears. That is not to have done all one's duty, and I wish to do mine.'

In court, he wore the simplest uniform of a Maréchal of France and the Medaille Militaire, the only decoration shared by simple soldiers and great commanders. His lawyer begged him to take his Maréchal's baton into court, only to receive the scornful reply: 'That would be theatrical.'

In his last words to the court before sentence, Pétain said: 'My thought, my only thought was to remain with the French on the soil of France, according to my promise, so as to protect them and to lessen their sufferings.'

Whether this was the simple truth or a desperate bid for sympathy, no one could tell. But it made no difference; the court remained unmoved. On 15 August, the ninety-year-old Maréchal was sentenced to death. President de Gaulle commuted the sentence to life imprisonment and the old man was confined on the Ile de Yeu off the Vendée coast. By June 1951, he had become almost totally senile and was released. Within a month he was dead, passing away within two days of the ex-Crown Prince Rupprecht of Bavaria, his old adversary at Verdun in the World War One.

Two months after the trial of Pétain, it was the turn of Pierre Laval, for whom the French reserved a special hatred. The proceedings in court could only be described as an undignified shambles; imprecations were hurled constantly from the public gallery. On 14 October, four days after being sentenced to death, Laval took poison. But France was determined to have its revenge and the stomach pumps went to work; the doctors kept him alive long enough to face the firing squad.

The men of the Glières who had perished in the German cleaning-up operations of February and March 1944 were avenged spectacularly the following August. The liberation of the Department of Haute-Savoie was to be down to the glory of the resistance alone.

German retreat did not mean that the enemy had done with Haute-Savoie. All those Germans stationed in the southeast were ordered to assemble in the area of the Rhône Valley, to stem the thrust that the Allies were bound to make to the north. In particular, the Germans were told to make their way quickly to the city of Lyons, which was to be fashioned as a strongpoint to delay the junction of both southern and northern Allied armies.

The key objective for the liberators was the town of Annecy, where most of the Wehrmacht and Gestapo had been stationed.

At the same time, the order went out to the maquis: attack all the enemy posts on the line of retreat.

Arms were distributed to the different camps. But it was not just the maquis who had caught the scene of battle. There was now a new people's army. An eyewitness, recalling the events a year later, wrote:

. . . This new people's army, though poor in weapons, held itself with pride. There were no uniforms, but there was faith. . . . Everyone joined in keenly; the butcher, the baker's apprentice, the postal employee, the schoolmaster, the factory worker and the peasant – everyone still in his working clothes, with a weapon different from his neighbours; all supporting the action of the maquisards, themselves so variously attired that the people's army made a very odd appearance. One would be wearing an old tin hat dating from the war of 1914–18; another had treasured his old French sailor's cap with a red pompom; a third had on a fireman's helmet. Many were in shorts, hair in the wind and chests bare. . . .

As the columns of maquis made their way down the mountain paths, they were held up at the farms by peasants who, leaving their field work, rolled out barrels of cider into the open to refresh the fighters.

The focal point for the twin assault of the maquis and the citizen army against the regrouping Germans was a sector between Marignier and Cluses, in a part of the valley of the Arve, to the east of Bonneville.

It was soon clear to the maquis that Cluses required its urgent attention. On the morning of 18 August, Bonneville signalled that a column of German lorries, reinforcements from Annecy, was moving up the main highway to Cluses, where the Germans already had a significant advantage of arms, including antitank weapons and captured French 75 mm guns.

The maquis, hidden in the fir forests, thickets and bushes which lined a road, opened up on the lorries loaded with men and guns. The Germans were forced to a halt in the vain effort to clean up an opposition which was virtually invisible. Their progress was inevitably slow; they were approaching two critical points, the Bridge at Vougy and the crossing at Scionzier, where the road snaked through a narrow street of houses bunched closely together.

The tactics of the maquis were to let the German column pass Vougy Bridge, so as to trap it between two bottlenecks at Cluses and Vougy. Of the 150 lorries that had left Annecy in convoy, only thirty managed to penetrate beyond Vougy Bridge. Along a thirty-mile stretch of road, the Germans were harassed by the maquis.

Bright flares and the path of tracer bullets from the dark heart of the mountains cut through the still of night at Cluses. The engagement went on until 2 a.m. In a sudden lull, the Germans attempted a bold move.

The inhabitants of Cluses remained huddled behind closed doors and windows. In silence, the Germans pushed their lorries to the point of exit from Cluses towards the national highway. No one risked switching on the engines of the vehicles, but, if the inhabitants of Cluses had snatched a few hours of sleep, the maquis had allowed themselves no such luxury.

They returned to the attack, firing into the convoy with the weapons supplied to them on previous Allied air drops. The progress of the German lorries, now making in the opposite direction towards Annecy, was even closer than the day before. Not a single vehicle or its occupants made the road crossing at Vougy. A well-placed machine-gun hidden in a roadside ditch sliced into one car that had tried to make a passage. Its five occupants, senior officers of the Gestapo at Cluses, were killed.

Other Germans made a bid to reach the Swiss frontier by crossing the Arve, but the foaming icy torrent proved too much. Many were drowned; those who managed the crossing had lost all will to fight and surrendered meekly enough.

By early evening, lorryloads of German prisoners, the vehicles churning up the hot dust of high summer, made their way to Marignier.

German casualties were put at around 500. Losses for the maquis were around thirty dead and a few wounded.

The final act in the liberation of Haute-Savoie took place the following day, 19 August, in front of Annecy, where all the maquis had assembled. Enemy strongholds were seized; the rump of the German garrison and members of the Vichy were arrested.

Partisans sported berets, military caps and open shirts, rounds of ammunition dangling from their belts. The atmosphere was festive. But it told only half the story. While one section of the resistance permitted itself to relax, another was on the move. Female collaborators were punched and kicked out of their houses, and stripped to the waist while their heads were shaved.

German prisoners fared comparatively well. It was the Milice that the partisans were seeking. There was not much discrimination about arrests; most people remembered only the brutality which the forces of Vichy had committed in Haute-Savoie, under the orders of the local Prefect, Charles Marion.

Now raw young recruits to the Milice were bracketed with hardened criminals. Many of them had not taken part in combat; nonetheless, they were arraigned in a series of field courts martial. Later, passions were to cool a little, but there were many cases where it was hard to tell vengeance and justice apart.

The more level-headed of the maquis, keen to preserve at least some trappings of legality, held villagers at gunpoint to prevent any bloodbath. Some 200 Milice in Annecy were hastily piled into trucks and taken up the mountain to the village of Grand-Bornand, where they were placed in the local dance hall.

Jean Comet, a regional prosecutor who had originally gone into hiding when the Germans rounded up court officials known to be hostile to collaboration, speedily offered his services as prosecutor at the forthcoming courts martial at Grand-Bornand.

The night before the trial, he drew up a list of responsibilities. The charges were fashioned in such a way as to avoid any future accusation of crude vengeance. Mere membership of the Milice was proclaimed to be the least heinous offence, followed by slightly more serious charges against those who had served but not taken part in actual combat against their fellow Frenchmen. But it was made clear to the resistance judges that the only possible verdicts on treason charges were Guilty or Not Guilty; the penalty was to be death.

It was calculated that at least three-quarters of the Milice would be found guilty of serious crimes; seventy-five coffins were ordered from a carpenter; local people were put to work digging a pit outside the village.

At 10 a.m. on 23 August, the Milice prisoners were mustered into the dock in groups of twenty, protected by armed partisans.

The trial went on all day and most of the night. Throughout, the judges were careful to give the defence fair play; lawyers for the accused made much of the fact that their clients were young and had been seduced by Vichy propaganda. Twenty-one of the defendants were acquitted, but that did not mean instant release: few of them would have left the court building alive. Besides, there were lesser charges to be answered. Seventy-six Milice were found guilty of crimes carrying the death penalty, and the judgment noted that 'present military circumstances require that these sentences be sanctioned with great energy'.

There was quick absolution from the village priest. Death certificates had been completed and coffins numbered. The convicted men had an opportunity to write a last letter and bequeath their possessions. Five stakes were set up at the execution site. The prisoners, led out in alphabetical order, were given the option of blindfolds. At the moment of execution they shouted: 'Long live the Maréchal!' or 'Long live France!'

The shootings, which began just after dawn, continued throughout the day.

29

The continent of Europe had been prostrated by war. In the centre of misery and destruction lay Germany. Bombing had gouged the heart out of her towns, cities and industries. For every ton of bombs dropped on Britain, 315 had descended on Hitler's Reich.

In 1945, the vast majority of Berliners were struggling to survive on about 800 calories a day.

Burst water mains and ruptured sewers spread typhoid. Mosquitoes fed on corpses rotting in the rubble and then spread dysentery. In July, six out of every ten babies born in Berlin perished.

In the rest of Europe, a feeling of anticlimax followed the euphoria of liberation. There was, of course, the very considerable consolation that a brutal occupation force had been driven out. These feelings were shared by the one section of the United Kingdom to be forced under the Nazi heel. As late as 7 May 1945, the Germans in Jersey, the largest of the Channel Islands, had made preparations to reinforce the fortifications. Six days later, after the surrender, a convoy of fifty ships arrived off the Channel Islands bringing with them luxuries only dimly remembered since 1940 – flour, meat, biscuits, tea, chocolate, tobacco, soap, coal and gas. Even the German workers cheered lustily as the first landing craft nosed its way into Jersey's port of St Helier.

For some members of the French maquis, there were still matters of uncompleted business.

Felix Plottier, the unrepentant resistant clapped in jail by the Swiss under his alias of Felix Fournier, was uneasy.

It was true that he had been released from prison, but the terms of the deportation order made it clear that he would be banned from Switzerland for life. Since he lived a mere twelve miles from the frontier, had many Swiss friends and needed to travel there for his business, the ban was more than mildly vexatious. Immediately on leaving jail, he sought out a senior Swiss official.

The man's demeanour was arctic; the ban must be allowed to stand. He intoned with heavy gravity: 'We cannot rescind the order prohibiting the entry of Monsieur Felix Fournier into Switzerland. If Monsieur Fournier attempts to enter our country again he will be arrested.'

There was a pause; the man's aura of disapproval filled the room. Without relaxing a muscle, he added: 'However, we have no record of a Felix Plottier and there is therefore no prohibition against such an individual entering Switzerland.'

Plottier played the game to the last; he gravely shook hands with the official and took his leave.

Felix and Joan Plottier, back in Bonneville, prepared to pick up the threads of their lives. But first they would give themselves a treat. In a barn near their home, buried beneath faggots of wood, lay their magnificent red and black Simca coupé.

They soon discovered that all it needed to be roadworthy was a new set of tyres.

Bestselling War Fiction and Non-Fiction

☐ Passage to Mutiny	Alexander Kent	£2.95
☐ Colours Aloft	Alexander Kent	£2.95
☐ Winged Escort	Douglas Reeman	£2.95
☐ Army of Shadows	John Harris	£2.50
☐ Decoy	Dudley Pope	£2.95
☐ Gestapo	Rupert Butler	£4.50
☐ Johnny Gurkha	E.D. Smith	£2.95
☐ Typhoon Pilot	Desmond Scott	£2.95
☐ The Rommel Papers	B.H. Liddel Hart	£5.95
☐ Hour of the Lily	John Kruse	£3.50
☐ Duel in the Dark	Peter Townsend	£3.95
☐ The Spoils of War	Douglas Scott	£2.99
☐ The Wild Blue	Walter J. Boyne & Steven L. Thompson	£3.95
☐ The Bombers	Norman Longmate	£4.99

Prices and other details are liable to change

ARROW BOOKS, BOOKSERVICE BY POST, PO BOX 29, DOUGLAS, ISLE OF MAN, BRITISH ISLES

NAME..

ADDRESS...

....

....

Please enclose a cheque or postal order made out to Arrow Books Ltd. for the amount due and allow the following for postage and packing.

U.K. CUSTOMERS: Please allow 22p per book to a maximum of £3.00.

B.F.P.O. & EIRE: Please allow 22p per book to a maximum of £3.00

OVERSEAS CUSTOMERS: Please allow 22p per book.

Whilst every effort is made to keep prices low it is sometimes necessary to increase cover prices at short notice. Arrow Books reserve the right to show new retail prices on covers which may differ from those previously advertised in the text or elsewhere.